AF783876

Measuring Race and Ethnicity

Larry E. Davis · Rafael J. Engel

Measuring Race and Ethnicity

Foreword by Patricia Y. Gurin

Springer

Larry E. Davis, Ph.D.
School of Social Work
University of Pittsburgh
2117 Cathedral of Learning
Pittsburgh, PA 15260, USA
ledavis@pitt.edu

Rafael J. Engel, Ph.D.
School of Social Work
University of Pittsburgh
2012 Cathedral of Learning
Pittsburgh, PA 15260, USA
rengel@pitt.edu

ISBN 978-1-4419-6696-4 e-ISBN 978-1-4419-6697-1
DOI 10.1007/978-1-4419-6697-1
Springer New York Dordrecht Heidelberg London

Library of Congress Control Number: 2010936824

© Springer Science+Business Media, LLC 2011
All rights reserved. This work may not be translated or copied in whole or in part without the written permission of the publisher (Springer Science+Business Media, LLC, 233 Spring Street, New York, NY 10013, USA), except for brief excerpts in connection with reviews or scholarly analysis. Use in connection with any form of information storage and retrieval, electronic adaptation, computer software, or by similar or dissimilar methodology now known or hereafter developed is forbidden.
The use in this publication of trade names, trademarks, service marks, and similar terms, even if they are not identified as such, is not to be taken as an expression of opinion as to whether or not they are subject to proprietary rights.

Printed on acid-free paper

Springer is part of Springer Science+Business Media (www.springer.com)

Foreword

Measuring Race and Ethnicity is a treasure trove of scales primarily developed by psychologists over the last quarter century that can be used to understand how individuals from various racial and ethnic groups think about themselves and members of other groups. It has numerous important features.

Most notably, this volume focuses on multiple groups, whereas most collections of scales in the past have generally covered only one or sometimes a couple of racial/ethnic groups. In this volume, the same criteria are applied to scales that pertain to Asian and Pacific Islanders, Hispanics, African Americans, Whites and to a lesser degree Native Americans. While the substantive content of the scales for each of these groups varies somewhat, the authors of this volume have managed to pull together scales that cover common themes across these groups. Ethnic/racial identity measures are evaluated for Asian and Pacific Islanders, Hispanics, African Americans, and Whites. Acculturation measures are evaluated for Asian and Pacific Islanders, Hispanics, African Americans, and Native Americans. Moreover, what is especially important is that the identity and acculturation scales are evaluated on the same criteria for each of these groups. A scholar who wants to measure one of these concepts across groups can readily turn to this volume for the most comprehensive measures with the strongest psychometric properties that apply to the groups of interest in specific research projects. That is a strong enough rationale for the value of this volume.

Perhaps an even stronger rationale is that this volume will decrease the tendency among researchers to create their own measures with little regard for assuring that research evidence accumulates over the time and across different samples of individuals. Of course, the study of race and ethnicity is not unique in too often failing to contribute to accumulated knowledge. Too many researchers have underestimated the importance of building scientific evidence through the use of common measures, and too often overestimated the importance of creating new measures even for concepts that have guided other studies as well. One would hope that this volume will provide a major corrective for this phenomenon, especially in the areas of ethnic/racial identity and acculturation.

This volume is a gift! Moreover, we are assured that the gift will re-occur. These authors are committed to updating *Measuring Race and Ethnicity* in a continuing fashion with the additional aim of including scales that are not covered in this volume as well as research evidence for scales that are covered here but not for specific racial/ethnic groups. We can thus look forward to an on-going resource because Larry Davis and Rafael Engel are dedicated to the continuity of this impressive compilation and evaluation of psychologically oriented measures of race and ethnicity.

Ann Arbor, MI Patricia Y. Gurin

Preface

Race and ethnicity are key dynamics at play in virtually every major issue America is facing. Educational inequities, crime and imprisonment, employment, health and mental health, inter-group conflict, family dysfunction, problems of youth and the aged all have significant racial and ethnic manifestations. Moreover, these concerns are likely to be with us for the foreseeable future. It is both surprising and disappointing to most scholars that America is still struggling with so many of the same race-related difficulties with which they struggled decades ago. Few of us who lived through the tumultuous 1960s and 1970s would have envisioned that after so many years, and after the passing of so much monumental legislation that race, color, and ethnicity would continue to be so powerful as predictors of life events. Still, most Americans would agree that our country has made significant race-related progress.

It is also the case that much has changed demographically in this country over the time. In the 1970s, when the idea for this book originated, one in five Americans was a person of color; today that figure is now roughly one in three (U.S. Census Bureau, 2008). Furthermore, this number is projected to increase to one in two by the middle of this century. America's rapidly changing racial and ethnic demography portends a future of increased cross racial/ethnic interaction. It is also likely to be the case that the disparities and differences which have historically occurred between racial and ethnic groups are likely to sustain themselves and be a cause of concern.

The idea for pulling together a collection of racial/ethnic group-specific instruments occurred to me in 1974. As a doctoral student at the University of Michigan, I came across a volume of scales, "Measures of Social Psychological Attitudes" by John P. Robinson and Phillip R. Shaver (1969). I found this collection of psychological instruments to be both interesting and of considerable use. But even at that time, I felt that a collection of instruments which focused on racial and ethnic groups would also be useful.

Fortunately, Dr. Ray Engel, formerly the associate dean of the School of Social Work here at the University of Pittsburgh agreed to be the co-editor of this volume. He possesses a wealth of expertise and interest in measurement, so together we attempted to bring about what we believe is a valuable collection of instruments. With the help a legion of capable and supportive students, we have created what we believe will be an important resource for those attempting to assess intra- and inter-social psychological group differences.

We are aware that ours is not the first endeavor to gather a collection of instruments having race and/or ethnicity as its focus (Jones, 1996). Yet most efforts to date have focused on but a single racial or ethnic group or addressed primarily health or mental health issues, or concerns of identity. In contrast, the focus of this volume is on intra- and inter-social psychological measures across a number of racial/ethnic groups. Specifically, we have elected to focus on Caucasians, Hispanics, Native Americans, Asian Americans and Pacific Islanders, and African Americans and their perceptions of self and interactions with others. We have also included "Generic" intra- and inter-group measures. Unlike the measures specific to certain racial/ethnic groups, these "Generic" measures are not targeted for use with a specific group. Hence, they can be used broadly and with groups for whom there exists no specific racial/ethnic measure. For example, a researcher may find these to be of value with Native Americans for whom specific measures are in short supply.

We did our best to collect the most up-to-date instruments available, but we are very much aware that there exist many more valuable scales, which for a variety of reasons, are not included here. Some we simply are unaware of and others we were unable to procure permission to use. We hope *Measuring Race and Ethnicity* will be well received by scholars from many disciplines. Clearly the scale development for racial and ethnic intra- and inter-group relations is more developed for some groups than in others. It is evident from the instruments listed here that scale development for some racial/ethnic groups is sorely needed. While these gaps in instrument development are very unfortunate, they highlight areas of significant opportunity for scale development. In particular, we strongly encourage greater development of scales for Native Americans.

Contents of This Volume

This volume contains six chapters as well as an appendix, which lists measurement scales that we are aware of, but have not received permission to list and review. We recognize that other racial or ethnic groups might have been included; for example, chapters on various Asian groups, Caribbean, or African immigrants would be beneficial given demographic trends. We have limited our efforts to chapters addressing the major racial/ethnic groupings in America, and have hopes to publish a more inclusive volume in the future.

About the Volume

The Chapter 1 focuses on Asian Americans and Pacific Islanders. It contains eight measurement scales. Each of these scales is an intra-group measure, and has as its goal the assessment of an individual's level of acculturation. That is, the extent to which individuals are inclined to identify with either Asian or American culture. There are no scales in this chapter which assess inter-group perceptions of Asians with other groups. For example, given the unfortunate recent history of inter-group conflict between Koreans and African Americans, it would be useful to have a measure assessing Korean/Black perceptions of relations (Hurh, 1998). It would also be worthwhile to have inter-group measures assessing the perceptions of attitudes and interactions between specific Asian ethnic groups, e.g., Chinese and Japanese, as it is the case that these groups have histories of inter-group conflict.

Chapter 2 focuses on Hispanics. Like the Asian American group, the Hispanic population is composed of a number of ethnic groups. There are 16 scales reviewed in the chapter. In our review of these measures, we found no measure that specifically focused on race-related relationships between Hispanics and other minority groups or between Hispanics and Whites. Therefore, this section focuses solely on intra-group measures that assess acculturation among Hispanic Americans.

Chapter 3 inspects African Americans. Because of its long history in America, this group has been researched and studied most pervasively. Research has been done on African Americans ranging from chronicling their history and culture to employment and crime. Researchers have studied between-group and within-group differences among African Americans. However to date, very little research attention has been given to group differences between African Americans and other minority groups of color. In this chapter, we review measures of intra-racial phenomena such as racial identity and acculturation. We also review instruments which attempt to assess inter-racial prejudice, prejudicial attitudes, cultural mistrust, and race-related stress. Fourteen scales are reviewed in this chapter.

Chapter 4 focuses on Caucasians. There are eight scales presented and reviewed in this chapter. All eight scales are inter-group assessment measures that focus on the inter-racial phenomena of racial prejudice and discriminatory attitudes. Most research in this area is focused on racism, discrimination practices, stereotyping, and prejudice. Additionally, some instruments focus specifically on perceived interactions between Caucasians and African Americans. But scales assessing race relations between Whites and other groups are scarce.

Chapter 5 is a compilation of generic scales. These scales are in principle suitable for use with any racial or ethnic group. They are the scales which researchers might employ when there is no known existing measure for a particular racial/ethnic group. There are 17 of these scales. Six of these scales measure intra-group phenomena focusing on ethnic identity and acculturation. Eleven scales measure inter-group racial phenomena focusing on issues ranging from attitudes toward diversity to racial attitudes/prejudice and cultural identification.

Chapter 6 is, clearly, an aspiration on our part. It focuses on Native Americans and has but one entry. We are certain that other scales exist, but we do not as yet have them. Still, scales assessing the perceptions and attitudes of Native Americans toward themselves as well as others are important. We, of course, view this as an area in great need of attention but one which, again, also presents tremendous opportunities for those who might construct such scales.

Finally, we have included an appendix listing measures for potential use across all racial/ethnic groups. We have neither reproduced the actual scales here, nor have we reviewed them for their psychometrics properties. Instead, we have merely listed them so that readers would be made aware of their existence and possible availability for use. At present, those wishing to use them will have to contact the authors to obtain the actual instrument and permission to use it.

Rationale for Selection of These Scales

The instruments were selected following a thorough review of the social science literature; in particular, we utilized psychological abstracts. Indeed most of our instruments were located in journals such as *Journal of Personality and Social Psychology*, *Journal of Hispanic Studies*, *Journal of Social Psychology*, *Black Psychology*, *Journal of Applied Social Psychology*, and the *Journal of Personality Assessment*.

The study of race and inter-group relations in America has a long history, Dubois (1903), Drake and Cayton (1945), Clark and Clark (1947), Franklin (1968) and Bennett (1962). Most of this early work focused almost exclusively on Blacks and their perceptions about themselves, or on Whites' attitudes or their perceptions. Rarely did these early measures address other racial or ethnic groups such as Asian Americans or Hispanics. Moreover, with respect to the procurement of race-focused instruments, we were unsure how far to go back in our inclusion of scales. Clearly, some measures of inter-racial interaction are classics such as the Bogardus (1932) scale. While many classic instruments such as the Bogardus scale warrant mention, many are no longer being used by present day researchers. The reasons for their discontinuation vary; some simply address topic areas in which there is presently little interest. Indeed, since the 1920s the study and thinking of race and ethnic relations in America has changed considerably (Duckitt, 1992). Researchers are asking different questions about different racial and ethnic groups. Furthermore, racial and ethnic groups over the time come to think about themselves differently, e.g., Colored versus Negroes versus African Americans. It is also true that significant racial and ethnic demographic changes have brought about new configurations of inter-group interactions. There is also an increasing group of Americans who view themselves as multiracial. That is, they report belonging to more than one racial/ethnic group and are classified by the census as being of mixed race. This is a potentially exciting and fruitful area of intra- and inter-racial/ethnic research.

Each of these changes has important implications for research scholars. We have tried to make the best decisions as to which scales were simply most important to the topics of interest for researchers today. Making these decisions as one might imagine were difficult and frequently dependent upon the availability of a specific scale. Again, this collection of instruments is very much a work in progress. It is our intent to revise this volume over time and add more newly developed scales, as well as some important ones which we were unaware of or were unable to get permission to use at the time of the publication of this volume.

Pittsburgh, Pennsylvania

Larry E. Davis
Rafael J. Engel

Acknowledgments

Over the course of working on this volume we have become indebted to many. A number of former doctoral students, all of whom are now holders of PhDs, were of major assistance in bringing this project into fruition. First among these is Eric Hadley-Ives who was the first student to be involved in this project. He was my Research Assistant at Washington University in St. Louis. He assisted in gathering the very first instruments. He managed to identify and help collect over 100 such scales. Secondly the efforts of Bongjae Lee and Kyaien Conner, both former doctoral students here at the University of Pittsburgh, should be acknowledged for their diligent contributions. In many respects they picked up where Eric left off several years ago, by scouring through the social science literature identifying and collecting additional instruments.

Drs. Jayashree Mohanty and Latika Davis-Jones are also former doctoral students here at the University of Pittsburgh who assisted us in the identification and procurement of many instruments which were ultimately included in this volume. We want to point out that the process of obtaining permission to use the instruments included in this volume was no easy task – indeed identifying an instrument is one thing, locating its author and getting the permission to use it is another! Both Latika Davis-Jones and Jayashree Mohanty played very important roles in this very labor-intensive effort. In addition to identifying, collecting, and procuring permission to use instruments, they were also very involved in reviewing of actual manuscripts in which the scales were imbedded. Each was also involved and contributed to the writing of early drafts of each of various sections. In particular, Jayashree was instrumental in assisting with the Asian and Hispanic sections, while Latika was similarly of assistance in helping to write the Generic, African American, and Caucasian sections. We also want to thank Rachelle Das, a Master's student, for her assistance. She was dutiful in reviewing all areas of the project as well as locating still more instruments and asking for permission to use them.

After her graduation Latika Davis-Jones became what was essentially the Project Manager for this effort – keeping up with all the new and old scales as well as all the many people who were or had been involved. Finally, we want to thank Nigel Smith, a Master's student, for assisting Latika with our final push to get this project done. And we want to thank Emily Penrose-McLaughlin whose secretarial talents and skills were invaluable in our efforts to bring the project to a close. Without the contributions of each of these individuals this project would still be years in "arriving".

References

Bennett, L. (1962). *Before the Mayflower: A history of Black Americans*. Chicago: Johnson.

Bogardus, E. S. (1932–1933). A social distance scale. *Journal of Sociology and Social Research, 17*, 165–271.

Clark, K. B. & Clark, M. P. (1947). Racist identification and preference in Negro Children. In T. Newcords & E. Hartley (Eds.), *Readings in soul psychology*. New York: Holt, Rinehart and Winston.

Drake, St. C. & Cayton, H. R. (1945). *Black metropolis: A study of Negro life in a Northern City*. New York: Harcourt, Brace and Jovanovich.

Dubois, W. E. B. (1903). *The souls of black folk: Essays and sketches*. Chicago: McClung.

Duckitt, J. (1992). *The social psychology of prejudice*. New York: Praeger.

Franklin, J. H. (1968). Introduction: Color and race in the modern world. In J. H. Franklin (Ed.), *Color of race* (p. vii). Boston: Houghton Mifflin Academy of Arts and Sciences.

Hurh, W. M. (1998). *Majority Americans' perceptions of Koreans in the United States: Implications of ethnic images and stereotypes. The Korean Americans*. Westport, CT: Greenwood Press.

Jones, R. L. (Ed.). (1996). *Handbook of tests and measurements for black populations* (Vol. 1 & 2). Hampton, VA: Cobb Henry Publishers.

Robinson, J. P. & Shaver, P. (1969). *Measures of social psychological attitudes*. Ann Arbor, MI: University of Michigan, Survey Research Center Institute for Social Research.

U.S. Census Bureau. (2008). *2006–2008 American Community Survey 3-year estimates*. http://factfinder.census.gov

Contents

Chapter 1
Asian Americans

Overview

Asian Americans are now the third largest minority group, numbering approximately 14 million of the US population in 2009 (U.S. Census Bureau, 2009). Over a quarter of all foreign-born persons in America are from Asia (Reeves & Bennett, 2003). While the term "Asian Americans" has been used to classify a single racial group, it includes members of many ethnic groups with different languages, cultures, values, and length of historical experiences in the United States. Some Asian groups, such as Chinese and Japanese Americans, have been in the United States for many generations with some of the earliest immigrants coming around the middle of the nineteenth century (Uba, 1994). Other groups, such as the Hmong, Vietnamese, Laotians, and Cambodians, are rather recent immigrants. The five largest Asian groups, Chinese, Asian Indian, Filipino, Vietnamese, and Korean, comprise 80% of the Asian population (U.S. Census Bureau, 2004). Overall, the median age of the Asian American population is slightly younger than the general population (35.7 years vs. 36.8 years) (U.S. Census Bureau, 2009).

Less research has been done on mental health and psychological functioning of Asian Americans in comparison to other ethnic groups. Researchers have rarely studied between-group or within-group differences among Asian Americans. Most studies have focused on differences between Asian Americans and Euro-Americans, while fewer studies have examined differences between Asian Americans and other minority groups of color. However, less is known about Asian American experiences of prejudice and discrimination in the majority society. Further, compared to other minority groups, the "model minority" image of Asian Americans has resulted in few efforts to assess or conduct applied research with this group (Uba, 1994).

Asian Americans are frequently viewed as the model minority group. But they, like other minorities of color, commonly experience racism, discrimination, and intra-/inter-group conflicts. Also, like other minority groups for whom many of their members are comparatively recent arrivals, they are in various stages of ethnic acculturation. Each of these factors suggests an increasing need for solid methods of psycho-social measurement.

L.E. Davis, R.J. Engel, *Measuring Race and Ethnicity*,

DOI 10.1007/978-1-4419-6697-1_1, © Springer Science+Business Media, LLC 2011

In this chapter, we will review measures of intra-racial phenomena such as racial identity and acculturation and inter-racial phenomena of racial prejudice and conflict among Asian Americans. There are eight scales reviewed in this chapter.

References

Pallasana, R. B. (2008, March). *Asian Americans overview, encyclopedia of social work* (20th ed., Vol. 1, pp. 153–160). Oxford: NASW Press/Oxford University Press.

Reeves, T., & Bennett, C. (2003) The Asian and Pacific Islanders population in the United States, March 2002 (Current Population Reports, pp. 20–540). Washington, DC: U.S. Census Bureau. U.S. Census Bureau, 2004.

Uba, L. (1994). *Asian Americans: Personality, patterns, identity, and mental health.* New York: Guilford Press.

U.S. Census Bureau. (2004). *American Community Survey*, Selected Population Profiles, S021.

U.S. Census Bureau. (2009). *2009 American Community Survey 1-year estimates.* http://factfinder.census.gov

Citations

Reeves and Bennett (2003)
Uba (1994)
U.S. Census Bureau (2004)
U.S. Census Bureau (2009)

Acculturation Scales

The Suinn-Lew Asian Self-Identity Acculturation (Suinn, Rickard-Figueroa, Lew, & Vigil, 1987)

The Suinn-Lew Asian Self-Identity Acculturation (SL-ASIA) measures six aspects of acculturation: language, identity, friendships, behaviors, generational/geographic background, and attitudes.

Description: The SL-ASIA is a 21-item multiple choice questionnaire. The scale includes six topics: language (items 1, 2, 17, 18), identity (items 3, 4, 5, 20), friendships (items 6, 7, 8, 9), behaviors (items 10, 11, 15, 16, 21), generational/geographic background (items 12, 13, 14), and attitudes (item 19). Each item is measured on a 5-point Likert scale from equivalent to a highly Asian response (1) to equivalent to a highly Western response (5). The total scale score is obtained by summing all responses and dividing by the number of items answered. Scores range from an indication of low acculturation or high Asian identity (1) to an indication of high acculturation or high Western identity (5); a score of 3 indicates biculturalism. The SL-ASIA is a self-administered questionnaire. The scale language is designed to be used with respondents having different Asian backgrounds.

Sample: The initial validation study included 82 Asian-American university students. The average age of the participants was 19 and nearly two-thirds (54) were females.

Reliability: Cronbach's alpha was .88.

Validity: Construct validity was established using generational level, length of residence, and self-identification. Mean scores were statistically significantly different for each generational level with scores increasing as generation in the United States increased; for example, the average score for first-generation respondents was 2.96, 3.78 for third-generation respondents, and 3.85 for fifth-generation respondents. Mean scores were also positively related to length of residence in the United States and self-identification.

Comments: The SL-ASIA has demonstrated reliability and validity. Subsequent research (e.g., Abe-Kim, Okazaki, & Goto, 2001; Chen & Kennedy, 2005; Cote & Bornstein, 2000; Johnson, Wall, Guanipa, Terry-Guyer, & Velasquez, 2002; Ownbey & Horridge, 1998; Suinn, Ahuna, & Khoo, 1992) has shown similar results with alpha coefficients ranging from .68 with Southeast Asian refugees (Lese & Robbins, 1994) to .92 with a Korean-American community sample (Kim & Chan, 2004). Test–retest reliabilities with an average of 87.6 days (SD = 47.0) between administrations was excellent (*r* –.92; Johnson, Wall, Guanipa, Terry-Guyer, & Velasquez, 2002). Additional studies support the scale's validity (Abe-Kim et al., 2001; Ownbey & Horridge, 1998; Suinn et al., 1992). The scale has been used both as a unidimensional scale (total score) and as a multidimensional scale (using categories of Asian Identity, Western Identity, and Bicultural).

Location: Suinn, R., Rickard-Figueroa, K., Lew, S., & Vigil, P. (1987). The Suinn-Lew Asian self-identify acculturation scale: An initial report. *Educational and Psychological Measurement, 47,* 401–407.

Selected Publications

Abe-Kim, J., Okazaki, S., & Goto, S. G. (2001). Unidimensional versus multidimensional approaches to the assessment of acculturation for Asian American populations. *Cultural Diversity and Ethnic Minority Psychology, 7,* 232–246.

Chen, J.-L., & Kennedy, C. (2005). Factors associated with obesity in Chinese-American children, *Pediatric Nursing, 31,* 110–115.

Cote, L. R., & Bornstein, M. H. (2000). Social and didactic parenting behaviors and beliefs among Japanese American and South American mothers of infants. *Infancy, 1,* 363–374.

Johnson, M. L., Wall, T. L., Guanipa, C., Terry-Guyer, L., & Velasquez, R. J. (2002). The psychometric properties of the orthogonal cultural identification scale in Asian Americans. *Journal of Multicultural Counseling and Development, 30,* 181–191.

Kim, J., & Chan, M. M. (2004). Acculturation and dietary habits of Korean Americans. *British Journal of Nutrition, 91,* 469–478.

Lese, K. P., & Robbins, S. B. (1994). Relationship between goal attributes and the academic acheivement of Southeast Asian adolescent refugees. *Journal of Counseling Psychology, 41*, 45–52.
Ownbey, S. F., & Horridge, P. E. (1998). The Suinn-Lew Asian self-identify acculturation scale: Test with a non-student, Asian American sample. *Social Behavior and Personality, 26*, 57–68.
Suinn, R. M., Ahuna, C., & Khoo, G. (1992). The Suinn-Lew Asian self-identity acculturation scale: Concurrent and factorial validation. *Educational and Psychological Measurement, 52*, 1041–1046.

Suinn-Lew Asian Self-Identity Acculturation (SL-ASIA) Scale

Instructions: The questions which follow are for the purpose of collecting information about your historical background as well as more recent behaviors which may be related to your cultural identity. Choose the one answer which best describes you.

Items 1–2: 1 = Asian only (for example, Chinese, Japanese, Korean, Vietnamese); 2 = Mostly Asian, some English; 3 = Asian and English about equally well (bilingual); 4 = Mostly English, some Asian; 5 = Only English

1. What language can you speak?
2. What language do you prefer?

Items 3–5: 1 = Oriental; 2 = Asian; 3 = Asian American; 4 = Chinese American, Japanese American, Korean American, etc.; 5 = American

3. How do you identify yourself?
4. Which identification does (did) your mother use?
5. Which identification does (did) your father use?

Items 6–9: 1 = Almost exclusively Asians, Asian Americans, Orientals; 2 = Mostly Asians, Asian Americans, Orientals; 3 = About equally Asian groups and Anglo groups; 4 = Mostly Anglos, Blacks, Hispanics, or other non-Asian ethnic groups; 5 = Almost exclusively Anglos, Blacks, Hispanics, or other non-Asian ethnic groups

6. What was the ethnic origin of the friends and peers you had, as a child up to age 6?
7. What was the ethnic origin of the friends and peers you had, as a child from age 6 to 18?
8. Whom do you now associate with in the community?

9. If you could pick, whom would you prefer to associate with in the community?

Items 10–11: 1 = Only Asian music (for example, Chinese, Japanese, Korean, Vietnamese); 2 = Mostly Asian, 3 = Equally Asian and English; 4 = Mostly English; 5 = English only

10. What is your music preference?
11. What is your movie preference?

Item 12: 1 = First generation = I was born in Asia or country other than United States; 2 = Second generation = I was born in United States, either parent was born in Asia or country other than United States, 3 = Third generation = I was born in United States, both parents were born in United States, and all grandparents born in Asia or country other than United States; 4 = Fourth generation = I was born in United States, both parents were born in United States, and at least one grandparent born in Asia or country other than United States and one grandparent born in United States; 5 = Fifth generation = I was born in United States, both parents were born in United States, and all grandparents also born in United States; 6 = Don't know what generation best fits since I lack some information

12. What generation are you? (Circle the generation that best applies to you.)

Item 13: 1 = In Asia only; 2 = Mostly in Asia, some in United States; 3 = Equally in Asia and United States; 4 = Mostly in United States, some in Asia; 5 = In United States only

13. Where were you raised?

Item 14: 1 = Raised 1 year or more in Asia; 2 = Lived for less than 1 year in Asia; 3 = Occasional visits to Asia; 4 = Occasional communications (letters, phone calls, etc.) with people in Asia; 5 = No exposure or communications with people in Asia

14. What contact have you had with Asia?

Items 15–16: 1 = Exclusively Asian food; 2 = Mostly Asian food, some American; 3 = About equally Asian and American; 4 = Mostly American food; 5 = Exclusively American food

15. What is your food preference at home?
16. What is your food preference in restaurants?

Items 17–18: 1 = Only in an Asian language; 2 = An Asian language better than English; 3 = Both Asian and English equally well; 4 = English better than an Asian language; 5 = Only English

17. Do you read
18. Do you write

Item 19: 1 = Extremely proud; 2 = Moderately proud; 3 = Little proud; 4 = No pride but do not feel negative toward group; 5 = No pride but do feel negative toward group

19. If you consider yourself a member of the Asian group (Oriental, Asian, Asian American, Chinese American, etc., whatever term you prefer), how much pride do you have in this group?

Item 20: 1 = Very Asian; 2 = Mostly Asian; 3 = Bicultural; 4 = Mostly westernized; 5 = Very westernized

20. How would you rate yourself?

Item 21: 1 = Nearly all; 2 = Most of them; 3 = Some of them; 4 = A few of them; 5 = None at all

21. Do you participate in Asian occasion, holidays, traditions, etc?

The Acculturation Scale for Vietnamese Adolescents (Nguyen & Von Eye, 2002)

The Acculturation Scale for Vietnamese Adolescents (ASVA) is a bidimensional scale measuring traditional attitudes, behaviors, and values across two dimensions.

Description: The revised ASVA consists of 50 items divided into two separate subscales: Involvement in Vietnamese Culture (IVN) and Involvement in American Culture (IUS). Each question asked on the IVN subscale is paired with a similar question on the IUS subscale (e.g., IVN: How often do you eat Vietnamese food? IUS: How often do you eat American food?) Both subscales contain 25 items and include statements about attitudes, behaviors, and values related to four life domains. These domains are as follows: Everyday Lifestyles, Group Interactions, Family Orientation, and Global Involvement. The Everyday Lifestyles domain includes eight items in each subscale (IVN: 5, 14, 32, 36, 39, 45, 48, 49; IUS: 3, 18, 25, 33, 34, 37, 40, 43) and assesses preferences for and participation in various cultural aspects of one's daily life. The Group Interactions domain includes seven items in each subscale (IVN: 21, 28, 30, 35, 41, 42, 44; IUS: 9, 10, 15, 38, 46, 47, 50) that measure the extent of one's interpersonal relationships, participation in gatherings, and level of comfort with other Vietnamese and/or Americans. There are seven items in each subscale that comprise the Family Orientation domain (IVN: 4, 8, 20, 22, 26, 27, 31; IUS: 2, 6, 7, 11, 17, 23, 29); these items measure the respondent's sense of collective values and gender roles common in traditional Vietnamese families and the respondent's sense of individualistic values and gender roles common among US families. The Global Involvement domain includes three items in each subscale (IVN: 1, 19, 24; IUS: 12, 13, 16) and is used to assess the overall sense of identification with the Vietnamese and/or American culture. A 5-point Likert scale is used for each item. Respondents are asked the extent they agree with each statement ranging from *strongly disagree* (1) to *strongly agree* (5) or engage in the behavior ranging from *never* (1) to *always* (5). Scores are computed for the IVN and IUS subscales by adding all responses in each subscale. The total scores for the IVN and IUS subscales range from 25 to 125. A high score on the IVN suggests high involvement with Vietnamese culture while a low score suggests low involvement with Vietnamese culture. Similarly, a high score on the IUS suggests high involvement with American culture and a low score suggests low involvement with American culture. Distinct cut-off points designating a high versus a low score were not provided. The scale is self-administered.

Sample: The validation sample consisted of 191 Vietnamese youth in grades 6 through 12. The average age was 15 years and ranged from 10 to 23; 56% of the participants were male. Most students (80%) were born in Vietnam and 19% were born in the United States. The average length of residence in the United States was 6 years.

Reliability: Coefficient alpha was .89 for the IVN subscale and .88 for the IUS subscale. Coefficient alpha for the life domains in the IVN and IUS subscales were .81/.85 (Group Interactions), .82/.77 (Everyday Lifestyles), .72/.49 (Family Orientation), and .63/.53 (Global Involvement).

Validity: The scale demonstrates concurrent validity. The IVN subscale was correlated in the expected directions with measures of the Vietnamese language ($r = .58$), overall involvement in Vietnamese life ($r = .52$), and overall importance of Vietnamese culture ($r = .41$) as well as years of US education ($r = -.48$), years of residence in the United States ($r = -.50$), age when first entered the United States ($r = .42$) and Vietnam as one's birthplace ($r = .36$). Similarly, the IUS was correlated in the expected directions with English language ($r = .60$), length of residence in the United States ($r = .57$), years of education in the United States ($r = .54$), preference for American ways ($r = .52$), age when first entered the United States ($r = -.39$), and overall involvement in United States ($r = .40$). Confirmatory factor analysis retained the four life domains for each subscale providing factorial validity.

Comments: This scale measures level of acculturation among Vietnamese adolescents. Overall, the scale demonstrated adequate to good internal consistency. Confirmatory factor analysis supported ASVA as a bidimensional scale for Vietnamese adolescents. The scale has been adapted for use with Chinese American adolescents with evidence of reliability and convergent validity (Juang & Nguyen, 2009).

Location: Nguyen, H. H., & von Eye, A. (2002). The Acculturation Scale for Vietnamese Adolescents (ASVA): A bidimensional perspective. *International Journal of Behavioral Development, 26*, 202–213.

Selected Publications

Juang, L. P., & Nguyen, H. H. (2009). Misconduct among Chinese American adolescents: The role of acculturation, family obligation, and autonomy expectations. *Journal of Cross-Cultural Psychology, 40*, 649–666.

The Acculturation Scale for Vietnamese Adolescents (Revised)

Below are statements about the Vietnamese and American culture. Please tell *us how strongly you agree or disagree* with each statement. There are no right or wrong/good or bad answers. We just want to know what you think. Use the following scale to circle the number that best applies to you. Answer all the items.

Items 1–32: 1 = Strongly disagree; 2 = Disagree; 3 = Neither agree or disagree; 4 = Agree; 5 = Strongly agree

1. I would like to retain (or keep) the Vietnamese way of life.
2. It is alright for boys/girls to choose their own career.
3. I want to speak English at home.
4. Children should follow their parents' wishes about dating (when and whom to date).
5. I like to eat Vietnamese food.
6. It is okay to question parents' authority/judgment/decisions.
7. I believe that I should do what is best for me.
8. Children should follow their parents' wishes about choosing a career.
9. Most of my closest friends are Americans
10. I feel at ease with American people.
11. Family matters should be handled democratically – where kids can also have a say.
12. As far as behaviors and values, I am "American."
13. I would like to adopt or take up the American way of life.
14. My room is decorated in Vietnamese style.
15. I enjoy going to American gatherings/parties.
16. It is important to me to incorporate American values.
17. I think that youthfulness in our society should be greatly valued.
18. I like to eat American food.

19. It is important to me to preserve my Vietnamese heritage.
20. Grandparents should have more influence than parents in the family.
21. I enjoy going to Vietnamese gatherings/parties.
22. Children should follow their parents' wishes about marriage (when and whom to marry).
23. Girls over the age of 18 should be allowed to move away from home to go to college and/or to take a job.
24. As far as behaviors and values, I am "Vietnamese."
25. My room is decorated in American style.
26. Parents always know what is best.
27. I believe that my actions should be based mainly on the well-being of the family.
28. Most of my closest friends are Vietnamese.
29. When a boy/girl reaches the age of 16, it is alright for him/her to date.
30. I feel at ease with Vietnamese people.
31. The eldest girl in the family should help her family take care of the house and the younger children whether she wants to or not.
32. I want to speak Vietnamese at home.

Items 33–50: 1 = Never; 2 = Rarely; 3 = Sometimes; 4 = Often; 5 = Always

33. How often do you listen to American music?
34. How often do you watch American movies or TV programs
35. How often do you go to Vietnamese gatherings/parties?
36. How often you eat Vietnamese food?
37. How often do you speak English?
38. How often do you participate in American groups (sports, hobbies, clubs, etc.)?
39. How often do you read Vietnamese newspapers or magazines?
40. How often do you eat American food?
41. How often do you interact with Vietnamese people?
42. How often do you hang out with Vietnamese friends?
43. How often do you read American newspapers and magazines?
44. How often do you participate in Vietnamese groups (sports, hobbies, clubs, etc.).
45. How often do you speak the Vietnamese language?
46. How often do you interact with American people?
47. How often do you go to American gatherings/parties?
48. How often do you listen to Vietnamese music?
49. How often do you watch Vietnamese movies or TV programs?
50. How often do you hang out with American friends?

Acculturation Scale for Southeast Asians (Anderson et al., 1993)

The Acculturation Scale for Southeast Asians (ASSA) measures language, social contacts, and food aspects of acculturation.

Description: The ASSA scale has 13 items. Ten items measure language proficiency: Four items (1–4) assess proficiency in English and are rated on a 4-point scale (1 = *very well* to 4 = *not at all*); three items (5–7) measure proficiency in language of origin and are rated on a 4-point scale (1 = *very well* to 4 = *not at all*); and three items (8–10) measure choice of language with social networks and are rated on a 5-point scale (1 = *only language of origin* to 5 = *only English*). Two items measure frequency of contact with friends (11) and neighbors (12) and are rated on a 3-point scale (1 = *from mostly origin* to 3 = *mostly American*). Item 13 assesses food preference on a 5-point scale (1 = *only origin* to 5 = *only American*). Factor analysis produced three factors: English proficiency factor (four items: 1–4), language, social, and food preference factor (LSF; six items: 8–13), and language of origin proficiency factor (three items: 5–7). For English proficiency, the score ranges from 4 to 16 and for proficiency in the language of origin, the score ranges from 3 to 12, with a higher score indicating higher proficiency. For social and food preference, the score ranges from 7.76 to 28.24 with a lower score indicating more cultural involvement with culture of origin and a higher score indicating more involvement with American culture. The authors derived two acculturation subscales: language proficiency (items 1–7) and preference factor (8–13). Participants can be classified using median scores into four groups: (1) low on both languages; (2) low on English but high on language of origin; (3) high on both languages; and (4) high on English, but low on language of origin. Respondents are interviewed.

Sample: The scale was developed and validated with 381 Cambodian, 250 Laotian, and 395 Vietnamese respondents. Nearly 70% of the subjects were male; the subject ages ranged from 35.5 to 41.0 years and the subjects had spent 5.4–7.9 years in the United States. The percentage of lifetime in the United States (calculated as number of years in United States divided by age) ranged from 17.8 to 24.7 years. The level of education for the sample ranged from 0 years of formal education to 21 years of formal education. However, the average number of years of formal education for the entire sample fell below 5 years. Vietnamese subjects were more highly educated than Cambodian and Laotian subjects. Females had less education than males.

Reliability: The alpha coefficients for the combined sample are English proficiency, 98; proficiency in the language of origin, 81; language, social, and food scale (LSF), 79. Within each ethnic group, alpha coefficients for English proficiency were .98 and higher. The alpha coefficients for language proficiency were .81 (Cambodians), .77 (Laotians), and .94 (Vietnamese). The alpha coefficients for the LSF factor were .76 (Cambodians), .81 (Laotians), and .84 (Vietnamese).

Validity: There is evidence to support the construct validity of the scale. Scores on the social and food preference scale were correlated in the expected directions for current age (Cambodians: $r = -.55$; Laotians: $r = -.38$; Vietnamese: $r = -.34$), length of residency in the United States (.32, .57, .24), years of education (.67, .53, .18), percent of lifetime in the United States (.60, .65, .41), and age when first entered the United States (–.60, –.51, –.40).

Comments: There is evidence to support the psychometric properties of the scale. Reliability of the total scale score has been reported in other studies (Kim & Sarna, 2001; Maxwell, Bastani, & Warda, 1998; Ngo-Metzger, Sorkin, Mangione, Gandek, & Hays, 2008). The scoring of the scale is not clear. The scale has been adapted for Korean Americans (Kim & Sarna, 2001; Maxwell et al., 1998) and older Chinese Americans (Lam, Pacala, & Smith, 1997).

Location: Anderson, J., Moeschberger, M., Chen, M. S., Kunn, P., Wewers, M. E., & Guthrie, R. (1993). An acculturation scale for Southeast Asians. *Social Psychiatry and Psychiatric Epidemiology*, *28*, 134–141.

Selected Publications

Kim, Y. H., & Sarna, L. (2001). An intervention to increase mammography use by Korean American women. *Oncology Nursing Forum, 31,* 105–110.

Lam, R. E., Pacala, J. T., & Smith, S. L. (1997). Factors related to depressive symptoms in an elderly Chinese American sample. *Clinical Gerontologist, 17,* 57–70.

Maxwell, A. E., Bastani, R., & Warda, U. S. (1998). Mammography utilization and related attitudes among Korean–American women. *Women and Health, 27,* 89–107.

Ngo-Metzger, Q., Sorkin, D. H., Mangione, C. M., Gandek, B., & Hays, R. D. (2008). Evaluating the SF-36 health survey (version 2) in older Vietnamese Americans. *Journal of Aging and Health, 20,* 420–436.

Acculturation Scale for Southeast Asians

Items 1–7: 1 = Very well; 2 = Pretty well; 3 = Not too well; 4 = Not at all

Proficiency in English language

1. Understand spoken English
2. Speak
3. Read
4. Write

Proficiency in language of origin

5. Speak
6. Read
7. Write

Items 8–10: 1 = Only origin; 2 = Mostly origin; 3 = Origin and English equally; 4 = Mostly English; 5 = Only English
Language usually used

8. With most of your friends
9. With most of your neighbors
10. At family gatherings

Items 11–12: 1 = Mostly origin; 2 = Equally origin and American; 3 = Mostly American
People

11. Close personal friends
12. Nearby neighbors

Item 13: 1 = Only origin; 2 = Mostly origin; 3 = Origin and American equally; 4 = Mostly American; 5 = Only American
Food

13. Food preferences

General Ethnicity Questionnaire (Tsai, Ying, & Lee, 2000)

General Ethnicity Questionnaire (GEQ) measures language and cultural aspects of acculturation.

Description: The GEQ may be used as both a unidimensional and bidimensional measure of acculturation as there are separate Chinese (GEQC) and American (GEQA) versions differing only in their cultural reference. Each scale includes the same 38 items and the GEQC includes an additional item. Respondents rate the extent of their agreement with statements about their cultural orientation on a 5-point scale (1 = *strongly disagree* to 5 = *strongly agree*) with higher numbers indicating a stronger cultural orientation. Items measuring language proficiency are rated on a 5-point scale (1 = *very much* to 5 = *not at all*), and these are reverse coded such that higher number reflects greater endorsement. Based on findings from a factor analysis, the authors concluded that the GEQC and GEQA consist of six dimensions. The GEQC and the GEQA are scored by summing item responses and dividing by the number of questions answered. Total scores on the GEQC and GEQA range from 38 to 190 if all questions are answered. Higher scores on the GEQC suggest a stronger identification with Chinese culture while lower scores suggest weaker identification with Chinese culture. The interpretation of scores on the GEQA is comparable with the frame of reference being American culture; a high score on the GEQA suggests that the respondent identifies more with American culture, while a low score suggests that the respondent identifies less with American culture. Use of the dimension scores was estimated by computing *z*-scores from regressions. Cut-off scores to designate between a high or low score were not specified for either the GEQC or the GEQA. The scale is self-administered.

Sample: The scales were evaluated with a sample of 353 Chinese-American college students. The sample was almost equally divided by gender and on an average was 20.23 years old. Participants were divided into three groups for analysis: (1) Chinese Americans born in the United States ($n = 122$); (2) "early immigrants" who arrived in the United States by age 12 ($n = 119$); and (3) "recent immigrants" who arrived in the United States after age 12 ($n = 112$).

Reliability: Cronbach's alphas for the GEQC and GEQA were .92. The 1-month test–retest reliability was .62 for the GEQC and .57 for the GEQA.

Validity: Convergent validity was established by correlating the average cultural orientation score with age of arrival (GEQC: $r = .56$; GEQA: $r = -.67$), generational status (GEQC: $r = -.50$; GEQA: $r = .58$), and length of residence in the United States (GEQC: $r = -.60$; GEQA: $r = .64$). The three subgroups' mean scores statistically significantly differed in the expected directions for Chinese language use and proficiency, affiliation with Chinese people, participation in Chinese-related activities, exposure to Chinese culture, English language use and proficiency, affiliation with American people, participation in American activities, participation in American culture, media preferences, and preferences for American food.

Comments: The scale assesses multiple cultural domains, supports both unidimensional and bidimensional models of acculturation, and has been shown to be reliable and valid with Chinese-American college students (e.g., Tsai, Semeonova, & Watanabe, 2004; Tsai, Ying, & Lee, 2001). Test–retest reliabilities were relatively low for a week period and given that the construct should be stable in a week period. The bidimensional structure has been supported in other research (Kang, 2006; Ying & Han, 2008). Some studies use factor analysis and then drop items (Ying & Han, 2008; Ying, Han, & Wong, 2008). The scale has been adapted to other ethnic groups including Vietnamese Americans, Cambodian Americans, Hmong Americans, and Korean Americans (Tsai-Chae & Nagata, 2008; Tsai, Mortensen, Wong, & Hess, 2002; Ying & Han, 2008), Asians in general (Kang, 2006), Latinos (Tsai, Pole, Levenson, & Munoz, 2003), and Caucasians (Tsai, Chentsova-Dutton, Freire-Bebeau, & Przymus, 2002). Reliability has been found with adults (Tsai-Chae & Nagata, 2008) and high-school students (Ying et al., 2008).

Location: Tsai, J. L., Ying, Y., & Lee, P. A. (2000). The meaning of "being Chinese" and "being American": Variation among Chinese American young adults. *Journal of Cross-Cultural Psychology, 31*, 302–332.

Selected Publications

Kang, S-M. (2006). Measurement of acculturation, scale formats, and language competence: Their implications for adjustment. *Journal of Cross-Cultural Psychology, 37*, 669–693.

Tsai, J. L., Mortensen, H., Wong, Y., & Hess, D. (2002). What does "Being American" mean? A comparison of Asian American and European American young adults. *Cultural Diversity and Ethnic Minority Psychology, 8*, 257–273.
Tsai, J. L., Pole, N., Levenson, R. W., & Munoz, R. F. (2003). The effects of depression on the emotional responses of Spanish-Speaking Latinos. *Cultural Diversity and Ethnic Minority Psychology, 9*, 49–63.
Tsai, J. L., Simeonova, D. I., & Watanabe, J. T. (2004). Somatic and social: Chinese Americans talk about emotion. *Personality and Social Psychology Bulletin, 30*, 1226–1238.
Tsai, J. L., Ying, Y., & Lee, P. A. (2001). Cultural predictors of self-esteem: A study of Chinese American female and male young adults. *Cultural Diversity and Ethnic Minority Psychology, 7*, 284–297.
Tsai, J. L., Chentsova-Dutton, Y., Freire-Bebeau, L., & Przymus, D. E. (2002). Emotional expression and physiology in European Americans and Hmong Americans. *Emotion, 2*, 380–397.
Tsai-Chae, A. H., & Nagata, D. K. (2008). Asian values and perceptions of intergenerational family conflict among Asian American students. *Cultural Diversity and Ethnic Minority Psychology, 14*, 205–314.
Ying, Y., & Han, M. (2008). Cultural orientation in Southeast Asian American young adults. *Cultural Diversity and Ethnic Minority Psychology, 14*, 29–37.
Ying, Y., Han, M., & Wong, S. L. (2008). Cultural orientation in Asian American adolescents: Variation by age and ethnic density. *Youth and Society, 4*, 507–523.

General Ethnicity Questionnaire (Abridged Versions)

Chinese Version

Please use the following scale to indicate how much you agree with the following statements. Circle your response.

1 = Strongly disagree; 2 = Disagree; 3 = Neutral; 4 = Agree; 5 = Strongly agree

1. I was raised in a way that was Chinese.
2. When I was growing up, I was exposed to Chinese culture.
3. Now, I am exposed to Chinese culture.
4. Compared to how much I negatively criticize other cultures, I criticize Chinese culture less.
5. I am embarrassed/ashamed of Chinese culture.
6. I am proud of Chinese culture.
7. Chinese culture has had a positive impact on my life.
8. I believe that my children should read, write, and speak Chinese.
9. I have a strong belief that my children should have Chinese names only.

10. I go to places where people are Chinese/Chinese Americans.
11. I am familiar with Chinese cultural practices and customs.
12. I relate to my partner or spouse in a way that is Chinese.
13. I admire people who are Chinese/Chinese American.
14. I would prefer to live in a Chinese/Chinese-American community.
15. I listen to Chinese music.
16. I perform Chinese dance.
17. I engage in Chinese forms of recreation.
18. I celebrate Chinese holidays.
19. At home, I eat Chinese food.
20. At restaurants, I eat Chinese food.
21. When I was a child, my friends were Chinese/Chinese American.
22. Now my friends are Chinese/Chinese America.
23. I wish to be accepted by Chinese/Chinese Americans.
24. The people I date are Chinese/Chinese American.
25. Overall, I am Chinese.

Please use the scale below to answer the following questions. Circle your response.

1 = Very much; 2 = Much; 3 = Somewhat; 4 = A little; 5 = Not at all

26. How much do you speak Chinese at home?
27. How much do you speak Chinese at school?
28. How much do you speak Chinese at work?
29. How much do you speak Chinese at prayer?
30. How much do you speak Chinese with friends?
31. How much do you view, read, or listen to Chinese on TV?
32. How much do you view, read, or listen to Chinese in film?
33. How much do you view, read, or listen to Chinese on the radio?
34. How much do you view, read, or listen to Chinese in literature?
35. How fluently do you speak Chinese?
36. How fluently do you read Chinese?
37. How fluently do you write Chinese?
38. How fluently do you understand Chinese?
39. Are you bilingual? (Please circle)

If yes, what language?

(1) ____________
(2) ____________American Version

Please use the following scale to indicate how much you agree with the following statements. Circle your response.

1 = Strongly disagree; 2 = Disagree; 3 = Neutral; 4 = Agree; 5 = Strongly agree

1. I was raised in a way that was American.
2. When I was growing up, I was exposed to American culture.
3. Now, I am exposed to American culture.
4. Compared to how much I negatively criticize other cultures, I criticize American culture less.
5. I am embarrassed/ashamed of American culture.
6. I am proud of American culture.
7. American culture has had a positive impact on my life.
8. I believe that my children should read, write, and speak English.
9. I have a strong belief that my children should have American names only.
10. I go to places where people are American.
11. I am familiar with American cultural practices and customs.
12. I relate to my partner or spouse in a way that is American.
13. I admire people who are American.
14. I would prefer to live in an American community.
15. I listen to American music.
16. I perform American dance.
17. I engage in American forms of recreation.
18. I celebrate American holidays.
19. At home, I eat American food.
20. At restaurants, I eat American food.
21. When I was a child, my friends were American.
22. Now, my friends are American.
23. I wish to be accepted by Americans.
24. The people I date are American.
25. Overall, I am American.

Please use the scale below to answer the following questions. Circle your response.

1 = Very much; 2 = Much; 3 = Somewhat; 4 = A little; 5 = Not at all

26. How much do you speak English at home?
27. How much do you speak English at school?
28. How much do you speak English at work?
29. How much to you speak English at prayer?
30. How much do you speak English with friends?
31. How much do you view, read, or listen to English on TV?
32. How much do you view, read, or listen to English in film?
33. How much do you view, read, or listen to English on the radio?
34. How much do you view, read, or listen to English in literature?
35. How fluently do you speak English?

36. How fluently do you read English?
37. How fluently do you write English?
38. How fluently do you understand English?

Intergenerational/Intercultural Conflict Scales

Intergenerational Congruence in Immigrant Families-Child Scale (Ying, Lee, & Tsai, 2004)

The Intergenerational Congruence in Immigration Families-Child Scale (ICIF-CS) measures the extent to which children of immigrants feel conflict with parents due to acculturation differences between parent and child. There is also a parent version of the scale reviewed in the next section.

Description: The ICIF-CS consists of eight items; seven items (items 1–7) assess the degree to which adult immigrant children agree with their parents on values and behaviors and item 8 measures overall satisfaction with the parent–child relationship. Items are answered with the either the father or mother as the referent. Item responses are coded on a 5-point Likert scale ranging from *strongly agree* (1) to *strongly disagree* (5). Scores for the ICIF-CS are obtained by summing the first seven items to yield an overall intergenerational congruence score with each parent. The eighth item is not included in the summed score because it is meant to be a stand-alone measure of satisfaction. Scores range from 7 to 49 with higher scores showing greater congruence between child and each parent. The scale is self-administered.

Sample: The original study sample consisted of 238 Chinese-American college students at a major public university in the western United States. All participants were children of immigrants; 46% of the participants were born in the United States and 54% were born outside the United States. The immigrant participants had lived in the United States for an average of 11.35 years. All participants were single and 52% were female. The respondents' average age was 19.83 years.

Reliability: The ICIF-CS had high internal consistency with a Cronbach's alpha of .85 for the items related to the father and .84 for the items related to the mother. The 1-month test–retest reliability estimates for the ICIF-CS (subsample $n = 51$) were .93 for the father items and .89 for the mother items.

Validity: A factor analysis for items 1 through 7 supported the unidimensional structure of the scale. Construct validity was evident as the ICIF-CS father total scale score was significantly related in the expected directions to Chinese language use ($r = .15$), Chinese cultural pride ($r = .24$), American affiliation ($r = -.13$), and American cultural activities ($r = -.17$). Similarly, the ICIF-CS mother total scale score was significantly related in the expected directions to Chinese affiliation ($r = .14$), Chinese cultural pride ($r = .21$) and endorsement of being Chinese ($r =.14$). The satisfaction with parent relationship items were also statistically significantly related to these constructs. Criterion validity was evaluated by correlating respondent scores on the Inventory of Parent and Peer Attachment parent attachment subscale with ICIF-CS father score ($r = .62$), ICIF-CS mother score ($r = .69$), satisfaction with father relationship ($r = .50$), and satisfaction with mother relationship ($r = .66$). Each of the first seven items were correlated with the satisfaction item demonstrating convergent validity.

Comments: The ICIF-CS is a unidimensional instrument that assesses intergenerational agreement; the factor structure has been replicated with a sample of Southeast Asian (Vietnamese, Cambodian, and Hmong) college students (Ying & Han, 2007). There is additional evidence of reliability and construct validity (Ying & Han, 2007). While the authors note the use of broad language to allow the scale to be applied to a variety of ethnic groups, we found psychometric studies of only Chinese Americans and Southeast Asian Americans.

Location: Ying, Y., Lee, P. A., & Tsai, J. L. (2004). Psychometric properties of the intergenerational congruence in immigrant families: Child scale in Chinese Americans. *Journal of Comparative Family Studies*, *35*, 91–103.

Selected Publications

Ying, Y., & Han, M. (2007). A test of the intergenerational congruence in immigrant families-child scale with Southeast Asian Americans. *Social Work Research, 31*, 35–43.

The Intergenerational Congruence in Immigrant Families: Child Scale

Response categories: 1 = Strongly disagree; 2 = Somewhat disagree; 3 = Neither agree nor disagree; 4 = Somewhat agree; 5 = Strongly agree

Father Items

1. My father and I agree on the aims, goals, and things believed to be important in life.
2. My father and I agree on friends.
3. My father and I agree on the amount of time we spend together.
4. My father and I agree on how we demonstrate our affection for each other.
5. My father and I generally talk things over together.
6. My father and I agree on how to behave in a predominantly American setting.
7. My father and I agree on how to behave in a predominantly Chinese setting.
8. I am satisfied with my relationship with father.

Mother Items

1. My mother and I agree on the aims, goals, and things believed to be important in life.
2. My mother and I agree on friends.
3. My mother and I agree on the amount of time we spend together.

4. My mother and I agree on how we demonstrate our affection for each other.
5. My mother and I generally talk things over together.
6. My mother and I agree on how to behave in a predominantly American setting.
7. My mother and I agree on how to behave in a predominantly Chinese setting.
8. I am satisfied with my relationship with mother.

Intergenerational Congruence in Immigrant Families-Parent Scale (Ying & Tracy, 2004)

The Intergenerational Congruence in Immigration Families-Parent Scale (ICIF-PS) measures the extent to which immigrant parents feel conflict with children due to acculturation differences between parent and child.

Description: The ICIF-PS consists of eight items; seven items (items 1–7) assess the degree to which immigrant parents agree with their children on values and behaviors and item 8 measures overall satisfaction with the parent–child relationship. The respondent chooses a child to be the referent. Item responses are coded on a 5-point Likert scale ranging from *strongly agree* (1) to *strongly disagree* (5). Scores for the ICIF-PS are obtained by summing the first seven items to yield an overall intergenerational congruence score. The eighth item is not included in the summed score and is intended as a stand-alone measure of intergenerational satisfaction. Scores range from 7 to 49 with higher scores showing greater congruence between child and each parent. The scale is self-administered.

Sample: The original study sample consisted of 787 Chinese-American immigrant parents; the sample was a subsample drawn from the Chinese American Psychiatric Epidemiology Study conducted in 1993 and 1994. Most participants were female (58%), married (86%), and employed (64%). Their average age was 46 years and they averaged 12.5 years of school. Nearly 60% of the participants responded to the scale with a son as the target.

Reliability: The ICIF-PS had high internal consistency with a Cronbach's alpha of .90.

Validity: A factor analysis for items 1 through 7 supported the unidimensional structure of the scale. Construct validity was evident as the ICIF-PS total scale score was statistically significantly related to greater satisfaction ($r = .07$) in the expected direction. Criterion validity was evaluated by correlating respondent problems with children with the ICIF-PS total score ($r = -.31$) and intergenerational satisfaction ($r = -.38$). Items 1–7 were correlated with the satisfaction item (ranging from $r = .42$ to $r = .52$) as was the total scale score ($r = .62$) providing evidence for convergent validity.

Comments: The ICIF-PS is a unidimensional instrument that assesses intergenerational agreement. There is evidence of reliability and validity. While the authors note the use of broad language to allow the scale to be applied to a variety of ethnic groups, we found psychometric studies of only Chinese Americans. The sample in this study was highly educated and may be unlike other samples. No analysis was conducted to determine if there were subgroup differences (e.g., gender of the parent; gender of the target child).

Location: Ying, Y., & Tracy, L. C. (2004). Psychometric properties of the intergenerational congruence in immigrant families-parent scale in Chinese Americans. *Social Work Research, 28*, 58–62.

Selected Publications

None

The Intergenerational Congruence in Immigrant Families: Parent Scale

These questions are about your relationship with your target child. Would you say

Response categories: 1 = Strongly disagree, 2 = Somewhat disagree, 3 = Neither agree nor disagree, 4 = Somewhat agree 5 = Strongly agree

1. My child and I agree on the aims, goals, and things believed to be important in life.
2. My child and I agree on friends.
3. My child and I agree on the amount of time spent together.
4. My child and I agree on how we demonstrate our affection for each other.
5. My child and I generally talk things over together.
6. My child and I agree on how we behave in a predominantly American setting.
7. My child and I agree on how we behave in a predominantly Chinese setting.
8. I am satisfied with my relationship with my child.

Asian American Family Conflicts Scale (Lee, Choe, Kim, & Ngo, 2000)

The Asian American Family Conflicts Scale measures Asian American family conflicts that arise from acculturation differences between late-adolescent and young adult children and their parents.

Description: The Asian American Family Conflicts Scale (FCS) includes 20 items drawn from 10 typical scenarios that cause conflict among Asian American families. The 10 items are written from the perspective of the child. The scale consists of two 10-item subscales: FCS-Likelihood (FCS-L) and FCS-Seriousness (FCS-S). For the FCS-L, respondents rate the likelihood of a conflict between the respondent and their parents occurring on a scale ranging from *almost never* (1) to *almost always* (5). The FCS-S subscale assesses how serious the conflict is on a scale ranging from *not at all* (1) to *extremely serious* (5). Scores on each subscale range from 10 to 50 with higher scores indicating a greater likelihood of a conflict occurring or the more serious the conflict. The scales are self-administered.

Sample: The initial psychometric study included three samples of Asian American college students. The first sample included 186 Asian American college students with different ethnic backgrounds. The sample included 99 males and 85 females and had an average age of 21.29 years. The second sample numbered 153 Asian American college students from a variety of ethnic backgrounds and different immigrant generations. Of these, 41 were males and 109 were females with an average age of 19.79 years. The third sample had 109 Asian American college students from different Asian backgrounds. The average age was 20.14 years. Forty-nine respondents were first-generation immigrants, 44 were second-generation, 12 were international, and 4 were third- or older generations.

Reliability: The Cronbach's alpha coefficients for FCS-Likelihood ranged from .84 to .89 and for FCS-Seriousness, .84 to .91 across the three samples. The test–retest correlations (sample 1) over the 3-week interval were .80 for FCS-L and .85 for FCS-S.

Validity: There is evidence of construct validity. The FCS-L and FCS-S scores for individual family situations were significantly correlated with the SAFE-Family ($r = .52$ and $r = -.53$) scale and the correlations were stronger than with the SAFE-Other ($r = .22$ and $r = -.32$), providing evidence of convergent validity. There is also evidence of concurrent validity. For Sample 2, the FCS-L was statistically significantly correlated in the expected directions with family income ($r = -.31$), father's educational level ($r = -.34$), participants' Asian orientation ($r = .22$), parents' Asian orientation ($r = .35$), and parents' Western orientation ($r = -.36$). FCS-S was positively correlated with participant's Western orientation ($r = .19$), and identification with non-Asians ($r = .24$). For Sample 3, the FCS-L was correlated with the Family Adaptation and Cohesions Evaluation Scales-II (FACES) Flexibility Scale ($r = -.38$), FACES-Cohesion Scale ($r = -.38$), Mother's Parent and Adolescent Communication Scale-Open (PAC) ($r = -.40$), Father's PAC-Open ($r = -.41$), Mother's PAC-Closed ($r = .42$) and Father's PAC-Closed ($r = .41$). Finally, from Sample 2, higher acculturated children with higher perceived acculturated parents were less likely to report family conflict than other parent–child interactions providing evidence of criterion validity. There is evidence that this outcome was due to acculturation differences and not generational differences. Additional evidence came from Sample 3. The authors used FACES to categorize respondents into four categories ranging from balanced families to unbalanced families. Mean FCS-L scores were linearly related to family type, with respondents having the lowest average FCS-L scores falling into the balanced family type and the highest average scores falling into the unbalanced family type.

Comments: There is evidence of reliability and ample evidence of the validity of the FCS-L scale in use with college-age and late-adolescent respondents. Similar findings of the scale's reliability have been reported for Asian-American college students (Lee & Liu, 2001; Lee, Su, & Yoshida, 2005), Hmong American college students (Su, Lee, & Vang, 2005) and Korean American college students (Ahn, Kim,

& Park, 2008). Several studies have computed an "intensity" score providing an overall score; this score is computed by averaging the item scores of the two scales (Ahn et al., 2008; Lee et al., 2005; Su et al., 2005). One study suggests their cultural equivalence with Hispanics and European Americans (Lee & Liu, 2001). All the reported studies have been with college students and therefore, there is a need for studies of other populations.

Location: Lee, R. M., Choe, J., Kim, G., & Ngo, V. (2000). Construction of the Asian American family conflict scale. *Journal of Counseling Psychology*, *47*, 211–222.

Selected Publications

Ahn, A. J., Kim, B. S. K., & Park, Y. S. (2008). Asian cultural values, gap, cognitive flexibility, coping strategies, and parent–child conflicts among Korean Americans. *Cultural Diversity and Ethnic Minority Psychology, 14,* 353–363.

Lee, R., & Liu, H. T. (2001). Coping with intergenerational family conflict: Comparison of Asian American, Hispanic, and European American college students. *Journal of Counseling Psychology, 48*, 410–419.

Lee, R. M., Su, J., & Yoshida, E. (2005). Coping with intergenerational family conflict among Asian American college students. *Journal of Counseling Psychology, 52*, 389–399.

Su, J., Lee, R., & Vang, S. (2005). Intergenerational family conflict and coping among Hmong American college students. *Journal of Counseling Psychology, 52*, 482–489.

Asian American Family Conflicts Scale

The following statements are parent–child situations that may occur in families. Consider how likely each situation occurs in your *present* relationship with your parents and how serious these conflicts are. Read each situation and answer the following questions using the following rating scales:

To each question, the respondents use the following two scales:

How likely is this situation to occur in your family? 1 = Almost never; 2 = Once in awhile; 3 = Sometimes; 4 = Often or frequently; 5 = Almost always

How serious a problem is this situation in your family? 1 = Not at all; 2 = Slightly; 3 = Moderately; 4 = Very much; 5 = Extremely

1. Your parents tell you what to do with your life, but you want to make your own decisions.
2. Your parents tell you that a social life is not important at this age, but you think that it is.
3. You have done well in school, but your parents' academic expectations always exceed your performance.

4. Your parents want you to sacrifice personal interests for the sake of the family, but you feel this is unfair.
5. Your parents always compare you to others, but you want them to accept you for being yourself.
6. Your parents argue that they show you love by housing, feeding, and educating you, but you wish they would show more physical and verbal signs of affection.
7. Your parents don't want you to bring shame upon the family, but you feel that your parents are too concerned with saving face.
8. Your parents expect you to behave like a proper Asian male or female, but you feel your parents are being too traditional.
9. You want to state your opinion, but your parents consider it to be disrespectful to talk back.
10. Your parents demand that you show respect for elders, but you believe in showing respect only if they deserve it.

Race-Related Stressor Scale for Asian American Veterans (Loo et al., 2001)

The Race-Related Stressor Scale (RRSS) was developed to measure negative race experiences of Asian American veterans who had served in the Vietnam War.

Description: The RRSS is a 33-item self-report questionnaire consisting of three subscales: Racial Prejudice and Stigmatization, Bicultural Identification and Conflict, and Racial Environment. The Racial and Prejudice Stigmatization subscale (19 items: 4, 7, 9, 10, 11 14, 15, 17, 18, 19, 20, 21, 22, 23, 29, 30, 31, 32, 33) measures perceptions of discrimination, harassment, belittling, stigmatization, and the like due to race; Bicultural Identification and Conflict (seven items: 3, 5, 13, 25, 26, 27, 28) measures conflicting feelings of identification with Vietnamese culture and identification with military enmity to the Vietnamese; and Racial Environment (seven items: 1, 2, 6, 8, 12, 16, 24) measures exposure to racial comments or behaviors. Each item has a 5-point, Likert response scale ranging from *never* (0) to *very frequently* (4). The total score ranges from 0 to 132; higher scores reflect more exposure to racism. Subscale scores are calculated by summing response items in the subscale and dividing by number of items answered. Subscale scores range from 0 to 4 with higher scores indicating stronger feelings of perceived negative raced-related experience.

Sample: The validation sample included 300 Asian American Vietnam veterans from a variety of ethnic backgrounds including Japanese-, Korean-, Chinese-, Filipino-, Okinawan-, Chamorro-, or Asian-mixed race participants. Their mean age was 55.

Reliability: The coefficient alpha for the entire RRSS was .97 and the coefficient alphas for the subscales were .97 (Racial Prejudice and Stigmatization),

.93 (Bicultural Identification and Conflict), and .93 (Racist Environment). The test–retest reliability conducted with a subsample was .85. Test–retest correlations for the subscales were .84 for Racial Prejudice and Stigmatization, .84 for Bicultural Identification and Conflict, and .69 for Racist Environment.

Validity: Construct validity was assessed using the Brief Symptom Inventory (BSI; a measure of generalized psychiatric symptoms), the Combat Exposure Scale (CES; measure of the degree of exposure to combat); Mississippi Scale for PTSD (MS), and military rank. Significant relations in the expected directions were found for the total scale score with the BSI ($r = .67$), CES ($r = .41$), MS ($r = .68$), and military rank ($r = -.37$). Similar relationships were found for the subscale scores with these constructs.

Comments: The RRSS was specifically designed to assess racism-related experiences among Asian Americans Vietnam veterans and therefore may not be applicable with other Asian Americans or with other experiences. The scale demonstrates good psychometric properties. There have been no factor analyses to support the subscale structure.

Location: Loo, C. M., Fairbank, J. A., Scurfield, R. M., Ruch, L. O., King, D. W., & Adams, L. J. (2001). Measuring exposure to racism: Development and validation of a Race-Related Stressor Scale (RRSS) for Asian American Vietnam veterans. *Psychological Assessment, 13*, 503–520.

Selected Publications

None

Race-Related Stressor Scale for Asian American Vietnam Veterans

Please answer the following questions about your experiences while you served in the Vietnam War or served in the military during the Vietnam War. These questions describe events that may have occurred in the field or in base camps or other rear areas. The term "military personnel" refers to American military personnel. The term "in Vietnam" refers to any duty on the ground, in the air over, or in the waters contiguous to South or North Vietnam or Cambodia, or in or over Laos. Please *circle the answer* that best describes your experiences.

Response categories: 0 = Never; 1 = Rarely; 2 = Sometimes; 3 = Frequently; 4 = Very frequently

In the military...

1. How often, if ever, did you *hear* military personnel describe Asian lives as having no value or lesser value than American lives?

2. Did you ever *observe* military personnel treat Asians as if their lives were of no value or of lesser value than while American lives?
3. How often, if ever, could you identify with the people or culture of Vietnam?
4. How often, if ever, were you concerned that other American soldiers might question your loyalty if you interacted with Vietnamese civilians?
5. As an American of Asian ancestry, did you ever feel a stronger identification with Vietnamese civilians than with American soldiers of White or Black ancestry?
6. How often, if ever, did military personnel refer to Asians as "gooks," "slant eyes," "slopes," or some other racially insulting or insensitive name?
7. Were you ever singled out for different or harsher treatment than persons of another race but of the same rank?
8. How often, if ever, did you hear military personnel express hatred toward Asians?
9. Were you ever pointed out as an example of what the enemy looked like?
10. Did other Americans ever keep their physical distance from you or tell you to get away from them because you were Asian?
11. Did other Americans ever say things that led you to believe that they thought you looked like a Vietnamese?
12. Did you ever observe Asian American military personnel being stared at in ways that non-Asian Americans were not?
13. How often, if ever, did you feel you were more like the Vietnamese than like the Americans?
14. Compared to persons of other races but of the same rank, were you ever ignored or treated disrespectfully?
15. How often, if ever, was your authority questioned for reasons you suspect had to do with your being Asian?
16. How often, if ever, did military personnel treat Asians as inferior?
17. How often, if ever, were you called a "gook," "slope," "slant eyes," "Jap," "kamikaze," "Chink," "boy," "pineapple," or "coconut head" in a way that felt hostile or insulting?
18. Did military personnel ever make racially insensitive remarks about your doing things like eating rice, using chopsticks, or squatting?
19. Did you ever feel like you "stood out" (in a negative way) or were looked at as if you did not belong there?
20. Were you ever in situations where you felt isolated because you were the only or one of few Asian Americans in your platoon or other small group?
21. How often, if ever, did other Americans treat you with racial hatred or hostility?

22. Were you ever denied access to certain areas or hassled before being given access to certain areas because you were Asian?
23. Did you ever feel like you did not really fit in with the rest of the Americans in your unit?
24. How often, if ever, did military personnel make insulting remarks about the South Vietnamese, related to their size, smell, intelligence, diet, or abilities?
25. How often, it ever, did a living Vietnamese *male* remind you of a family member, relative, or friend?
26. How often, if ever, did a *living* Vietnamese *woman or child* remind you of a family member, relative, or friend?
27. How often, if ever, did a *wounded or dead* Vietnamese *male* remind you of a family member, relative, or friend?
28. How often, if ever, did any *wounded or dead* Vietnamese *woman or child* remind you of a family member, relative, or friend?
29. Did you ever feel like you had to express anti-Asian sentiments in front of other Americans even if you did not really feel that way?
30. How often, if ever, aid you feel your presence in the military was resented because you were Asian?
31. How often, if ever, did you feel you were treated unfairly because of your race or ethnicity?
32. Did other Americans ever treat you like an outsider or a foreigner?
33. How often, if ever, did you try to prove, or feel the need to prove, that you were American?

Original Scale References

Anderson, J., Moeschberger, M., Chen, M. S., Kunn, P., Wewers, M. E., & Guthrie, R. (1993). An acculturation scale for Southeast Asians. *Social Psychiatry and Psychiatric Epidemiology, 28*, 134–141.

Lee, R. M., Choe, J., Kim, G., & Ngo, V. (2000). Construction of the Asian American family conflict scale. *Journal of Counseling Psychology, 47*, 211–222.

Loo, C. M., Fairbank, J. A., Scurfield, R. M., Ruch, L. O., King, D. W., & Adams, L. J. (2001). Measuring exposure to racism: Development and validation of a Race-Related Stressor Scale (RRSS) for Asian American Vietnam veterans. *Psychological Assessment, 13*, 503–520.

Nguyen, H. H., & von Eye, A. (2002). The Acculturation Scale for Vietnamese Adolescents (ASVA): A bidimensional perspective. *International Journal of Behavioral Development, 26*, 202–213.

Suinn, R., Rickard-Figueroa, K., Lew, S., & Vigil, P. (1987). The Suinn-Lew Asian self-identify acculturation scale: An initial report. *Educational and Psychological Measurement, 47*, 401–407.

Tsai, J. L., Ying, Y., & Lee, P. A. (2000). The meaning of "being Chinese" and "being American": Variation among Chinese American young adults. *Journal of Cross-Cultural Psychology, 31*, 302–332.

Ying, Y., & Tracy, L. C. (2004). Psychometric properties of the intergenerational congruence in immigrant families-parent scale in Chinese Americans. *Social Work Research, 28*, 58–62.

References

Abe-Kim, J., Okazaki, S., & Goto, S. G. (2001). Unidimensional versus multidimensional approaches to the assessment of acculturation for Asian American populations. *Cultural Diversity and Ethnic Minority Psychology*, *7*, 232–246.

Ahn, A. J., Kim, B. S. K., & Park, Y. S. (2008). Asian cultural values, gap, cognitive flexibility, coping strategies, and parent–child conflicts among Korean Americans. *Cultural Diversity and Ethnic Minority Psychology*, *14*, 353–363.

Chen, J.-L., & Kennedy, C. (2005). Factors associated with obesity in Chinese-American children. *Pediatric Nursing*, *31*, 110–115.

Cote, L. R., & Bornstein, M. H. (2000). Social and didactic parenting behaviors and beliefs among Japanese American and South American mothers of infants. *Infancy*, *1*, 363–374.

Johnson, M. L., Wall, T. L., Guanipa, C., Terry-Guyer, L., & Velasquez, R. J. (2002). The psychometric properties of the orthogonal cultural identification scale in Asian Americans. *Journal of Multicultural Counseling and Development*, *30*, 181–191.

Juang, L. P., & Nguyen, H. H. (2009). Misconduct among Chinese American adolescents: The role of acculturation, family obligation, and autonomy expectations. *Journal of Cross-Cultural Psychology*, *40*, 649–666.

Kang, S.-M. (2006). Measurement of acculturation, scale formats, and language competence: Their implications for adjustment. *Journal of Cross-Cultural Psychology*, *37*, 669–693.

Kim, J., & Chan, M. M. (2004). Acculturation and dietary habits of Korean Americans. *British Journal of Nutrition*, *91*, 469–478.

Kim, Y. H., & Sarna, L. (2001). An intervention to increase mammography use by Korean American women. *Oncology Nursing Forum*, *31*, 105–110.

Lam, R. E., Pacala, J. T., & Smith, S. L. (1997). Factors related to depressive symptoms in an elderly Chinese American sample. *Clinical Gerontologist*, *17*, 57–70.

Lee, R. M., Su, J., & Yoshida, E. (2005). Coping with intergenerational family conflict among Asian American college students. *Journal of Counseling Psychology*, *52*, 389–399.

Lee, R., & Liu, H. T. (2001). Coping with intergenerational family conflict: Comparison of Asian American, Hispanic, and European American college students. *Journal of Counseling Psychology*, *48*, 410–419.

Lese, K. P., & Robbins, S. B. (1994). Relationship between goal attributes and the academic acheivement of Southeast Asian adolescent refugees. *Journal of Counseling Psychology, 41*, 45–52.

Maxwell, A. E., Bastani, R., & Warda, U. S. (1998). Mammography utilization and related attitudes among Korean-American women. *Women and Health*, *27*, 89–107.

Ngo-Metzger, Q., Sorkin, D. H., Mangione, C. M., Gandek, B., & Hays, R. D. (2008). Evaluating the SF-36 health survey (version 2) in older Vietnamese Americans. *Journal of Aging and Health*, *20*, 420–436.

Ownbey, S. F., & Horridge, P. E. (1998). The Suinn-Lew Asian self identify acculturation scale: Test with a non-student, Asian American sample. *Social Behavior and Personality*, *26*, 57–68.

Su, J., Lee, R., & Vang, S. (2005). Intergenerational family conflict and coping among Hmong American college students. *Journal of Counseling Psychology*, *52*, 482–489.

Suinn, R. M., Ahuna, C., & Khoo, G. (1992). The Suinn-Lew Asian self-identity acculturation scale: Concurrent and factorial validation. *Educational and Psychological Measurement*, *52*, 1041–1046.

Tsai, J. L., Chentsova-Dutton, Y., Freire-Bebeau, L., & Przymus, D. E. (2002). Emotional expression and physiology in European Americans and Hmong Americans. *Emotion*, *2*, 380–397.

Tsai, J. L., Mortensen, H., Wong, Y., & Hess, D. (2002). What does "Being American" mean? A comparison of Asian American and European American young adults. *Cultural Diversity and Ethnic Minority Psychology*, *8*, 257–273.

Tsai, J. L., Pole, N., Levenson, R. W., & Munoz, R. F. (2003). The effects of depression on the emotional responses of Spanish-Speaking Latinos. *Cultural Diversity and Ethnic Minority Psychology*, *9*, 49–63.

Tsai, J. L., Simeonova, D. I., & Watanabe, J. T. (2004). Somatic and social: Chinese Americans talk about emotion. *Personality and Social Psychology Bulletin*, *30*, 1226–1238.

Tsai, J. L., Ying, Y., & Lee, P. A. (2001). Cultural predictors of self-esteem: A study of Chinese American female and male young adults. *Cultural Diversity and Ethnic Minority Psychology*, *7*, 284–297.

Tsai-Chae, A. H., & Nagata, D. K. (2008). Asian values and perceptions of intergenerational family conflict among Asian American students. *Cultural Diversity and Ethnic Minority Psychology*, *14*, 205–314.

Uba, L. (1994). *Asian Americans: Personality, patterns, identity, and mental health*. New York: Guilford Press.

U.S. Census Bureau. (2004). *American Community Survey*, Selected Population Profiles, S021.

U.S. Census Bureau. (2009). *2009 American Community Survey 1-year estimates*. http://factfinder.census.gov

Ying, Y., & Han, M. (2008). Cultural orientation in Southeast Asian American young adults. *Cultural Diversity and Ethnic Minority Psychology*, *14*, 29–37.

Ying, Y., Han, M., & Wong, S. L. (2008). Cultural orientation in Asian American adolescents: Variation by age and ethnic density. *Youth and Society*, *4*, 507–523.

Ying, Y., & Han, M. (2007). A test of the intergenerational congruence in immigrant families-child scale with Southeast Asian Americans. *Social Work Research*, *31*, 35–43.

Chapter 2
Hispanics

Overview

The Hispanic population in 2008 included 45.5 million (15.1%) of the estimated US population (U.S. Census Bureau, 2008). Hispanics represent the largest and fastest growing minority group. Hispanics come from more than 20 countries sharing a common language. The three largest ethnic identity groups of Hispanics in the United States are Mexican, Puerto Rican, and Cuban. Hispanics, with a median age of 27.6 years, are younger than the general population as a whole at 36.6 years. Hispanics may be of any race. In 2007, most Hispanics described themselves as White while a substantial number reported some other race (U.S. Census Bureau, 2008).

With the rapid increase of Hispanic groups entering the United States and interacting with the mainstream culture, the issues associated with acculturation are very relevant. While some individuals retain the language, behaviors, and values close to their culture of origin, others identify strongly with the values and standards of the mainstream culture. Most research on Hispanic Americans has focused on these acculturation processes. However, little attention has been paid to how the contextual factors such as immigration context, individual factors, and settlement affect the acculturation experience of Hispanic Americans (Cabassa, 2003). Further, a large number of studies have examined the relationship between psychosocial variables and acculturation. A few have focused on how the perceived discrimination and racism among Hispanic Americans related to the acculturation process.

In our review of measures, we did not find any measure that specifically focuses on race-related relationships between Hispanics and other minority groups or between Hispanics and members of the majority group. Therefore, this section will focus solely on intra-group measures that assess acculturation among Hispanic Americans. In a broad sense, acculturation is defined as the psychological and social changes that groups and individuals experience when they enter a new and different cultural context. Conceptually, two major theoretical frameworks dominate the acculturation patterns: unidimensional and bidimensional. Proponents of acculturation as a unidimensional construct consider the acculturating process as a zero-sum behavior or "linear" in which individuals move along a single continuum, ranging

L.E. Davis, R.J. Engel, *Measuring Race and Ethnicity*,
DOI 10.1007/978-1-4419-6697-1_2, © Springer Science+Business Media, LLC 2011

from the immersion in one's culture of origin to the immersion in the dominant or host culture (Cabassa, 2003; Cuellar, Arnold, & Maldonado, 1995). Those who support the bidimensional perspective argue acculturation consists of two independent dimensions: maintenance of the native culture and adherence to the host culture (Cuellar et al., 1995; Marín & Gamba, 1996). Our review of acculturation scales is organized primarily by these dimensional structures. A third section deals with acculturative stress. A total of 16 scales are reviewed in this section.

Citations

Cabassa (2003)
Cuellar et al. (1995)
Marín and Gamba (1996)
U.S. Census Bureau (2008)

Unidimensional Scales

1. Short Acculturation Scale for Hispanics (Marin, Sabogal, Marin, Otero-Sabogal, & Perez-Stable, 1987)
2. Short Acculturation Scale for Hispanic Youth (SASH-Y) (Barona & Miller, 1994)
3. A Brief Acculturation Scale for Hispanics (Norris, Ford, & Bova, 1996)
4. Acculturation Index for Mexican Americans (Mainous, 1989)
5. The Los Angeles Epidemiologic Catchment Area (LAECA) Acculturation Scale (Burnman, Hough, Telles, & Escobar, 1987)
6. Acculturation Scale for Mexican Americans (Deyo Diehl, Hazuda, & Stern, 1985)
7. Children's Acculturation Scale (CAS) (Franco, 1983)

Bidimensional Scales

1. Bidimensional Acculturation Scale for Hispanics (BAS) (Marín & Gamba, 1996)
2. American and Puerto Rican Cultural Involvement Scales (Cortes, Rogler, & Malgady, 1994)
3. The Abbreviated Multidimensional Acculturation Scale (AMAS-ZABB) (Zea, Asner-Self, Birman, & Buki, 2003)
4. Acculturation Rating Scale (Montgomery, 1992)
5. Cultural Life Styles Inventory (Mendoza, 1989)
6. Acculturation Rating Scale for Mexican Americans-II: A Revision of the Original ARSMA Scale (Cuellar, Arnold, & Maldonado, 1995)
7. Psychological Acculturation Scale (PAS) (Tropp, Erkut, Coll, Alarcon, & Vazquez-Garcia, 1999)
8. Bicultural Involvement Questionnaire (Szapocznik, Kurtines, & Fernandez, 1980)

Acculturative Stress

1. The Societal, Attitudinal, Familial, and Environmental Acculturative Stress Scale (Chavez, Moran, Reid, & Lopez, 1997).

Unidimensional Scales

Short Acculturation Scale for Hispanics (Marin, Sabogal, Marin, Otero-Sabogal, & Perez-Stable, 1987)

The Short Acculturation Scale for Hispanics (SASH) assesses the behavioral and cultural values aspects of acculturation.

Description: The 12-item SASH consists of three factors: (1) language use (five items: 1–5); (2) media (three items: 6–8); and (3) ethnic social relations (four items: 9–12). The scale utilizes a 5-point Likert scale. For items assessing language and media preference, the score ranges from *only Spanish* (1) to *only English* (5). For items assessing ethnic social relations, the score ranges from *all Latinos/Hispanics* (1) to *all Americans* (5). Items are summed across the 12 items and divided by the number of items answered to achieve an overall average score. Total scores range from 1 to 5. An overall average of 2.99 should be used to differentiate the less acculturated respondents and the more acculturated respondents; a respondent is less acculturated if the average score is between 1 and 2.99 and is more acculturated if the average score is greater than 2.99. The mid-point in the scale should not be interpreted to represent biculturalism. The authors do not provide instructions for scoring subscales separately. Both English and Spanish versions were developed in the original study. The scale is a self-administered questionnaire.

Sample: The original validation study conducted by the author included a sample of 363 Hispanics and 228 non-Hispanic Whites. Sixty-two percent of the Hispanic respondents were females and 57% of the non-Hispanics were females. The Hispanic sample was younger (31.2 years) than the non-Hispanic sample (38.8 years). The majority (70%) of the Hispanic respondents were foreign born.

Reliability: The coefficient alpha for the 12 items was .92. The alphas for the subscales were: .90 for language, .86 for media, and .86 for ethnic social relations.

Validity: The 12-item scale has construct validity with the respondents' generation ($r = .65$), the length of residence in the United States ($r = .70$), ethnic self-identification ($r = .76$), and the age at arrival ($r = -.69$). The language use factor correlated positively with the respondent's generation ($r = .69$), the length of residence in the United States ($r = .76$), ethnic self-identification ($r = .74$), and negatively with the age of arrival ($r = -.72$). The media factor correlated positively with the respondents' generation ($r = .43$), the length of residence in the United States ($r = .46$), ethnic self-identification ($r = .52$), and negatively with the age at arrival ($r = -.58$). The ethnic social relations factor correlated positively with the respondents' generation ($r = .53$), the length of residence in the United States

($r = .50$), ethnic self-identification ($r = .66$), and negatively with the age at arrival ($r = -.46$). Discriminant validity was established using group mean differences; non-Hispanics ($x = 4.63$) differed significantly from Hispanics ($x = 2.72$) on the 12-item scale.

Comments: Other studies have found evidence that the scale has good psychometric properties with Hispanics of different origins. For example, the language subscale has good psychometric properties with alpha coefficient of .80 and higher across various Hispanic groups including Mexican Americans, Cuban Americans, Puerto Ricans, Dominicans, and Central and South Americans (Kali, Zayas, & Malgady, 2000; Norris et al., 1996; Wallen, Feldman, & Anliker, 2002; Alvelo, Collazo, & Rosario, 2001) as well as older Hispanics (Goodman & Silverstein, 2005; Juarbe, Turok, & Perez-Stable, 2002). The scale has been adapted for other populations (e.g., Dela Cruz, Padilla, & Agustin, 2000; Yoshioka, Gilbert, El-Bassel, & Baig-Amin, 2003).

Location: Marin, G., Sabogal, F., Marin, B.V., Otero-Sabogal, R., & Perez-Stable, E.J. (1987). Development of a short acculturation scale for Hispanics. *Hispanic Journal of Behavioral Sciences, 9*, 183–205.

Selected Publications

Alvelo, J., Collazo, A. A., & Rosario, D. (2001). Comprehensive assessment tools for Hispanics: Validation of the multi-problem screening inventory (MPSI) for Puerto Ricans. *Research on Social Work Practice, 11,* 699–724.

Cruz, F. A., Padilla, G. V., & Agustin, E. O. (2000). Adapting a measure of acculturation for cross-cultural research. *Journal of Transcultural Nursing, 11*, 191–198.

Goodman, C. C., & Silverstein, M. (2005). Latina grandmothers raising grandchildren: acculturation and psychological well-being. *International Journal of Aging and Human Development, 60*, 305–316.

Juarbe, T., Turok, X. P., & Perez-Stable, E. J. (2002). Perceived benefits and barriers to physical activity among older Latina women. *Western Journal of Nursing Research, 24,* 868–886.

Kali, B., Zayas, L. H., & Malgady, R. G. (2000). Depression, acculturation, and motivations for alcohol use among young Colombian, Dominican, and Puerto Rican men. *Hispanic Journal of Behavioral Sciences*, *22*, 64–67.

Norris, A. E., Ford, K., & Bova, C. A. (1996). Psychometrics of a brief acculturation scale for Hispanics in a probability sample of urban Hispanic adolescents and young adults. *Hispanic Journal of Behavioral Sciences, 18*, 29–28.

Wallen, G. R., Feldman, R. H., & Anliker, J. (2002). Measuring acculturation among Central American women and the use of a brief language scale. *Journal of Immigrant Health, 4,* 95–102.

Yoshioka, M. R., Gilbert, L., El-Bassel, N., & Baig-Amin, M. (2003). Social support and disclosure of abuse: Comparing south Asian, African American, and Hispanic battered women. *Journal of Family Violence, 18*, 171–180.

Short Acculturation Scale for Hispanics – English Version

Response categories: *Items 1–8*: 1 = Only Spanish; 2 = Spanish better than English; 3 = Both equally; 4 = English better than Spanish; 5 = Only English

1. In general, what language(s) do you read and speak?
2. What was the language(s) you used as a child?
3. What language(s) do you usually speak at home?
4. In which language(s) do you usually think?
5. What language(s) do you usually speak with your friends?
6. In what language(s) are the TV programs you usually watch?
7. In what language(s) are the radio programs you usually listen to?
8. In general, in what language(s) are the movies, TV, and radio programs you *prefer* to watch and listen to?

Response categories: *Items 9–12*: 1 = All Latinos/Hispanics; 2 = More Latinos than Americans; 3 = About half and half; 4 = More Americans than Latinos; 5 = All Americans

9. Your close friends are;
10. You prefer going to social gatherings/parties at which the people are;
11. The persons you visit or who visit you are;
12. If you could choose your children's friends, you would want them to be.

Short Acculturation Scale for Hispanic Youth (SASH-Y) (Barona & Miller, 1994)

The Short Acculturation Scale for Hispanic Youth (SASH-Y) is a brief self-report acculturation scale designed specifically for use with Hispanic youth.

Description: The SASH-Y includes 12 items assessing three domains: Extra-familial language use (items 2, 3, 9), familial language use (items 1, 4, 5, 6, 7, 8), and ethnic social relations (items 10–12). The scale utilizes a 5-point Likert scale. The response options for item 1 are *only Spanish* (1), *Spanish better than English* (2), *both equally* (3), *English better than Spanish* (4), and *only English* (5). The response options for items 2 through 9 are *only Spanish* (1), *more Spanish than English* (2), *both equally* (3), *more English than Spanish* (4), and *only English* (5); the response options for items 10 through 12 are *all Hispanics* (1), *more Hispanic than White* (2), *about half and half* (3), *more White than Hispanic* (4), and *all White* (5). Responses are summed across all 12 items to form a composite score ranging from 12 to 60, with higher scores indicating higher acculturation to US society. The author recommends a single composite score be computed for the SASH-Y. The scale is a self-administered questionnaire.

Sample: The validation study conducted by the author included 141 Hispanic and 230 non-Hispanic White children. The authors did not distinguish specific ethnic groups within the Hispanic sample. The sample consisted of 194 males with a mean age of 13.2 years and 177 females with a mean age of 13 years. Of the sample, 20% were in fifth grade, 22% were in sixth grade, 22% were in seventh grade, and 35% were in eighth grade. The mean score on the SASH-Y for the total sample was 49.5 and the standard deviation was 9.9.

Reliability: The SASH-Y produced an alpha coefficient of .94 when calculated for the total sample. The alpha coefficient for the Hispanic sample was .92 while the alpha coefficient for the non-Hispanic sample was .85. The overall split-half reliability was .96; it was .95 for the Hispanic sample and .87 for the non-Hispanic sample.

Validity: To establish factorial validity, the authors used factor analysis and a chi-square test of fit. The resulting factor analysis suggested three factors. The chi-square test suggested a 4-factor solution; however, the authors decided to use the three factors suggested by the factor analysis since the three factors would be easier to interpret. The authors ran an ANOVA test that successfully discriminated between Hispanic and non-Hispanic White responses to acculturation items on the scale providing evidence for the scale's discriminant validity.

Comments: The scale demonstrates excellent internal consistency for the total sample as well as for the Hispanic and non-Hispanic samples. Similar internal consistency scores for the total scale have been found elsewhere (Guilamo-Ramos et al., 2009; Ruiz, 2009; Serrano & Anderson, 2003). Some studies have also reported adequate internal consistency scores for the three subscales (Guilamo-Ramos, Bouris, Jaccard, Lesesne, & Ballan, 2009; Serrano & Anderson, 2003). A three-factor structure has been reported elsewhere, though with different items loading on the factors suggesting that more work needs to be done to assure use of subscales. Although three-factor solutions from the exploratory analysis provide evidence for factorial validity, confirmatory factor analysis still needs to be conducted. The scale requires additional evidence for other forms of validity. In studies not focused on the psychometric properties of the scale, the acculturation construct measured by the SASH-Y has been found to be related to other constructs as hypothesized (Guilamo-Ramos et al., 2009). Younger children (fourth and fifth graders), may have difficulty with some of the questions regarding ethnic identity (Serrano & Anderson, 2003).

Location: Barona, A., & Miller, J. (1994). Short acculturation scale for Hispanic youth (SASH-Y): A preliminary report. *Hispanic Journal of Behavioral Sciences, 16,* 155–62.

Selected Publications

Guilamo-Ramos, V., Bouris, A., Jaccard, J., Lesesne, C., & Ballan, M. (2009). Familial and cultural influences on sexual risk behaviors among Mexican, Puerto

Rican, and Dominican youth. *AIDS Education and Prevention, 21*(Suppl. B), 61–79.
Guilamo-Ramos, V., Bouris, A., Jaccard, J., Lesesne, C., Gonzalez, B., & Kalogerogiannis, K. (2009). Family mediators of acculturation and adolescent sexual behavior among Latino youth. *Journal of Primary Prevention, 30,* 395–419.
Ruiz, Y. (2009). Predictors of academic achievement for Latino middle schoolers. *Journal of Human Behavior in the Social Environment, 19,* 419–433.
Serrano, E., & Anderson, J. (2003). Assessment of a refined short acculturation scale for Latino preteens in rural Colorado. *Hispanic Journal of Behavioral Sciences, 25,* 240–253.

Short Acculturation Scale for Hispanics Youth – English Version

Response categories: *Item 1*: 1 = Only Spanish; 2 = Spanish better than English; 3 = Both equally; 4 = English better than Spanish; 5 = Only English

1. What languages do you read and speak?

Response categories: *Items 2–9*: 1 = Only Spanish; 2 = Spanish better than English; 3 = Both Equally; 4 = English better than Spanish; 5 = Only English

2. What languages do your parents speak to you in?
3. What languages do you usually speak at home?
4. In which language do you usually think?
5. What languages do you usually speak with your friends?
6. In what languages are the TV programs you usually watch?
7. In what languages are the radio programs you usually listen to?
8. In what languages are the movies, TV, and radio programs you *prefer* to watch and listen to?
9. In what languages do your parents speak with their parents?

Response categories: *Items 10–12*: 1 = All Latinos/Hispanics; 2 = More Latinos than Americans; 3 = About half and half; 4 = More Americans than Latinos; 5 = All Americans

10. Your close friends are;
11. You prefer going to parties at which the people are;
12. The persons you visit or who visit you are.

A Brief Acculturation Scale for Hispanics (Norris, Ford, & Bova, 1996)

The Brief Acculturation Scale for Hispanics (BASH) uses language use as a measure of acculturation.

Description: The 4-item Brief Acculturation Scale includes four items from Marin and Sabogal's Language Use subscale of the Short Acculturation Scale for Hispanics (see scale #1). Response options are: *Only Spanish* (1), *more Spanish than English* (2), *both equally* (3), *more English than Spanish* (4), *only English* (5). An acculturation score is created by summing the values of the item responses and dividing this sum by the number of items with responses. A dichotomous level of acculturation (low, high) can be created; scores less than or equal to 3 indicate a low level of acculturation and scores greater than 3 indicate of a high level of acculturation. The scale is administered as a structured face-to-face interview.

Sample: Respondents were recruited from a household probability sample of Hispanic adolescents and young adults, ages 15–24, from a low-income area of Detroit. The sample included 519 Mexican Americans and 165 Puerto Rican participants. Fifty-one percent of the Mexican Americans and 56% of the Puerto Ricans were female.

Reliability: The alpha coefficient for the entire sample was .90. The alpha coefficient was .92 for Mexican American respondents and .80 for Puerto Rican respondents.

Validity: To assess construct validity, scale scores were compared to generational status, length of time in the United States, a subjective measure of acculturation, place of birth, and language which respondent chose to take the scale (Spanish or English). Each of the variables was related to scale scores in the expected direction for the overall sample and the two subgroups: Generation status ($r = .67$), Length of time in the United States ($r = .50$), subjective measure of acculturation ($r = -.43$ Mexican American; $r = -.18$ Puerto Rican). The mean score for respondents born in the United States was 16.5 while the mean score for respondents born outside of the United States was 9.03. Respondents who chose to take the scale in English had a higher mean score (16.00) in contrast to those who chose to take the scale in Spanish (6.85).

Comments: This scale provides a brief measure of acculturation with evidence of reliability and validity for two groups: Mexican Americans and Puerto Ricans. In another study of Latina women, Unger and Molina (2000) report a Cronbach's alpha of .89. The brief nature of this scale makes it easy to use. There is no evidence to support the dichotomization of subject scores into a high level versus a low level of acculturation. There is a need for additional studies of the scale's validity; one report found some relationship between acculturation and use of contraception (Unger & Molina, 2000).

Location: Norris, A. E., Ford, K., & Bova, C. A. (1996). Psychometrics of a brief acculturation scale for Hispanics in a probability sample of urban Hispanic adolescents and young adults. *Hispanic Journal of Behavioral Sciences, 18*, 29–38.

Selected Publications

Unger, J. B., & Molina, G. B. (2000). Acculturation and attitudes about contraceptive use among Latina women. *Health Care for Women International, 21*, 235–49.

Brief Acculturation Scale for Hispanics

Response categories: 1 = Only Spanish; 2 = More Spanish than English; 3 = Both equally; 4 = More English than Spanish; 5 = Only English

1. In general what language do you read and speak?
2. What language do you usually speak at home?
3. In what language do you usually think?
4. What language do you usually speak with your friends?

Acculturation Index for Mexican Americans (Mainous, 1989)

The Acculturation Index for Mexican Americans (AIMA) assesses role identity or the extent to which the respondent identifies as an "outsider" or "insider" in relation to mainstream American culture (Mainous, 1989).

Description: The Acculturation Index for Mexican Americans consists of eight items measuring three dimensions of acculturation: (1) Language (three items: 1–3), (2) Self-definition as an Insider (three items: 4–7), and (3) Self-definition as an Outsider (two items: 8 and 9). The items assess language use, based on the interviewer's observations of language use during the interview, the language spoken within the family, and the language spoken with friends. The response options for the language use items are: *English only* (1), *mostly English* (2), *both languages about equal* (3), *mostly Spanish* (4), and *Spanish only* (5). Response options for self-definition as an insider include *American of Mexican descent* (1), *Mexican American* (2), *US citizen* (3), and *US native* (4). Self-definition as an outsider is defined as *Foreigner* (1) or *Immigrant* (2). The scale is administered by interview, conducted in English or Spanish. The author does not explain how to score the scale or whether individual items or dimension scores should be used. An index was used based on the factor scores: Language use, self-definition as an insider and self-definition as an outsider.

Sample: The scale was developed and evaluated using a sample of 991 Mexican American individuals, 60% of whom were female. The respondents ranged from ages 17 to 93 years, with the median age being 20 years. Sixty-two percent of the respondents were US born and 38% were Mexican born.

Reliability: None reported.

Validity: The factor analysis yielded the three expected factors providing evidence for factorial validity. Construct validity was demonstrated as the measure correlates with previously employed indicators of acculturation such as generational distance ($r = .74$), length of time spent in the United States ($r = .45$), ratio of time in the United States divided by the age of the respondent, ($r = .75$), and discrimination ($r = -.23$).

Comments: Use of the scale is not adequately explained, particularly the scoring. There is support for the validity of the scale but no evidence of reliability. We found no additional studies of the scale's psychometric properties.

Location: Mainous, A. (1989). Self-concept as an indicator of acculturation in Mexican Americans. *Hispanic Journal of Behavioral Sciences, 11*, 178–89.

Selected Publications

None

Acculturation Index for Mexican Americans

Response categories: *Items 1–3*: 1 = English only; 2 = Mostly English; 3 = Both languages about equal; 4 = Mostly Spanish; 5 = Spanish only

1. Language spoken with friends
2. Language spoken with siblings
3. Language of interview

Response categories: *Items 4–7*: 1 = American of Mexican descent; 2 = Mexican American; 3 = US Citizen; 4 = US Native

4. Self-definition as an American of Mexican descent
5. Self-definition as a Mexican American
6. Self-definition as a US Native
7. Self-definition as a US citizen

Response categories: *Items 8–9*: 1 = Foreigner; 2 = Immigrant

8. Self-definition as a foreigner
9. Self-definition as an immigrant

The Los Angeles Epidemiologic Catchment Area Acculturation Scale (Burnam, Hough, Telles, & Escobar, 1987)

The Los Angeles Epidemiologic Catchment Area (LAECA) Acculturation Scale is designed to measure different aspects of acculturation such as language preference and use, ethnic background and identification, culturally linked customs and habits, and ethnic interaction.

Description: The 26-item LAECA Acculturation Scale consists of three factors: (1) language, (2) social activities, and (3) ethnic background. The authors suggest using the total score composed of 26 items rather than computing subscale scores. The LAECA Acculturation Scale was conceived as a continuous scale with values ranging from completely Hispanic to equally Hispanic and Anglo (bicultural) to completely Anglo. A 5-point response scale was used. Total scale scores are created by summing item values and dividing by the number of items for which there are responses. The average total scale score may range from 1 to 5, with 5 indicating higher levels of acculturation to the host culture and 1 indicating no acculturation. Scores between 1 and 1.75 are defined as low acculturation, scores of 1.76–3.25 are defined as medium acculturation, and scores of 3.26–5 are defined as high acculturation. The scale is administered as a structured interview. Respondents can choose to have the interview conducted in either English or Spanish.

Sample: The scale was evaluated with a sample of 1,245 adult Mexican Americans residing in Los Angeles. There were 568 males and 628 females; 59% were first-generation ($N = 707$), 27% were second-generation ($N = 323$), and 15% were third- or later generation ($N = 178$).

Reliability: Cronbach's alpha for the entire scale was .97. Cronbach's alpha for males and females was .97; obtained education level ranged from .94 to .96; and language spoken by respondent ranged from .91 to .93. Corrected item-total correlations for the scale ranged from .41 (ethnicity of people in the neighborhood) to .92 (language spoken).

Validity: Findings from the factor analysis suggests that the items composing three factors are highly inter-correlated, supporting a unidimensional approach to measurement of acculturation. Construct validity was established by comparing mean LAECA Acculturation scores across generational groups. Mean level of acculturation increased from first to second to later generation groups. In addition, among the first generation, level of acculturation was positively correlated with the number of years individuals had lived in the United States. The relation of acculturation to age showed that younger persons acculturate more rapidly than older, which is consistent with acculturation theory.

Comments: The LAECA Acculturation scale demonstrated a high degree of internal reliability for the entire sample, and for specific sex, educational, and language sub-samples. High internal consistency has been reported elsewhere (Clark, 2002). The scale discriminated between generational groups. Scores on the scale were positively correlated with the number of years the respondent was exposed to Anglo-American culture.

Location: Burnam, M. A. Hough, R. L., Telles, C. A., & Escobar, J. I. (1987). Measurement of acculturation in a community population of Mexican Americans. *Hispanic Journal of Behavioral Sciences, 9*, 105–130.

Selected Publications

Clark, L. (2002). Mexican-Origin mothers' experiences using children's health care services. *Western Journal of Nursing Research, 24*, 159–179.

LAECA Acculturation Scale Items

Response categories: *Item 1*: 1 = First; 2 = Second; 3 = Third; 4 = Fourth; 5 = Fifth

1. Generation

Response categories: *Item 2–3*: 1 = Spanish only; 2 = Mostly Spanish; 3 = Both Equally; 4 = Mostly English; 5 = English only

2. Language spoken
3. Language preferred

Response categories: *Items 4–14*: 1 = Spanish only; 2 = Spanish better; 3 = Both equally; 4 = English better; 5 = English only

4. Language use with spouse
5. Language use with children
6. Language use with parents
7. Language use with co-workers
8. Language use with friends
9. Language of TV viewing
10. Language of radio listening
11. Language of thinking
12. Language reads better
13. Language used when reading
14. Language writes better

Response categories: *Items 15–17*: 1 = All Hispanic; 2 = Most Hispanic; 3 = Half Hispanic; 4 = Few Hispanic; 5 = None Hispanic

15. Ethnicity of people in neighborhood
16. Ethnicity of co-workers
17. Ethnicity of close friends

Response categories: *Items 18–20*: 1 = All of the time; 2 = Most of the time; 3 = Half of the time; 4 = Sometimes; 5 = Never

18. Proportion of time spent eating Hispanic foods
19. Proportion of time spent listening to Latin music
20. Proportion of time spent celebrating Hispanic traditions

Response categories: *Item 21*: 1 = All Hispanic; 2 = Most Hispanic; 3 = Half Hispanic; 4 = Few Hispanic; 5 = None Hispanic

21. Ethnicity of leisure time social environment

Response categories: *Items 22–24*: 1 = Mexican; 2 = Chicano; 3 = Mexican American; 4 = Latin American, other Hispanic American; 5 = Anglo American or other

22. Ethnic background
23. Mother's ethnic background
24. Father's ethnic background

Response categories: *Item 25*: 2 = Other; 4 = United States

25. Country spent childhood

Response categories: *Item 26*: 2 = Mostly Hispanic, partly United States; 3 = Equal; 4 = Mostly United States, partly Hispanic; 5 = United States only

26. Proportion of life lived in United States versus Hispanic country

Acculturation Scale for Mexican Americans (Deyo, Diehl, Hazuda, & Stern, 1985)

The Acculturation Scale for Mexican Americans (ASMA) is a unidimensional measure using language use.

Description: The ASMA includes four items. Items are scored by assigning 1 point for each response favoring English and 0 for each response favoring Spanish. The scale score is calculated by summing the points for the four items. Scores range from 0 to 4 with higher scores indicating higher acculturation. The scale has both English and Spanish versions. The scale is administered as a structured interview.

Sample: Two studies were conducted to develop and validate the scale. Study 1: This was a clinical study on lower back pain and included 97 Mexican American patients. Study 2: The sample included 1,685 Mexican Americans and 1,103 non-Hispanic Whites. Participants ranged from age 24 to 64 years.

Reliability: In the clinical study, the Guttman coefficient of reproducibility for the four language questions was .97 and the coefficient of scalability was .89. In the validation study, the coefficient of reproducibility was .97 and the coefficient of scalability was .90. Among Mexican Americans, the coefficient of reproducibility was .96 and the coefficient of scalability was .81.

Validity: In the clinical study, construct validity was established by correlating the language scale with patient ethnicity and the interviewer's rating of the respondent's English fluency. Non-Hispanics had a mean language scale score of 4.0, while Mexican Americans had a mean score of 1.6. Scores for Mexican Americans were compared with an interviewer's report of the respondent's English fluency on a five-point scale. The Spearman rank correlation between the two rating methods was .79. In the validation study, the authors provided evidence of construct validity by showing statistically significant associations between the scale and ethnicity, place of birth, generation within the United States, and type of neighborhood.

Comments: The scale's brevity makes it suitable for incorporation into other research instruments. There is evidence of reliability and validity of the scale. Ruiz, Dolbier, and Fleschler (2006) report strong internal consistency. The scale is associated with other constructs such as timing of sexual initiation (Gilliam, Berlin, Kozloski, Hernandez, & Grundy, 2007), birth outcome risk factors, and perceived stress (Ruiz et al., 2006) and depression (Escalante, del Rincon, & Mulrow, 2000). In some studies, the wording for Questions 1 and 4 has been shortened to just ask about language (e.g., Gilliam et al., 2007; Ruiz et al., 2006). Psychometric evaluation with other subgroups of Hispanics is needed.

Location: Deyo, R. A., Diehl, A. K., Hazuda, H., & Stern, M. P. (1985). A simple language-based scale for Mexican Americans: Validation and application to health care research. *American Journal of Public Health*, *75*, 51–55.

Selected Publications

Escalante, A., del Rincon, I., & Mulrow, C. D. (2000). Symptoms of depression and psychological distress among Hispanics with rheumatoid arthritis. *Arthritis Care and Research, 13,* 156–167.

Gilliam, M. L., Berlin, A., Kozloski, M., Hernandez, M., & Grundy, M. (2007). Interpersonal and personal factors influencing sexual debut among Mexican-American young women in the United States. *Journal of Adolescent Health, 41,* 493–503.

Ruiz, R. J., Dolbier, C. L., & Fleschler, R. (2006). The relationships among acculturation, bio-behavioral risk, stress, corticotrophin-releasing hormone, and poor birth outcomes in Hispanic women. *Ethnicity and Disease, 16,* 926–931.

Acculturation Scale for Mexican Americans

1. Some of our patients speak both English and Spanish, but many speak only one or the other. To improve our future contacts with you, we would like to know what language you prefer to speak.

   1 = English 2 = Spanish 3 = Both equally

2. What language is most often spoken in your home?

   1 = English 2 = Spanish 3 = Both equally

3. What was your first language as a child?

   1 = English 2 = Spanish 3 = Other

4. Many of our patients have difficulty reading in either English or Spanish. Do you read any English?

   1 = Yes, anything 2 = Some 3 = Very little 4 = None

   Scoring:

   Question 1: 1 point for English; 0 points for Spanish or both
   Question 2: 1 point for English or both; 0 points for Spanish
   Question 3: 1 point for English; 0 points for Spanish or other
   Question 4: 1 point for 1, 2, or 3; 0 points for Answer 4

   Summary Score = sum of points for the four items.

Children's Acculturation Scale (Franco, 1983)

The Children's Acculturation Scale (CAS) is designed to measure values and behavioral aspects of acculturation in Mexican-American children.

Description: The Children's Acculturation Scale is a 10-item scale. The scale is completed by someone who can assess the child's language usage, perceived discrimination, religion, education, parental occupation, food preferences, entertainment preferences, knowledge of Mexican and American history, and ethnic identity. The scale requires the rater (teacher or parent) to respond on a 5-point Likert scale ranging from *very Mexican* (1) to *very Anglicized* (5). The scale score is calculated by summing and averaging across the 10 multiple-choice items. The total scale score ranges from 1 to 5. A total scale score of 1 suggests the respondent is very Mexican, and a total score of 5 suggests the respondent is very Anglicized. A rating near 3 is considered to be bicultural. The scale takes approximately 5 minutes to complete.

Sample: The original validation study included an assessment by teachers and parents of 141 Mexican American and 34 White, first-, third-, and sixth-grade children. The Mexican American sample consisted of 74 males and 67 females while the Anglo sample was almost equally divided by gender.

Reliability: The coefficient alpha for the scale was .77. Inter-rater reliability was .93, $p < .001$. Test–retest reliability, assessed in a sample of 14 first graders with 5 weeks between the tests, was .97.

Validity: Construct validity was established as the CAS correlates strongly (.76) with the Acculturation Rating Scale for Mexican Americans. Using a factor analysis, the CAS yielded three factors: (1) language proficiency, preference, and peer associations; (2) parental occupations and educational level; and (3) music preference. The mean acculturation score was highest among sixth graders, followed by third and first graders consistent with the theory that children become more acculturated the longer they are exposed to Anglo-American culture.

Comments: The scale demonstrates a moderate level of internal consistency though high-rater reliability. The author does not specify if training is required for the raters. A modified version read to participants had moderate internal consistency, alpha = .65 (Hess & D'Amato, 1996).

Location: Franco, J. N. (1983). An acculturation scale for Mexican-American children. *The Journal of General Psychology, 108*, 175–181.

Selected Publications

Hess, R. S., & D'Amato, R. C. (1996). High school completion among Mexican-American children: Individual and family background variables. *School Psychology Quarterly, 11*, 353–368.

Children's Acculturation Scale

Circle the appropriate response for this child:

Item 1: 1 = Poor; 2 = Below average; 3 = Average; 4 = Above average; 5 = Excellent

1. The student's English proficiency for a student at his/her grade level is

Items 2–3: 1 = Unemployed; 2 = Laborer; 3 = Blue collar; 4 = White collar; 5 = Professional

2. Father's occupation
3. Mother's occupation

Items 4–5: 1 = Spanish only; 2 = Mostly Spanish; 3 = Both Spanish and English; 4 = Mostly English; 5 = English only

4. To the best of your knowledge, which language is spoken at this child's home?
5. In your opinion, which language does the child prefer to use?

Item 6: 1 = Mexican; 2 = Chicano; 3 = Mexican American; 4 = Spanish American, Latin American, Hispanic American; 5 = Anglo American or White

6. In your opinion, would this child prefer to be identified as

Item 7: 1 = Hispanics only; 2 = mostly with Hispanics; 3 = Hispanics and Anglos equally; 4 = mostly Anglos; 5 = Anglos only

7. In your opinion, does this child associate with

Item 8: 1 = 1–5 years; 2 = 4–9 years; 3 = Some high school; 4 = High school graduate; 5 = Post high school

8. Educational level of head of household

Item 9: 1 = Spanish music; 2 = Mostly Spanish; 3 = Spanish and English equally; 4 = Mostly English; 5 = English only

9. In your opinion, would this child's music preference be

Item 10: 1 = Not an American citizen; 2 = A first-generation American; 3 = A second-generation American; 4 = A third-generation American; 5 = A fourth or more generation American

10. To the best of your knowledge, is this child

Bidimensional Scales

Bidimensional Acculturation Scale for Hispanics (Marín & Gamba, 1996)

The Bidimensional Acculturation Scale for Hispanics (BAS) measures acculturation to both Hispanic and non-Hispanic cultures.

Description: The BAS includes 24 items with 12 items measuring acculturation to Hispanic culture and 12 items measuring acculturation to Anglo-American culture. The 12 items that measure Hispanic or non-Hispanic acculturation are divided as Language Use (three items), Linguistic Proficiency (six items), and Electronic Media (three items). Participants rate their agreement with statements about the frequency of their language use and their proficiency using a 4-point Likert-type format. Each respondent is assigned two scores: a score for the 12 items making up the Hispanic domain (items 4, 5, 6, 13, 14, 15, 16, 17, 18, 22, 23, 24) and a score for the 12 items forming the non-Hispanic domain (items 1, 2, 3, 7, 8, 9, 10, 11, 12, 19, 20, 21). These scores are calculated by summing item values and dividing by the number of response items answered. The possible total score range is from 1 to 4 for each cultural domain. The two scores are used to define the level of acculturation of the respondent. A score of 2.5 can be used as a cut-off score to indicate low or high level of adherence to each cultural domain. A low score (<2.5) on either 12-item domain suggests low acculturation to that culture while a high score (>2.5) on either domain suggests high acculturation to the culture in question. For example, scores above 2.5 in both cultural domains can be interpreted as indicating biculturalism on the part of the participant whereas a high score on the Hispanic domain and a low score on the Anglo-American domain would suggest low acculturation to Anglo-American culture and a high degree of acculturation to Hispanic culture. The scale has both English and Spanish versions. The scale is administered as a structured interview.

Sample: The scale was developed using a sample of 254 adult Hispanic residents of San Francisco, California. Most respondents (79.5%) were born in Central America (52.8%) or in Mexico (24%). The average age of the respondents was 37.3 years, 54% were females, and the sample averaged 10.4 years of formal education. Most of the respondents (74%) answered the questionnaire in Spanish.

Reliability: The Cronbach's alpha was .90 for the Hispanic domain and .96 for the non-Hispanic domain.

Validity: All of the language-based subscales showed high correlations with generation status, length of residence in the United States, amount of formal education, age at arrival in the United States, proportion of respondent's life lived in the United States, and ethnic self-identification demonstrating construct validity. There is evidence of convergent validity as the Hispanic and non-Hispanic domains of the scale correlate with the Short Acculturation Scale for Hispanics (SASH) (0.79 for the non-Hispanic Domain and –0.64 for Hispanic domain).

Comments: This scale measures acculturation to both Hispanic and non-Hispanic American culture. The scale has evidence of both reliability and validity. There is other evidence of internal consistency with other populations groups such as high-school students (Guinn, 1998), Hispanic women from a community sample (Rojas-Guyler, Ellis, & Sanders, 2005), immigrant men (Cabassa, 2007), women from the Dominican Republic (Dawson, 2009), and college students both with the English and Spanish versions (Singelis et al., 2006). There is also evidence of satisfactory test retest reliability within the same language of administration and if the language of administration changes (Singelis et al., 2006). The BAS does relate as hypothesized to other variables (e.g., Christenson, Zabriske, Eggett, & Freeman, 2006; Dawson, 2009; Rojas-Guyler et al., 2005). The authors suggest that the Linguistic Proficiency items could be used separately as a quick measure of acculturation (e.g., Edwards & Romero, 2008). In its present form, the scale appears best used with Mexican Americans and Central Americans; psychometric evaluation is required with other Hispanic groups.

Location: Marín, G., & Gamba, R. J. (1996). A new measurement of acculturation for Hispanics: The bidimensional acculturation scale for Hispanics (BAS). *Hispanic Journal of Behavioral Sciences, 18*, 297–316.

Selected Publications

Cabassa, L. J. (2007). Latino immigrant men's perceptions of depression and attitudes toward help seeking. *Hispanic Journal of Behavioral Sciences, 29,* 492–509.

Christenson, O. D., Zabriske, R. B., Eggett, D. L., & Freeman, P. A. (2006). Family acculturation, family leisure involvement, and family functioning among Mexican-Americans. *Journal of Leisure Research, 38,* 475–495.

Dawson, B. A. (2009). Discrimination, stress, and acculturation among Dominican immigrant women. *Hispanic Journal of Behavioral Sciences, 31,* 96–111.

Edwards, L. M., & Romero, A. J. (2008). Coping with discrimination among Mexican descent adolescents. *Hispanic Journal of Behavioral Sciences, 30,* 24–39.

Guinn, B. (1998). Acculturation and health locus of control among Mexican American adolescents. *Hispanic Journal of Behavioral Sciences, 20,* 492–499.

Rojas-Guyler, L., Ellis, N., & Sanders, S. (2005). Acculturation, health protective sexual communication, and HIV/AIDS risk behavior among Hispanic women in a large Midwestern city. *Health Education and Behavior, 32,* 767–779.

Singelis, T. M., Yamada, A. M., Barrio, C., Laney, J. H., Her, P., Ruiz-Anaya, A., & Lennertz, S. T. (2006). Metric equivalence of the bidimensional acculturation scale, the satisfaction with life scale, and the self-construal scale across Spanish and English language versions. *Hispanic Journal of Behavioral Sciences, 28,* 231–244.

The Bidirectional Acculturation Scale for Hispanics (BAS): English Version

Response categories: *Items 1–6*: 1 = Almost never; 2 = Sometimes; 3 = Often; 4 = Almost always

Language Use Subscale

1. How often do you speak English?
2. How often do you speak in English with your friends?
3. How often do you think in English?
4. How often do you speak Spanish?
5. How often do you speak in Spanish with your friends?
6. How often do you think in Spanish?

Response categories: *Items 7–18*: 1 = Very poorly; 2 = Poorly; 3 = Well; 4 = Very well

Linguistic Proficiency Subscale

7. How well do you speak English?
8. How well do you read in English?
9. How well do you understand TV programs in English?
10. How well do you understand radio programs in English?
11. How well do you write in English?
12. How well do you understand music in English?
13. How well do you speak Spanish?
14. How well do you read in Spanish?
15. How well do you understand TV programs in Spanish?
16. How well do you understand radio programs in Spanish?
17. How well do you write in Spanish?
18. How well do you understand music in Spanish?

Response categories: *Items 19–24*: 1 = Almost never; 2 = Sometimes; 3 = Often; 4 = Almost always
Electronic Media Subscale

19. How often do you watch TV programs in English?
20. How often do you listen to radio programs in English?
21. How often do you listen to music in English?
22. How often do you watch TV programs in Spanish?
23. How often do you listen to radio programs in Spanish?
24. How often do you listen to music in Spanish?

American and Puerto Rican Cultural Involvement Scales (Cortes, Rogler, & Malgady, 1994)

The American and Puerto Rican Cultural Involvement Scales (APRCIS) measures acculturation to both Puerto Rican and Anglo-American cultures.

Description: To measure acculturation to both of these cultures, the items focus on language use, values, ethnic pride, food preferences, and child-rearing practices. The scale includes a total of 18 items. Nine items measure acculturation to and involvement with Anglo-American culture (items 1–9) and nine items assess acculturation to and involvement with Puerto-Rican culture (items 10–18). Respondents are asked to rate their agreement with a particular behavior, value, or belief on a 4-point scale ranging from *not at all* (1) to *very much* (4). Scores for each dimension are based on the average score of the items and range from 1 to 4, with higher scores suggesting a high degree of acculturation to the culture measured in that dimension and lower scores suggesting low acculturation to the culture measured in that dimension. No specific cut-off scores are given by the authors to distinguish between a high versus low degree of acculturation. The scale is administered by a structured interview. The scale can be administered in either English or Spanish.

Sample: The sample size for the validation study was 403 participants. Among them, 254 were born in Puerto Rico and 149 were born in the United States. The average age of the respondents was 38.93 and their average education was 9.8 years of school. The scale was administered in a structured interview format with both Spanish and English versions available.

Reliability: Coefficient alpha for the nine items measuring involvement in American culture was .78, and the alpha coefficient for the nine items measuring involvement in Puerto Rican culture was .73.

Validity: There is evidence for construct validity. The scale measuring involvement in American culture was inversely related to place of birth and age at arrival in the United States, and was positively related to number of years in the United States. The scale measuring involvement in Puerto Rican culture showed the opposite pattern of relationships.

Comments: The two scales demonstrate adequate internal consistency. Similar findings have been found for other Puerto Rican respondents (Contreras, 2004; Cortes et al., 2003; Lopez & Contreras, 2005) and Hispanic women with the *Hispanic* replacing *Puerto Rican* (McKee, Zayas, & Jankowski, 2004). There is additional evidence of construct validity such as the relationship of response language to scores on both scales, American cultural involvement, generation in the US, years of US residence, and years of US schooling (Lopez & Contreras, 2005). The scale has been adapted and evaluated to assess "original culture" versus "mainstream culture" for Latinos, Korean Americans, and Chinese Americans (Mezzich, Ruiperez, Yoon, Liu, & Zapata-Vega, 2009). Note that some studies include two deleted items (see scale note; see for example Mezzich et al., 2009).

Location: Cortes, D. E., Rogler, L. H., & Malgady, R. G. (1994). Biculturality among Puerto Rican adults in The United States. *American Journal of Community Psychology, 22*, 707–721.

Selected Publications

Contreras, J. M. (2004). Parenting behaviors among mainland Puerto Rican adolescent mothers: The role of grandmother and partner involvement. *Journal of Research on Adolescence, 14,* 341–368.

Cortes, D. E., Deren, S., Andia, J., Colon, H., Robles, R., & Kang, S. (2003). The use of the Puerto Rican biculturality scale with Puerto Rican drug users in New York and Puerto Rico. *Journal of Psychoactive Drugs, 35*, 197–207.

Lopez, I. R., & Contreras, J. M. (2005). The best of both worlds: Biculturality, acculturation, and adjustment among young mainland Puerto Rican mothers. *Journal of Cross-Cultural Psychology, 36,* 192–208.

McKee, M. D., Zayas, L. H., & Jankowski, K. R. B. (2004). Breastfeeding intention and practice in an urban minority population: Relationship to maternal depressive symptoms and mother-infant closeness. *Journal of Reproductive and Infant Psychology, 22,* 167–181.

Mezzich, J. E., Ruiperez, M. A., Yoon, G., Liu, J., & Zapata-Vega, M. I. (2009). Measuring cultural identity: Validation of a modified Cortez, Rogler, and

Malgady bicultural scale in three ethnic groups in New York. *Culture, Medicine, & Psychiatry, 33,* 451–472.

American and Puerto Rican Cultural Involvement Scales

Response categories: 1 = Not at all; 4 = Very much

1. How important is it to you to celebrate holidays in the American way?
2. How much are American values a part of your life?
3. How comfortable would you be in a group of Americans who don't speak Spanish?
4. How important is it to you to raise your children with American values?
5. How proud are you of being American?
6. Do you think Americans are kind and generous?
7. How much do you enjoy American TV programs?
8. How much do you enjoy speaking English?
9. How many days a week would you like to eat American food?
10. How much are Puerto Rican values a part of your life?
11. How important is it to you to celebrate holidays in the Puerto Rican way?
12. How important is it to you to raise your children with Puerto Rican values?
13. How comfortable would you be in a group of Puerto Ricans who don't speak English?
14. How proud are you of being Puerto Rican?
15. How much do you enjoy speaking Spanish?
16. How much do you enjoy Spanish TV programs?
17. How many days a week would you like to eat Puerto Rican food?
18. Do you think Puerto Ricans are kind and generous?

Deleted items:

How important would it be to you for your children to have all American friends?
How important would it be to you for your children to have all Puerto Rican friends?

The Abbreviated Multidimensional Acculturation Scale (Zea, Asner-Self, Birman, & Buki, 2003)

The Abbreviated Multidimensional Acculturation Scale (AMAS-ZABB) scale measures acculturation to both Anglo-American culture and the respondent's culture of origin by including items on language preference, cultural competence, and self-identified ethnicity.

Description: The Abbreviated Multidimensional Acculturation Scale is a 42-item scale designed to assess three factors associated with acculturation in the United

States and in the country of origin: Identity (US American and culture of origin; items 1–6 and items 7–12), Language Competence (mastery of English and mastery of Spanish or other native language; items 13–21 and items 22–30), and Cultural Competence (knowledge of United States and country of origin cultures; items 31–36 and items 37–42). The scale options for items 1–12 range from *strongly* disagree (1) to *strongly agree* (4) and the scale options for items 12–42 range from *not at all* (1) to *extremely well/like a native* (4). For each subscale and ethnic group, item scores are averaged to form a total subscale score potentially ranging from 1 to 4. The total score for the US-American dimension on the AMAS-ZABB is calculated by averaging the three US-American subscales of cultural identity, language, and cultural competence, with higher scores indicating greater US acculturation. Similarly, the AMAS-ZABB culture-of-origin dimension is calculated by averaging the equivalent three (Latino/Latina in this study) subscales, with higher scores indicating greater retention of one's culture of origin. This scale is administered in two different ways: Respondents can take the survey as a self-administered scale available only in English or the scale can be offered as a structured interview in either Spanish or English.

Sample: Two initial studies were conducted to examine the psychometric properties of the Abbreviated Multidimensional Acculturation Scale. Study 1: The sample included 156 Latino/Latina students from mid-Atlantic urban institutes of higher education. The average age of participants was 23.5 years and nearly 60% were women. Study 2: The sample included 90 Central American immigrants living in the Washington, DC; the average age of the participants was 38.92 years, the average educational attainment was 10.54 years and about 52% were women.

Reliability: In Study 1, Cronbach's alpha coefficients ranged from .90 to .97 on the subscales while in Study 2, Cronbach's alpha coefficients ranged from .83 to .97 on the subscales.

Validity: Content validity was established by conducting 15 focus groups and asking the groups to examine the relevance of each scale item. Criterion validity was established as participants born in the United States scored higher on US-American subscales and lower on culture-of-origin subscales while participants born in Latin America scored higher on the culture-of-origin subscales and lower on the US-American subscales. Discriminant and convergent validity was tested using the Bicultural Involvement Questionnaire (BIQ-B) (Birman, 1991) and the Multigroup Ethnic Identity Measure (MEIM) (Phinney, 1992). The US-American identity scale was significantly related to BIQ-B Americanism, English language; US-American cultural competence; and overall AMAS-ZABB American dimension, while the AMAS-ZABB Latino subscales were not related to the BIQ-B Americanism scale. Conversely, the AMAS-ZABB subscales were significantly positively related to the BIQ-B Hispanicism scale: Latino ethnic identity; Spanish language; and overall AMAS-ZABB culture of origin dimension. Ethnic identity measured by the Multigroup Ethnic Identity Measure (MEIM) was positively related to Latino/Latina ethnic identity. There is evidence of factor validity because both the college and the community samples indicated that the proposed six subscales emerged as six factors.

Comments: The AMAS-ZABB demonstrated good internal consistency, a finding that has been replicated in other studies with Mexican American and Latina college students (Lechuga, 2008; Schiffner & Buki, 2006), parents from a variety of Hispanic countries of origin and their children (Davidson & Cardemil, 2009; both in English and Spanish versions), Latino males with HIV-positive status (Zea, Reisen, Poppen, Echeverry, & Bianchi, 2004), and Latinos in general (Morandi & Risco, 2006). The scale shows evidence of adequate concurrent, convergent, divergent, and constructs validity. The scale is fairly long.

Location: Zea, M. C., Asner-Self, K. K., Birman, D., & Buki, L. P. (2003). The abbreviated multidimensional acculturation scale: Empirical validation with two Latino/Latina samples. *Cultural Diversity and Ethnic Minority Psychology, 9*, 107–126.

Selected Publications

Davidson, T. M., & Cardemil, E. V. (2009). Parent-child communication and parental involvement in Latino adolescents. *Journal of Early Adolescence, 29*, 99–121.

Lechuga, J. (2008). Is acculturation a dynamic construct? The influence of method of priming culture on acculturation. *Hispanic Journal of Behavioral Sciences, 30*, 324–339.

Morandi, B., & Risco, C. (2006). Perceived discrimination experiences and mental health of Latina/o American persons. *Journal of Counseling Psychology, 53*, 411–421.

Phinney, J. S. (1992). The multigroup ethnic identity measure: A new scale for use with diverse groups. *Journal of Adolescent Research, 7*, 156–176.

Schiffner, T., & Buki, L. (2006). Latina college students' sexual health beliefs about human Papillomavirus infection. *Cultural Diversity and Ethnic Minority Psychology, 12*, 687–696.

Zea, M. C., Reisen, C. A., Poppen, P. J., Echeverry, J. J., & Bianchi, F. T. (2004). Disclosure of HIV-positive status to Latino gay men's social networks. *American Journal of Community Psychology, 3*, 107–116.

Abbreviated Multidimensional Acculturation Scale

Instructions: Please mark the number from the scale that best corresponds to your answer.

Response categories: 1 = Strongly disagree; 2 = Disagree somewhat; 3 = Agree somewhat; 4 = Strongly agree

1. I think of myself as being US American.
2. I feel good about being US American.

3. Being US American plays an important part in my life.
4. I feel that I am part of US-American culture.
5. I have a strong sense of being US American.
6. I am proud of being US American.
7. I think of myself as being (a member of my culture of origin).
8. I feel good about being (a member of my culture of origin).
9. Being (a member of my culture of origin) plays an important part in my life.
10. I feel that I am part of culture (culture of origin).
11. I have a strong sense of being (culture of origin).
12. I am proud of being (culture of origin).

Please answer the questions below using the following responses:

Response categories: 1 = Not at all; 2 = A little; 3 = Pretty well; 4 = Extremely well

How well do you speak English:

13. at school or work
14. with American friends
15. on the phone
16. with strangers
17. in general

How well do you understand English:

18. on TV or in movies
19. in newspapers and magazines
20. words in songs
21. in general

How well, do you speak your native language:

22. with family
23. with friends from the same country as you
24. on the phone
25. with strangers
26. in general

How well do you understand your native language:

27. on TV or in movies
28. in newspapers and magazines
29. words in songs
30. in general

How well do you know:

31. American national heroes
32. popular American TV shows
33. popular American newspapers and magazines
34. popular American actors and actresses

35. American history
36. American political leaders

How well do you know:

37. national heroes from your native culture
38. popular TV shows in your native language
39. popular newspapers and magazines in your native language
40. popular actors and actresses from your native culture
41. history of your native culture
42. political leaders from your native culture

Acculturation Rating Scale (Montgomery, 1992)

The Acculturation Rating Scale (ARS) was designed to measure acculturation to Mexican and Anglo-American culture and comfort with one's culture.

Description: The ARS is a 28-item scale assessing five domains including (1) comfort with Spanish language and Mexican traditions and comfort with thinking and speaking Spanish (10 items: 5, 6, 7, 11, 12, 13, 14, 15, 16, 17); (2) comfort with English language and Anglo-American tradition (7 items: 18, 19, 20, 21, 22, 23, 24); (3) one's preference for ethnic identity (5 items: 4, 25, 26, 27, 28); (4) self-rated ethnic identity (4 items: 1, 2, 3, and an item about generation in United States not on the scale), and (5) comfort with speaking English (3 items: 8, 9, 10). The items are rated on different scales depending on question (see scale for specifics). Several questions are reverse coded (items 5, 6, 7, 11, 12, 13, 14, 15, 16, and 17). The total acculturation score is calculated by summing and averaging the subject's ratings on the 28 items. Lower scores reflect a Mexican cultural orientation while higher scores reflect higher acculturation to Anglo-American culture. The authors used subscale scores in their psychometric tests, but did not provide a metric for measuring the subscales outside of these psychometric tests. The scale is self-administered and is available in both Spanish and English versions.

Sample: The scale was evaluated using a sample of 844 students enrolled in high school, college, or the English Language Institute at a local university. Fifty-five percent of the respondents were female; the average age of the subjects was 18.8, and 84% reported their surname as Mexican American.

Reliability: The alpha coefficient for the total scale score was .94. The alpha coefficients for the 5-factor subscales were .92, .86, .92, .90, and .92, respectively.

Validity: There is evidence of construct validity as significant relationships in the expected directions were found for the total acculturation score and its five subscales with subjects' surname, school, and generation status. Generational status in the United States was associated with the total acculturation scores. Anglo-surnamed individuals were more Anglo oriented than Mexican-surnamed individuals. Subjects who took the questionnaire in English had a stronger Anglo orientation than those who took the questionnaire in Spanish.

Comments: This scale assesses Anglo and Mexican orientation with separate questions. While the scale has internal consistency and construct validity, we could identify no additional studies assessing the psychometric properties. The findings are limited to a narrow sample of students.

Location: Montgomery, G. T. (1992). Comfort with acculturation status among students from south Texas. *Hispanic Journal of Behavioral Sciences, 14*, 201–223.

Acculturation Rating Scale: English Version

Response categories: *Items 1–3*: 1 = Mexican/Medicano; 2 = Chicano; 3 = Mexican American; 4 = Spanish, Hispanic, Latin American, American; 5 = Anglo American/other

1. Which ethnic identification does (did) your mother use?
2. Which ethnic identification does (did) your father use?
3. How do you identify yourself?

Response categories: *Item 4*: 1 = Almost exclusively Mexicans, Chicanos, Mexican Americans; 2 = Mostly Mexicans, Chicanos, Mexican Americans; 3 = About equally Mexicans, Chicanos, Mexican Americans, and Anglos or other ethnic groups; 4 = Mostly Anglos, Blacks, or other ethnic groups; 5 = Almost exclusively Anglos, Blacks, or ethnic groups.

4. What has been (or was) the ethnic origin of your friends from ages 6 to 18?

Response categories: *Items 5–10*: 1 = Very Uncomfortable; 2 = A Little Uncomfortable; 3 = Comfortable; 4 = Mostly Comfortable; 5 = Very Comfortable

5. How comfortable do you feel speaking Spanish at home? (R)
6. How comfortable do you feel speaking Spanish with friends, such as during free time at school? (R)
7. How comfortable do you feel thinking in Spanish? (R)
8. How comfortable do you feel speaking English at home?
9. How comfortable do you feel speaking English with friends, such as during free time at school?
10. How comfortable do you feel thinking in English?

Response categories: *Items 11–24*: 1 = Not at all; 2 = Very little; 3 = A little; 4 = A lot; 5 = Very much
How much do you enjoy:

11. listening to Spanish music? (R)
12. watching TV programs in Spanish? (R)
13. watching Spanish language movies? (R)
14. celebrating holidays according to Mexican tradition? (R)
15. reading books/magazines in Spanish? (R)
16. eating Mexican food? (R)
17. traveling and visiting in Mexico? (R)
18. listening to English music?
19. watching TV programs in English?
20. watching English language movies?
21. celebrating holidays according to Anglo-American tradition?
22. reading books/magazines in English?
23. eating Anglo-American food?
24. traveling and visiting in the United States?

Response categories: *Items 25–28*: 1 = Almost exclusively Mexicans, Chicanos, Mexican Americans; 2 = Mostly Mexicans, Chicanos, Mexican Americans; 3 = About equally Mexicans, Chicanos, Mexican Americans, and Anglos or other ethnic groups; 4 = Mostly Anglos, Blacks, or other ethnic groups; 5 = Almost exclusively Anglos, Blacks, or ethnic groups. Sometimes life is not as we really want it. If you could have your way, how would you like the following aspects of your life to be?

25. How would you like the ethnic identify of your friends to be?
26. How would you like your father's ethnic identify to be?
27. How would you like your mother's ethnic identity to be?
28. How would you like your own ethnic identity to be?

Cultural Life Style Inventory (Mendoza, 1989)

The Cultural Life Style Inventory (CLSI) assesses acculturation by identifying the level at which respondents identify with their native versus their new culture.

Description: The CLSI consists of 29 items and identifies three categories of acculturation: (1) Cultural Resistance (CR) refers to clinging to native culture and refusing to adopt a new culture; (2) Cultural Shift (CS) refers to adopting the new culture and almost letting go of native culture and values; and (3) Cultural Incorporation (CI) refers to adopting customs and values from both cultures. There are five domains: intra-family language, extra-family language, social affiliation and activities, cultural familiarity and activities, and cultural identification and pride. These domains are intermixed within the three dimensions of acculturation defined above. Items are rated with a letter; an *a* or *b* response is considered as cultural resistance, a *c* or *d* response is considered as cultural shift, and *e* is considered cultural incorporation. The CLSI can be used to generate two scores. The Cultural Life Style Profile is an indicator of the extent to which an individual's cultural lifestyle reflects cultural resistance, cultural incorporation, and cultural shift tendencies and is calculated by determining how many questions are answered in a resistance, incorporation or shift direction, then dividing these by the total number of valid responses. The second, Dominant and Non-dominant Cultural Life Style Tendencies is determined by statistically comparing an individual's two highest scores on the three acculturation choices (i.e., CR, CI, and CS scores); if statistically significant differences are found between the two most frequent cultural lifestyle tendencies, the individual is said to be predominantly in the acculturation pattern on which he or she scored highest. When the two proportions are not significantly different, the person is classified as culturally eclectic with respect to his or her acculturation pattern. The instrument is available in both English and Spanish, and may be administered individually or in a group setting. The interview is self-administered.

Sample: Two different samples were used to create and test the scale. One sample consisted of 97 first-generation Mexican Americans and 82 Anglo Americans ranging in age from 17 to 55. The second sample consisted of 68 first-generation, 76 second-generation, and 41 third-generation Mexican Americans ranging from age 16 to 52 years.

Reliability: Sample 2 was used to determine reliability. Cronbach's alpha for each of the five factors were .87 for intra-familial language use; .91 for extra-familial language use; .89 for social affiliation and activities; .84 for cultural familiarity and activities; and .89 for cultural identification and pride. Test–retest was assessed with a sample of 88 Mexican American and 59 Anglo Americans. The correlation across all groups was $r = .91$, for Mexican Americans who took the inventory in English; $r = .88$, for Mexican Americans who completed it in Spanish, and $r = .95$, for Anglo Americans. A test of equivalence for parallel forms yielded significant correlations between the two groups of bilingual Mexican Americans: $r = .80$ for the former group and $r = .77$ for the latter group.

Validity: There is evidence of construct validity. The study results showed that with successive generations, certain customs from the Mexican culture disappear from the respondent's habits (eta = .54), certain customs from the Anglo-American culture are adopted (eta = .61), and certain customs from both cultures coexist across generations. A significant positive correlation was found between exposure to the mainstream culture and cultural shift ($r = .66$) and significant negative correlations with cultural resistance and incorporation ($r = -.60$ and $r = -.25$). The test of the Cultural Life Styles Inventory for concordance shows a significant correlation between the self-reported responses of the target individuals and reports given by relatives ($r = .71$).

Comments: By linking the multidimensional factors and the styles of acculturation within a single instrument, the scale provides an approach to measuring different levels of acculturation. The scoring for this instrument is complicated. There is evidence of reliability. Moderate to high internal consistency for the five factors has been found in a study with Puerto Rican undergraduate students

(De Leon & Mendez, 1996). High internal consistency has been found for the total scale score, though the scale is bidimensional (Managa et al., 1996). The five factor model has been found in a study of Puerto Rican undergraduates, though the item composition is somewhat different, offering evidence of factorial validity (De Leon & Mendez, 1996). A 10-item adaptation of the scale has been evaluated by Lerman, Maldonado, and Luna (2009). Note that the scale has been modified since its original publication.

Location: Mendoza, R. H. (1989). An empirical scale to measure type and degree of acculturation in Mexican-American adolescents and adults. *Journal of Cross-Cultural Psychology, 20*, 372–385.

Selected Publications

DeLeon, B., & Mendez, S. (1996). Factorial structure of a measure of acculturation in a Puerto Rican population. *Educational and Psychological Measurement, 56*, 155–165.

Lerman, D., Maldonado, R., & Luna. D. (2009). A theory-based measure of acculturation: The shortened cultural life style inventory. *Journal of Business Research, 62*, 399–406.

Magana, J. R., Rocha, O. D., Amsel, J., Magana, H. A., Fernandez, M. I., & Rulnick, S. (1996). Revisiting the dimensions of acculturation: Cultural theory and psychometric practice. *Hispanic Journal of Behavioral Sciences, 18*, 444–468.

Mendoza, R. (1994). *Cultural life styles inventory. Version 2.0.* Author.

Cultural Life Styles Inventory (Version 2.0; Mendoza, 1994)

1. What language do you use when you speak with your *grandparents*?
    ____a. Only Spanish
    ____b. More Spanish than English
    c. More English than Spanish
    ____d. Only English
    ____e. Both English and Spanish about equally
    ____f. Other language (please specify:________________)
    ____g. I do not have any grandparents
2. What language do you use when you speak with your *parents*?
    ____a. Only Spanish
    ____b. More Spanish than English
    ____c. More English than Spanish
    ____d. Only English
    ____e. Both English and Spanish about equally
    ____f. Other language (please specify:________________)
    ____g. I do not have any parents

3. What language do you use when you speak with your *brothers* and *sisters*?
____a. Only Spanish
____b. More Spanish than English
____c. More English than Spanish
____d. Only English
____e. Both English and Spanish about equally
____f. Other language (please specify:______________)
____g. I do not have any brothers or sisters
4. What language do you use when you speak with your *spouse* or *person you live with*?
____a. Only Spanish
____b. More Spanish than English
____c. More English than Spanish
____d. Only English
____e. Both English and Spanish about equally
____f. Other language (please specify:______________)
____g. I am not married
5. What language do you use when you speak with your *children*?
____a. Only Spanish
____b. More Spanish than English
____c. More English than Spanish
____d. Only English
____e. Both English and Spanish about equally
____f. Other language (please specify:______________)
____g. I do not have any children
6. What language do you use when you speak with your *closet friends*?
____a. Only Spanish
____b. More Spanish than English
____c. More English than Spanish
____d. Only English
____e. Both English and Spanish about equally
____f. Other language (please specify:______________)
7. What language *records*, *tapes*, or *compact discs* do you own?
____a. Only Spanish-speaking records, tapes, and compact discs
____b. Mostly Spanish-speaking records, tapes, and compact discs
____c. Mostly English-speaking records, tapes, and compact discs
____d. Only English-speaking records, tapes, and compact discs
____e. Both English- and Spanish-speaking records, tapes, and compact discs about equally
____f. Records tapes and compact discs in other language (please specify: ______________)
____g. I do not own any records, tapes, or compact discs
8. What kind of *radio* stations do you listen to?
____a. Only Spanish-speaking radio stations
____b. Mostly Spanish-speaking radio stations

____c. Mostly English-speaking radio stations
____d. Only English-speaking radio stations
____e. Both English- and Spanish-speaking radio stations about equally
____f. Radio stations in other language (please specify: ______________)

9. What kind of *TV* programs do you watch?
____a. Only Spanish-speaking TV programs
____b. Mostly Spanish-speaking TV programs
____c. Mostly English-speaking TV programs
____d. Only English-speaking TV programs
____e. Both English- and Spanish-speaking TV programs about equally
____f. TV programs in other language (please specify: ______________)

10. What kind of *newspapers* and *magazines* do you read?
____a. Only newspapers and magazines in Spanish
____b. Mostly newspapers and magazines in Spanish
____c. Mostly newspapers and magazines in English
____d. Only newspapers and magazines in English
____e. Both newspapers and magazines in English and Spanish about equally
____f. Newspapers and magazines in other language (please specify: ______________)

11. In what language do you *pray*?
____a. Only Spanish
____b. More Spanish than English
____c. More English than Spanish
____d. Only English
____e. Both English and Spanish about equally
____f. Other language (please specify:______________)
____g. I do not pray

12. In what language are the *jokes* with which you are familiar?
____a. All are in Spanish
____b. More are in Spanish than in English
____c. More are in English than in Spanish
____d. All are in English
e. Some are in English and some are in Spanish about equally
____f. Other language (please specify:______________)

13. What kind of *foods* do you typically eat *at home*?
____a. Only Mexican foods
____b. Mostly Mexican foods
____c. Mostly American (US) foods
____d. Both American (US) and Mexican foods about equally
____e. Other types of foods (please specify:______________)

14. What kind of *restaurants* do you typically eat?
____a. Only at Mexican restaurants
____b. Mostly at Mexican restaurants
____c. Mostly at non-Mexican restaurants
____d. Only at non-Mexican restaurants

____e. Both at non-Mexican and Mexican restaurants about equally
____f. Other types of restaurants (please specify:_______________)

15. What is the ethnic background of your *closet friends*?
____a. All are Mexican or Mexican American
____b. Most are Mexican or Mexican American
____c. Most are Anglo American
____d. All are Anglo American
____e. Both Anglo American and Mexican/Mexican American about equally
____f. Other ethnic group (please specify:_______________)

16. What is the ethnic background of the people that you have *dated*?
____a. All are Mexican or Mexican American
____b. Most are Mexican or Mexican American
____c. Most are Anglo American
____d. All are Anglo American
____e. Both Anglo American and Mexican/Mexican American about equally
____f. Other ethnic group (please specify:_______________)
____g. I have never dated anyone

17. When you go to *social functions* such as parties, dances, picnics, or sports events, what is the ethnic background of the people that you tend to go with?
____a. Always with Mexicans or Mexican Americans
____b. Mostly with Mexicans or Mexican Americans
____c. Mostly with Anglo Americans
____d. Always with Anglo Americans
____e. Both with Anglo Americans and Mexicans/Mexican Americans about equally
____f. Other ethnic group (please specify:_______________)

18. What is the ethnic composition of the *neighborhood* where you *live*?
____a. Only Mexican or Mexican American
____b. Mostly Mexican or Mexican American
____c. Mostly Anglo American
____d. Only Anglo American
____e. Both Anglo American and Mexican/Mexican American about equally
____f. Other ethnic group (please specify:_______________)

19. Which *national anthem* do you know?
____a. Only the Mexican National anthem
____b. Mostly the Mexican national anthem
____c. Mostly the American (US) national anthem
____d. Only the American (US) national anthem
____e. Both the American (US) and Mexican national anthems about equally
____f. Neither the American (US) nor the Mexican national anthems

20. Which *national* or *cultural heritage* do you feel *most proud* of?
____a. Unquestionably my Mexican heritage
____b. Primarily my Mexican heritage
____c. Primarily my American (US) heritage
____d. Unquestionably my American (US) heritage

____e. Both my American (US) and Mexican heritage about equally
____f. Other national or cultural heritage (please specify:______________)

21. What types of *national* or *cultural holidays* (such as Fourth of July and Dieciséis De Septiembre) do you typically celebrate?
____a. Only Mexican holidays
____b. Mostly Mexican holidays
____c. Mostly American (US) holidays
____d. Only American (US) holidays
____e. Both American (US) and Mexican holidays about equally
____f. Other national or cultural holidays (please specify:______________)
____g. I do not celebrate any national or cultural holidays

22. What is the ethnic background of the *movie stars* and *popular singers* that you *most admire*?
____a. All are Mexican, Mexican American, or Latino
____b. Most are Mexican, Mexican American, or Latino
____c. Most are Anglo American
____d. All are Anglo American
____e. Some are Anglo American and some are Mexican, Mexican American, or Latino about equally
____f. Other ethnic group (please specify:______________)

23. If you had a choice, what is the ethnic background of the person that you would *marry*?
____a. Most definitely a Mexican or Mexican American
____b. Preferably a Mexican or Mexican American
____c. Preferably an Anglo American
____d. Most definitely an Anglo American
____e. Either an Anglo American or a Mexican/Mexican American, it would not matter to me
____f. Other ethnic group (please specify:______________)

24. If you had *children*, what types of *names* would you give them?
____a. Most definitely Spanish or Mexican names
____b. Probably Spanish or Mexican names
c. Probably English or Anglo-American names
____d. Most definitely English or Anglo-American names
____e. Either English/Anglo-American or Spanish/Mexican names, it would not matter to me
____f. Other ethnic names (please specify:______________)

25. If you had children, in what language would you *teach* them to *read*, *write,* and *speak*?
____a. Only in Spanish (with no English)
____b. Primarily in Spanish (with some English)
____c. Primarily in English (with some Spanish)
____d. Only in English (with no Spanish)
____e. Equally in both English and Spanish
____f. Other language (please specify:______________)

26. Which culture and way of life do you believe is *responsible* for the *social problems* (such as poverty, teenage pregnancies, and gangs) found in some Mexican American communities?
____a. Only the Mexican culture
____b. Mostly the Mexican culture
____c. Mostly the American (US) culture
____d. Only the American (US) culture
____e. Both American (US) and Mexican cultures about equally
____f. Other (please specify:______________)
27. At what kind of *stores* do you *typically shop*?
____a. Only in stores that have Spanish-speaking workers
____b. Primarily at stores that have Spanish-speaking workers
____c. Primarily at stores that have English-speaking workers
____d. Only in stores that have English-speaking workers
____e. Both, at stores that have English-speaking workers and at stores that have Spanish-speaking workers about equally
____f. Other types of stores (please specify:______________)
28. How do you prefer to be *identified*?
____a. Most definitely as a Mexican, Mexican American, Chicano, Latino, or Hispanic
____b. Preferably as a Mexican, Mexican American, Chicano, Latino, or Hispanic
____c. Preferably as an American, Anglo American, or Caucasian
____d. Most definitely as an American, Anglo American, or Caucasian
____e. Either as an American/Anglo American/Caucasian or as a Mexican/Mexican American/Chicano/Latino/Hispanic, I have no preference
____f. Other group (please specify:______________)
29. Which culture and way of life would you say has had the *most positive influence* on your life?
____a. Most definitely the Mexican culture
____b. Probably the Mexican culture
____c. Probably the American (US) culture
____d. Most definitely the American (US) culture
____e. Both American (US) and Mexican cultures about equally
____f. Other culture (please specify:______________)

Acculturation Rating Scale for Mexican Americans-II (Cuellar, Arnold, & Maldonado, 1995)

The Acculturation Rating Scale for Mexican Americans-II (ARSMA-II) assesses behavioral and affective aspects of acculturation.

Description: ARSMA-II assesses four domains: (a) language use and preference, (b) ethnic identity and classification, (c) cultural heritage and ethnic behaviors, and (d) ethnic interaction. ARSMA-II consists of two scales. Scale 1 (Acculturation Scale) measures integration (how well the respondent adopts aspects of both cultures) and assimilation (degree to which respondents adopts dominant culture by dropping their Mexican culture). Scale 2 (Marginality Scale) assesses marginalization (the degree to which a respondent that tries to assimilate is rejected by the dominant group) and separation (the degree to which the respondent refuses to adopt the dominant culture.). The scales need not be used together. The ARSMA-II is a self-administered questionnaire and there are English and Spanish versions.

Scale 1 is a 30-item scale. The Anglo Orientation Subscale (AOS) includes 13 items (2, 4, 7, 9, 10, 13, 15, 16, 19, 23, 25, 27, 30) and the Mexican Orientation Subscale (MOS) includes 17 items (1, 3, 5, 6, 8, 11, 12, 14, 17, 18, 20, 21, 22, 24, 26, 28, 29). Responses range from *not at all* (1) to *extremely often or almost always* (5). The AOS score is calculated by summing the items and dividing by 13; the MOS score is the sum of the items divided by 17. The overall acculturation score is calculated by subtracting the MOS score from the AOS score. The degree of acculturation is based on cut-off scores: *very Mexican oriented* (<-1.33); *Mexican oriented to approximately bicultural* (≥ -1.33 to $\leq -.07$); *slightly Anglo oriented bicultural* ($> -.07$ to 1.19); *strongly Anglo oriented* ($\geq$ 1.19 to 2.45); and *very Assimilated* ($>$ 2.45).

Scale 2 includes 18 items and includes three subscales: Anglo Marginality (ANGMAR; items 1–6), Mexican Marginality (MEXMAR; items 7–12), and Mexican American marginality (MAMARG; items 13–18). An overall marginality score is computed by summing the 18 items and subscale scores are the sum of the relevant six items.

Sample: The validation sample consisted of 379 undergraduates including Mexican, Mexican American or non-Hispanic White. The sample was almost equally divided by gender (males = 43% and females = 48% with 9% missing data). The average educational level was between 1 and 2 years of college.

Reliability: Coefficient alphas and 1-week test–retest reliabilities for the scales were .83/.94 for Anglo Orientation Scale, .88/.96 for Mexican Orientation Scale, .87/.78 for Marginality Scale, .90/.72 for Anglo Marginality Subscale, .68/.80 for Mexican Marginality Subscale, and .91/.81 for Mexican American Marginality Subscale

Validity: ARSMA and ARSMA-II were correlated ($r = .89$) demonstrating concurrent validity. The correlation between acculturation and generational status was .61 and the mean differences between generations are significant, supporting the construct validity of ARSMA-II.

Comments: There is evidence of reliability and validity with a college sample both using scores and levels of acculturation. Similar findings have been found with college students and the relationship of acculturation scores (Scale 1) with ethnic identity (Cueller, Nyberg, & Maldonado, 1997) and substance abusing adults (Lessinger, 1997). There is evidence that the Marginality scale (Scale 2) is not a valid indicator of marginality (Gutierrez, Franco, Powell, Peterson, & Reid, 2009). Scale 1 has been adapted for use with Asian American college students (Lee, Yoon, & Liu-Tom, 2006) and Asian American middle school aged youth (Schaefer et al., 2009) with satisfactory evidence of reliability and validity. A brief version using 12 items from Scale 1 has been adapted for children and adolescents with mixed results for reliability and validity (Bauman, 2005; Lopez, 2009).

Location: Cuellar, I., Arnold, B., & Maldonado, R. (1995). Acculturation rating scale for Mexican Americans-II: A revision of the original ARSMA scale. *Hispanic Journal of Behavioral Sciences, 17*, 275–304.

Selected Publications

Bauman, S. (2005). The reliability and validity of the brief acculturation rating scale for Mexican Americans-II for children and adolescents. *Hispanic Journal of Behavioral Sciences, 27*, 426–441.

Cuellar, I., Nyberg, B., & Maldonado, R. E. (1997). Ethnic identity and acculturation in a young adult Mexican-origin population. *Journal of Community Psychology, 25*, 535–549.

Gutierrez, M. A., Franco, L. M., Powell, K. G., Peterson, N. A., & Reid, R. J. (2009). Psychometric properties of the Acculturation Rating Scale for Mexican Americans-II: Exploring dimensions of marginality among a diverse Latino population. *Hispanic Journal of Behavioral Sciences, 31*, 340–356.

Lee, R. M., Yoon, E., & Liu-Tom, H.-T. T. (2006). Structure and measurement of acculturation/enculturation for Asian Americans using the ARSMA-II. *Measurement and Evaluation in Counseling and Development, 39*, 42–55.

Lessenger, L. H. (1997). Use of acculturation rating scale for Mexican Americans-II with substance abuse patients. *Hispanic Journal of Behavioral Sciences, 19*, 387–398.

Lopez, F. A. (2009). Developmental considerations and acculturation of children: Measures and issues. *Hispanic Journal of Behavioral Sciences, 31*, 57–72.

Schaefer, S. E., Salazar, M., Bruhn, C., Saviano, D., Boushey, C., & Van Loan, M. D. (2009). Influence of race, acculturation, and socioeconomic status on tendency toward overweight in Asian-American and Mexican-American early adolescent females. *Journal of Immigrant and Minority Health, 11*, 188–197.

Acculturation Rating Scale for Mexican Americans-II: English Version

Note: (B) indicates used in Brief ARSMA-II for Children.

Scale 1: 1 = Not at all; 2 = Very little or not very often; 3 = Moderately; 4 = Much or very often; 5 = Extremely often or almost always

1. I speak Spanish (B)
2. I speak English (B)
3. I enjoy speaking Spanish (B)
4. I associate with Anglos (B)
5. I associate with Mexicans and/or Mexican Americans
6. I enjoy listening to Spanish language music
7. I enjoy listening to English language music
8. I enjoy Spanish language on TV (B)
9. I enjoy English language on TV
10. I enjoy English language movies (B)
11. I enjoy Spanish language movies (B)
12. I enjoy reading (e.g., books in Spanish) (B)
13. I enjoy reading (e.g., books in English)
14. I write letters in Spanish
15. I write letters in English (B)
16. My thinking is done in the English language (B)
17. My thinking is done in the Spanish language (B)
18. My contact with Mexico has been
19. My contact with the USA has been
20. My father identifies or identified himself as 'Mexicano'
21. My mother identifies or identified herself as 'Mexicana'
22. My friends, while I was growing up, were of Mexican origin
23. My friends, while I was growing up, were of Anglo origin
24. My family cooks Mexican foods
25. My friends now are of Anglo origin (B)
26. My friends now are of Mexican origin
27. I like to identify myself as an Anglo American
28. I like to identify myself as a Mexican American
29. I like to identify myself as a Mexican
30. I like to identify myself as an American

Scale 2: 1 = Not at all; 2 = Very little or not very often; 3 = Moderately; 4 = Much or very often; 5 = Extremely often or almost always

1. I have difficulty accepting some ideas held by Anglos
2. I have difficulty accepting some attitudes held by Anglos
3. I have difficulty accepting some behaviors exhibited by Anglos
4. I have difficulty accepting some values held by some Anglos
5. I have difficulty accepting certain practices and customs found in some Anglos
6. I have, or think I would have, difficulty accepting Anglos as close personal friends
7. I have difficulty accepting ideas held by some Mexicans
8. I have difficulty accepting certain attitudes held by Mexicans
9. I have difficulty accepting some behaviors exhibited by Mexicans

10. I have difficulty accepting some values held by some Mexicans
11. I have difficulty accepting certain practices and customs found in some Mexicans
12. I have, or think I would have difficulty accepting Mexicans as close personal friends
13. I have difficulty accepting ideas held by Mexican Americans
14. I have difficulty accepting certain attitudes held by Mexican Americans
15. I have difficulty accepting some behaviors exhibited by Mexican Americans
16. I have difficulty accepting some values help by Mexican Americans
17. I have difficulty accepting certain practices and customs commonly found in Mexican Americans
18. I have, or think I would have difficulty accepting Mexican Americans as close personal friends

The Psychological Acculturation Scale (Tropp, Erkut, Coll, Alarcon, & Vazquez-Garcia, 1999)

The Psychological Acculturation Scale (PAS) assesses individual's sense of attachment to and understanding of Anglo-American and Latino/Hispanic cultures.

Description: The PAS is a 10-item scale. Responses are offered on a 9-point Likert-type scale ranging from *only Hispanic/Latino* (1) to *only Anglo/American* (9). The midpoint represents a bicultural orientation. A mid-point score (4.5) suggests that the respondent is bicultural, that is, both Latino/a and American. Scores lower than 4.5 suggest a higher Latino/a orientation and scores higher than 4.5 suggest a greater Anglo-American identification. The scale can either be self-administered or administered through a structured interview format. The scale is available in both English and Spanish.

Sample: Three studies were performed to determine the psychometric properties of the PAS. Study 1: The sample included 36 participants who identified themselves as Latinos, 26 were women, and the respondents' average age was 28.6. Study 2: The sample included 107 Puerto Rican, of whom 64 were female and had an average age of 27.9 years. Study 3: The sample included 247 Puerto Rican adolescents, ages 13 and 14 and 228 mothers of the adolescents. The majority of the adolescent sample (52%) was female, 98 were born in Puerto Rico, and 146 were born on the US mainland. The average age of the parents was 39 years.

Reliability: In Studies 1 and 2, Cronbach's alphas were .83 and .90 for the Spanish version and .85 and .83 for the English version. In Study 1, item total correlation ranged from .22 and .68 for scores on the Spanish version and from .27 and .71 for the English version. In Study 2, item total correlations ranged from .55 to

.81 for the Spanish version, and from .36 to .67 for the English version. Cronbach's alphas for the adolescent and parent samples were .91.

Validity: There is evidence of construct validity since the PAS correlated with percentage of lifetime in the United States ($r = .43$) indicating a stronger Anglo/American orientation the longer the time spent on the US mainland. Respondents born in Puerto Rico had lower PAS scores than did respondents born on the US mainland (Studies 2 and 3). PAS also correlated positively with use of English at home during the respondent's childhood (Studies 2 and 3). Respondents who chose to complete the questionnaire in Spanish tended to have lower scores on the PAS than did respondents who completed the questionnaire in English.

Comments: The PAS measures individuals' psychological responses to cultural exposure. Overall, the scale demonstrates excellent internal consistency; this finding has been found in other studies (Beeber, Perreira, & Schwartz, 2008; Castillo, Cano, Chen, Blucker, & Olds, 2008; Cintron, Carter, & Sbrocco, 2005). There is evidence of validity across different samples and across two different modes of administration; other research finds the scale relating to other constructs as hypothesized (Castillo et al., 2008; Ghorpade, Lackritz, & Singh, 2004). The scale has been used with different ethnic groups in the United States, with excellent internal consistency (Ghorpade et al., 2004) and adapted to other ethnic groups and languages (Miglietta & Tartaglia, 2008).

Location: Tropp, L. R., Erkut, S., Coll, C. G., Alarcon, O., & Vazquez-Garcia, H. A. (1999). Psychosocial acculturation: Development of a new measure for Puerto Ricans on the U.S. mainland. *Educational and Psychological Measurement, 59*, 351–367.

Selected Publications

Beeber, L. S., Perreira, K. M., & Schwartz, T. (2008). Supporting the mental health of mothers raising children in poverty: How do we target them for intervention studies. *Annals of the New York Academy of Science, 1136;* 86–100.

Castillo, L. G., Cano, M. A., Chen, S. W., Blucker, R. T., & Olds, S. O. (2008). Family conflict and intragroup marginalization as predictors of acculturative stress in Latino college students. *International Journal of Stress Management, 15,* 43–52.

Cintron, J. A., Carter, M. M., & Sbrocco, T. (2005). *Ataques de Nervios* in relation to anxiety sensitivity among island Puerto Ricans. *Culture, Medicine, and Psychiatry, 29,* 415–431.

Ghorpade, J., Lackritz, J., & Singh, G. (2004). Psychological acculturation of ethnic minorities into White Anglo American culture: Consequences and predictors. *Journal of Applied Social Psychology, 34,* 1208–1228.

Miglietta, A., & Tartaglia, S. (2008). The influence of length of stay, linguistic competence, and media exposure in immigrants' adaptation. *Cross-Cultural Research, 20,* 1–16.

Psychological Acculturation Scale – English Version

Response categories:

1———2———3———4———5———6———7———8———9

Only with Hispanics/Latinos	Equally with Hispanics/Latinos	Only with Anglos (Americans)

1. With which group of people do you feel you share most of your beliefs and values?
2. With which group of people do you feel you have the most in common?
3. With which group of people do you feel most comfortable?
4. In your opinion, which group of people best understands your ideas (your way of thinking)?
5. Which culture do you feel proud to be a part of?
6. In what culture do you know how things are done and feel that you can do them easily?
7. In what culture do you feel confident you know how to act?
8. In your opinion, which group of people do you understand best?
9. In what culture do you know what is expected of a person in various situations?
10. Which culture do you know the most about (for example: its history, traditions, and customs)?

Bicultural Involvement Questionnaire (Szapocznik, Kurtines, & Fernandez, 1980)

The Bicultural Involvement Questionnaire (BIQ) assesses the degree to which an individual participates and feels comfortable in Hispanic and American culture.

Description: The BIQ consists of 42 items (note that items 25–33 are scored twice and differently to create a 42-item scale) to assess two dimensions: (1) Biculturalism ranging from high Hispanic acculturation to high Anglo acculturation, with a middle score representing a bicultural orientation and (2) Cultural Involvement ranging from no cultural involvement with Hispanic or Anglo-American culture to cultural involvement with Hispanic or Anglo-American culture. Items are scored on a 5-point Likert scale with responses varying depending on item. The scale questions are divided into involvement in American culture, Americanism, and includes 21 questions (items 6–10, 18–24, and 25–33) and involvement in Hispanic culture, Hispanicism, and includes 21 questions (items 1–5, items 11–17, and the reverse score of items 25–33). Americanism and Hispanicism scores are calculated by summing the appropriate item responses. The Biculturalism scale score is calculated by subtracting the total Americanism scores from the total Hispanicism scores. A score of zero reflects biculturalism, less than zero reflects a tendency toward Americanism and greater than zero reflects a tendency toward Hispanicism. The Cultural Involvement scale score is calculated by summing the Hispanic items and American items together. A higher score represents more involvement in both cultures while a lower score reflects less involvement in either of the two cultures. The scale is self-administered. There are both English and Spanish versions.

Sample: Three samples were used to assess the scale's psychometric properties. Sample 1 consisted of 93 Cuban-American youth with an average age of 13.7 years; 51 (54.8%) were males. Sample 2 included 47 non-Cuban Hispanic-American youth with an average age of 14.1; 25 (53.2%) were males. Sample 3 included 16 participants, 11 Cuban-Americans and 5 non-Cuban Hispanic-Americans. The participants' average age was 14 years and 10 (62.5%) were males.

Reliability: The combined Samples 1 and 2 alpha coefficients for the scales were .93 Hispaniscism and .89 for Americanism. The reliability of the difference scores for the Biculturalism Scale was .94, and of the composite scores for Cultural Involvement Scale was .79. Sample 3's 6-week test–retest reliability scores were .50 Hispanicism, .54 Americanism, .79 Biculturalism, and .14 (ns) Cultural Involvement.

Validity: To establish criterion validity, biculturalism of Samples 1 and 2 participants was rated by teachers. Teacher ratings of biculturalism were statistically significantly related to Biculturalism Scale scores ($r = .42$) and Cultural Involvement Scale scores ($r = .22$) for Sample 1 (Cuban Hispanics) but not for Sample 2 (non-Cuban Hispanics). Teacher ratings (Sample 1) of adjustment were also related to Biculturalism and both Biculturalism and Cultural Involvement distinguished the most adjusted from the least adjusted students.

Comments: There is evidence of reliability and validity. Excellent internal consistency has been found in other studies with broader samples of Hispanic youth (Birman, 1998; Coatsworth, Maldonado-Molina, Pantin, & Szapocznik, 2005; Martinez, 2006; Schwartz, Pantin, Sullivan, Prado, & Szapocznik, 2006), Hispanic college students (Gomez & Fassinger, 1994) and Hispanic adults (Martinez, 2006; Schwartz et al., 2006). Construct validity has been found as the scales, in particular, the Americanism, Hispanicism, and the Bicultural scales, are related to other constructs such as styles of achieving one's goals (Gomez & Fassinger, 1994), length of residence in the United States (Rivera-Sinclair, 1997; Schwartz et al., 2006), generation in the United States (Perez & Padilla, 2000), and anxiety (Rivera-Sinclair, 1997). Respondents may be classified into categories that provide meaningful differences (Coatsworth et al., 2005). There is evidence of factorial validity; Guo, Suarez-Morales, Schwartz, & Szapocznik (2009) report a four-factor structure of Spanish language, Hispanic activity, English language, and American activity.

Location: Szapocznik, J., Kurtines, W. M., & Fernandez, T. (1980). Bicultural involvement and adjustment in Hispanic-American youths. *International Journal of Intercultural Relations, 4*, 353–365.

Selected Publications

Birman, D. (1998). Biculturalism and perceived competence of Latino immigrant adolescents. *American Journal of Community Psychology, 26*, 335–354.

Coatsworth, J. D., Maldonado-Molina, M., Pantin, H., & Szapocznik, J. (2005). A person-centered and ecological investigation of acculturation strategies in Hispanic immigrant youth. *Journal of Community Psychology, 33*, 157–174.
Gomez, M. J., & Fassinger, R. E. (1994). An initial model of Latina achievement: Acculturation, biculturalism and achieving styles. *Journal of Counseling Psychology, 41,* 205–215.
Guo, X., Suarez-Morales, L., Schwartz, S. J., & Szapocznik, J. (2009). Some evidence for multidimensional biculturalism: Confirmatory factor analysis and measurement invariance analysis on the Bicultural Involvement Questionnaire-Short Version. *Psychological Assessment, 21,* 22–31.
Martinez, C. R. (2006). Effects of differential family acculturation on Latino adolescent substance abuse. *Family Relations, 55,* 306–317.
Perez, W., & Padilla, A. M. (2000). Cultural orientation across three generations of Hispanic adolescents. *Hispanic Journal of Behavioral Sciences, 22,* 390–398.
Rivera-Sinclair, E. A. (1997). Acculturation/biculturalism and its relationship to adjustment in Cuban-Americans. *International Journal of Intercultural Relations, 21*, 379–391.
Schwartz, S. J., Pantin, H., Sullivan, S., Prado, G., & Szapocznik, J. (2006). Nativity and years in the receiving culture as markers of acculturation. *Journal of Cross-Cultural Psychology, 37,* 345–353.

Bicultural Involvement Questionnaire

Response categories: *Items 1–10*: 1 = Not at all comfortable to 5 = Very comfortable

A. How comfortable do you feel speaking *Spanish*

1. at home
2. in school
3. at work
4. with friends
5. in general

B. How comfortable you feel speaking English

6. at home
7. in school
8. at work
9. with friends
10. in general

Items 11–24: 1 = Not at all; 5 = Very much

C. How much do you enjoy

11. Hispanic music

12. Hispanic dances
13. Hispanic-oriented places
14. Hispanic-type recreation
15. Hispanic TV programs
16. Hispanic radio stations
17. Hispanic books and magazines

D. How much do you enjoy

18. American music
19. American dances
20. American-oriented places
21. American-type recreation
22. American TV programs
23. American radio stations
24. American books and magazines

Items 25–33: 1 = I would wish this to be completely Hispanic; 2 = I would wish this to be mostly Hispanic; 3 = I would with this to be both Hispanic and American; 4 = I would wish this to be mostly American; 5 = I would wish this to be completely American

E. Sometimes life is not as we really want it. If you could have your way, how would you like the following aspects of your life to be?

25. Food
26. Language
27. Music
28. TV programs
29. Books/magazines
30. Dances
31. Radio programs
32. Way of celebrating birthdays
33. Way of celebrating weddings

Acculturative Stress

The Societal, Attitudinal, Familial, and Environmental Acculturative Stress Scale – Children (Chavez, Moran, Reid, & Lopez, 1997)

The Societal, Attitudinal, Familial, and Environmental Acculturative Stress Scale-Children (SAFE-C) measures both general and ethnicity specific acculturative stress in children.

Description: SAFE-C consists of 36 items measuring three domains: (1) General Social Stressors that are generally common to youth (16 items: 2, 6, 7, 10, 11, 13, 16, 17, 19, 21, 23, 25, 26, 30, 31, 36); (2) Process-oriented Stressors (14 items: 3, 4, 5, 8, 9, 14, 15, 18, 20, 22, 27, 28, 29, 35); and (3) Perceptions of Discrimination (6 items: 1, 12, 41, 32, 33, 34). The latter two domains can be combined into a single score. Each response is based on a 5-point Likert scale with response options being: *does not bother me* (1); *almost never bothers me* (2); *sometimes bothers me* (3); *often bothers me* (4); *bothers me a lot* (5). A statement that does not apply to the subject is scored as zero. A statement that does not apply to the subject response is not used to compute scores (though at least one study counted it as a *does not bother me* response). A total score for the SAFE-C is obtained by summing the individual items and subtracting 36; scores can also be generated for any of the domains in the same way. Total SAFE-C scores range from 0 to 180, higher scores indicate higher level of perceived stress. For general social stress, the possible scores range from 0 to 80; process-oriented stress scores, 0 to 70; and for perceived discrimination, 0 to 30. The scale is administered in a standardized interview format.

Sample: The scale was developed using a sample of 71 children; 45 were Euro-Americans and 26 were Latino/as. The average age of the participants was 9.43 years.

Reliability: Cronbach's alpha for the overall SAFE-C was .86. No subscale alphas were provided.

Validity: The Latino children had a mean score of 44.31 on Acculturation Process items, 14.19 on Perceived Discrimination items, 43.27 on general Social Stress items, and 101.77 on the total Safe-C. The Euro-American sample had a mean score of 27.04 on Acculturative process items; 9.36 on Perceived Discrimination items; 34.87 on General Social Stress items; and 71.27 on the Total Safe-C. Results from the comparisons of the Latino and Euro-American SAFE-C mean scores suggest that Latinos scored significantly higher than Euro-Americans in all stress domains as expected.

Comments: There is limited evidence for reliability and just for the total scale score. Other studies have found satisfactory internal consistency for the Process-Oriented Subscale (Schwartz, Zamboanga, & Jarvis, 2007) or the 20 item unique stressors domain (Hawley, Chavez, & St. Romain, 2007). There is less evidence for validity; psychometric studies have found mixed results about the hypothesized relationship of scale scores to other constructs (Hawley et al., 2007; Schwartz et al., 2007; Weisskirch & Alva, 2002). There is no evidence of factorial validity bringing into question the actual use of subscale scores. A factor analysis of the 20 items reflecting ethnic-related stressors found that only 12 of the items should be retained and some items identified as process were related to discrimination (Suarez-Morales, Dillon, & Szapocznik, 2007).

Location: Chavez, D. V., Moran, V. R., Reid, S. L., & Lopez, M. (1997). Acculturative stress in children: A modification of the SAFE scale. *Hispanic Journal of Behavioral Sciences, 19*, 34–44.

Selected Publications

Hawley, S. R., Chavez, D. V., & St. Romain, T. (2007). Developing a bicultural model for academic achievement: A look at acculturative stress, coping, and self-perception. *Hispanic Journal of Behavioral Sciences, 29,* 283–299.

Schwartz, S. J., Zamboanga, B. L., & Jarvis, L. H. (2007). Ethnic identify and acculturation in Hispanic early adolescents: Mediated relationships to academic grades, prosocial behaviors, and externalizing symptoms. *Cultural Diversity and Ethnic Minority Psychology, 13,* 364–373.

Suarez-Morales, L., Dillon, F. R., & Szapocznik, J. (2007). Validation of the acculturative stress inventory for children. *Cultural Diversity and Ethnic Minority Psychology, 13,* 216–224.

Weisskirch, R. S., & Alva, S. A. (2002). Language brokering and the acculturation of Latino children. *Hispanic Journal of Behavioral Sciences, 24,* 369–378.

Societal, Academic, Familial, and Environmental Acculturative Stress Scale: Children

Response categories: 0 = Doesn't apply; 1 = Doesn't bother me; 2 = Almost never bothers me; 3 = Sometimes bothers me; 4 = Often bothers me; 5 = Bothers me a lot

1. I feel bad when others make jokes about people who are in the same group as me.
2. It's hard for me to talk to new kids.
3. I have more things that get in my way than most people do.
4. It bothers me that people in my family who I am close to don't understand the things that I think are important, that are new to them.
5. People in my family who I am close to have plans for when I grow up that I don't like.
6. It bothers me when someone in my family is very sick.
7. It bothers me when my parents argue.
8. It's hard for me to tell my friends how I really feel.
9. I don't have any close friends.
10. It's hard for me to ask questions in class.
11. I worry about what other kids think about me.
12. Many people believe certain things about the way people in my group act, think, or are, and they treat me as if those things are true.
13. I worry about having to take tests in school.
14. I don't feel at home here in the United States.
15. People think I am shy, when I really just have trouble speaking English.
16. I worry about being sick.

17. The thought of my family and I moving to a new place bothers me.
18. I often feel that people purposely try to stop me from getting better at something.
19. I worry that other kids won't like me.
20. It bothers me when people force me to be like everyone else.
21. I worry that other kids are making fun of me.
22. I often feel like people who are supposed to help are really not paying any attention to me.
23. It bothers me when I am not with my family.
24. Because of the group I am in, I don't get the grades I deserve.
25. It bothers me when I argue with my brother/sister.
26. I worry about getting my report card.
27. It bothers me that I have an accent.
28. It's hard to be away from the country I used to live in.
29. I think a lot about my group and its culture.
30. It bothers me when some countries of the world don't get along.
31. It's hard to talk with my teacher.
32. Because of the group I am in, I feel others don't include me in some of the things they do, games they play, etc.
33. It's hard for me to "show off" my family.
34. People think badly of me if I practice customs or I do the "special things" of my group.
35. I have a hard time understanding what others say when they speak.
36. I worry about having enough money.

Original Scale References

Barona, A., & Miller, J. (1994). Short acculturation scale for Hispanic youth (SASH-Y): A preliminary report. *Hispanic Journal of Behavioral Sciences*, *16*, 155–162.

Burnam, M. A., Hough, R. L., Telles, C. A., & Escobar, J. I. (1987). Measurement of acculturation in a community population of Mexican Americans. *Hispanic Journal of Behavioral Sciences*, *9*, 105–130.

Chavez, D. V., Moran, V. R., Reid, S. L., & Lopez, M. (1997). Acculturative stress in children: A modification of the SAFE scale. *Hispanic Journal of Behavioral Sciences*, *19*, 34–44.

Cortes, D. E., Rogler, L. H., & Malgady, R. G. (1994). Biculturality among Puerto Rican adults in the United States. *American Journal of Community Psychology*, *22*, 707–721.

Cuellar, I., Arnold, B., & Maldonado, R. (1995). Acculturation rating scale for Mexican Americans-II: A revision of the original ARSMA scale. *Hispanic Journal of Behavioral Sciences*, *17*, 275–304.

Deyo, R. A., Diehl, A. K., Hazuda, H., & Stern, M. P. (1985). A simple language-based scalefor Mexican Americans: Validation and application to health care research. *American Journal of Public Health*, *75*, 51–55.

Franco, J. N. (1983). An acculturation scale for Mexican-American children. *The Journal of General Psychology*, *108*, 175–181.

Mainous, A. (1989). Self-concept as an indicator of acculturation in Mexican Americans. *Hispanic Journal of Behavioral Sciences*, *11*, 178–189.

Marin, G., Sabogal, F., Marin, B. V., Otero-Sabogal, R., & Perez-Stable, E. J. (1987). Development of a short acculturation scale for Hispanics. *Hispanic Journal of Behavioral Sciences, 9*, 183–205.

Marín, G., & Gamba, R. J. (1996). A new measurement of acculturation for Hispanics: The bidimensional acculturation scale for Hispanics (BAS). *Hispanic Journal of Behavioral Sciences, 18*, 297–316.

Mendoza, R. H. (1989). An empirical scale to measure type and degree of acculturation in Mexican-American adolescents and adults. *Journal of Cross-Cultural Psychology, 20*, 372–385.

Montgomery, G. T. (1992). Comfort with acculturation status among students from south Texas. *Hispanic Journal of Behavioral Sciences, 14*, 201–223.

Norris, A. E., Ford, K., & Bova, C. A. (1996). Psychometrics of a brief acculturation scale for Hispanics in a probability sample of urban Hispanic adolescents and young adults. *Hispanic Journal of Behavioral Sciences, 18*, 29–38.

Szapocznik, J., Kurtines, W. M., & Fernandez, T. (1980). Bicultural involvement and adjustment in Hispanic-American youths. *International Journal of Intercultural Relations, 4*, 353–365.

Tropp, L. R., Erkut, S., Coll, C. G., Alarcon, O., & Vazquez-Garcia, H. A. (1999). Psychosocial acculturation: Development of a new measure for Puerto Ricans on the U.S. mainland. *Educational and Psychological Measurement, 59*, 351–367.

Zea, M. C., Asner-Self, K. K., Birman, D., & Buki, L. P. (2003). The abbreviated multidimensional acculturation scale: Empirical validation with two Latino/Latina samples. *Cultural Diversity and Ethnic Minority Psychology, 9*, 107–126.

References

Alvelo, J., Collazo, A. A., & Rosario, D. (2001). Comprehensive assessment tools for Hispanics: Validation of the Multi-Problem Screening Inventory (MPSI) for Puerto Ricans. *Research on Social Work Practice, 11*, 699–724.

Bauman, S. (2005). The reliability and validity of the brief acculturation rating scale for Mexican Americans-II for children and adolescents. *Hispanic Journal of Behavioral Sciences, 27*, 426–441.

Beeber, L. S., Perreira, K. M., & Schwartz, T. (2008). Supporting the mental health of mothers raising children in poverty: How do we target them for intervention studies. *Annals of the New York Academy of Science, 1136*, 86–100.

Birman, D. (1998). Biculturalism and perceived competence of Latino immigrant adolescents. *American Journal of Community Psychology, 26*, 335–354.

Cabassa, L. J. (2003). Measuring acculturation: Where we are and where we need to go. *Hispanic Journal of Behavioral Sciences, 25*, 127–146.

Cabassa, L. J. (2007). Latino immigrant men's perceptions of depression and attitudes toward help seeking. *Hispanic Journal of Behavioral Sciences, 29*, 492–509.

Castillo, L. G., Cano, M. A., Chen, S. W., Blucker, R. T., & Olds, S. O. (2008). Family conflict and intragroup marginalization as predictors of acculturative stress in Latino college students. *International Journal of Stress Management, 15*, 43–52.

Christenson, O. D., Zabriske, R. B., Eggett, D. L., & Freeman, P. A. (2006). Family acculturation, family leisure involvement, and family functioning among Mexican-Americans. *Journal of Leisure Research, 38*, 475–495.

Cintron, J. A., Carter, M. M., & Sbrocco, T. (2005). *Ataques de Nervios* in relation to anxiety sensitivity among island Puerto Ricans. *Culture, Medicine, and Psychiatry, 29*, 415–431.

Clark, L. (2002). Mexican-Origin mothers' experiences using children's health care services. *Western Journal of Nursing Research, 24*, 159–179.

Coatsworth, J. D., Maldonado-Molina, M., Pantin, H., & Szapocznik, J. (2005). A person-centered and ecological investigation of acculturation strategies in Hispanic immigrant youth. *Journal of Community Psychology*, *33*, 157–174.

Contreras, J. M. (2004). Parenting behaviors among mainland Puerto Rican adolescent mothers: The role of grandmother and partner involvement. *Journal of Research on Adolescence*, *14*, 341–368.

Cortes, D. E., Deren, S., Andia, J., Colon, H., Robles, R., & Kang, S. (2003). The use of the Puerto Rican biculturality scale with Puerto Rican drug users in New York and Puerto Rico. *Journal of Psychoactive Drugs*, *35*, 197–207.

Cuellar, I., Nyberg, B., & Maldonado, R. E. (1997). Ethnic identity and acculturation in a young adult Mexican-origin population. *Journal of Community Psychology*, *25*, 535–549.

Davidson, T. M., & Cardemil, E. V. (2009). Parent-child communication and parental involvement in Latino adolescents. *Journal of Early Adolescence*, *29*, 99–121.

Dawson, B. A. (2009). Discrimination, stress, and acculturation among Dominican immigrant women. *Hispanic Journal of Behavioral Sciences*, *31*, 96–111.

Dela Cruz, F. A., Padilla, G. V., & Agustin, E. O. (2000). Adapting a measure of acculturation for cross-cultural research. *Journal of Transcultural Nursing*, *11*, 191–198.

DeLeon, B., & Mendez, S. (1996). Factorial structure of a measure of acculturation in a Puerto Rican population. *Educational and Psychological Measurement*, *56*, 155–165.

Edwards, L. M., & Romero, A. J. (2008). Coping with discrimination among Mexican descent adolescents. *Hispanic Journal of Behavioral Sciences*, *30*, 24–39.

Escalante, A., del Rincon, I., & Mulrow, C. D. (2000). Symptoms of depression and psychological distress among Hispanics with rheumatoid arthritis. *Arthritis Care and Research*, *13*, 156–167.

Ghorpade, J., Lackritz, J., & Singh, G. (2004). Psychological acculturation of ethnic minorities into White Anglo American culture: Consequences and predictors. *Journal of Applied Social Psychology*, *34*, 1208–1228.

Gilliam, M. L., Berlin, A., Kozloski, M., Hernandez, M., & Grundy, M. (2007). Interpersonal and personal factors influencing sexual debut among Mexican-American young women in the United States. *Journal of Adolescent Health*, *41*, 493–503.

Gomez, M. J., & Fassinger, R. E. (1994). An initial model of Latina achievement: Acculturation, biculturalism and achieving styles. *Journal of Counseling Psychology*, *41*, 205–215.

Goodman, C. C., & Silverstein, M. (2005). Latina grandmothers raising grandchildren: Acculturation and psychological well-being. *International Journal of Aging and Human Development*, *60*, 305–316.

Guilamo-Ramos, V., Bouris, A., Jaccard, J., Lesesne, C., & Ballan, M. (2009). Familial and cultural influences on sexual risk behaviors among Mexican, Puerto Rican, and Dominican youth. *AIDS Education and Prevention*, *21*(Suppl. B), 61–79.

Guilamo-Ramos, V., Bouris, A., Jaccard, J., Lesesne, C., Gonzalez, B., & Kalogerogiannis, K. (2009). Family mediators of acculturation and adolescent sexual behavior among Latino youth. *Journal of Primary Prevention*, *30*, 395–419.

Guinn, B. (1998). Acculturation and health locus of control among Mexican American adolescents. *Hispanic Journal of Behavioral Sciences*, *20*, 492–499.

Guo., X., Suarez-Morales, L., Schwartz, S. J., & Szapocznik, J. (2009). Some evidence for multidimensional biculturalism: Confirmatory factor analysis and measurement invariance analysis on the bicultural involvement questionnaire-short version. *Psychological Assessment*, *21*, 22–31.

Gutierrez, M. A., Franco, L. M., Powell, K. G., Peterson, N. A., & Reid, R. J. (2009). Psychometric properties of the acculturation rating scale for Mexican Americans-II: Exploring dimensions of marginality among a diverse Latino population. *Hispanic Journal of Behavioral Sciences*, *31*, 340–356.

Hawley, S. R., Chavez, D. V., & St. Romain, T. (2007). Developing a bicultural model for academic achievement: A look at acculturative stress, coping, and self-perception. *Hispanic Journal of Behavioral Sciences*, *29*, 283–299.

Hess, R. S., & D'Amato, R. C. (1996). High school completion among Mexican-American children: Individual and family background variables. *School Psychology Quarterly, 11*, 353–368.

Juarbe, T., Turok, X. P., & Perez-Stable, E. J. (2002). Perceived benefits and barriers to physical activity among older Latina women. *Western Journal of Nursing Research, 24*, 868–886.

Kali, B., Zayas, L. H., & Malgady, R. G. (2000). Depression, acculturation, and motivations for alcohol use among young Colombian, Dominican, and Puerto Rican men. *Hispanic Journal of Behavioral Sciences, 22*, 64–77.

Lechuga, J. (2008). Is acculturation a dynamic construct? The influence of method of priming culture on acculturation. *Hispanic Journal of Behavioral Sciences, 30*, 324–339.

Lee, R. M., Yoon, E., & Liu-Tom, H.-T. T. (2006). Structure and measurement of acculturation/enculturation for Asian Americans using the ARSMA-II. *Measurement and Evaluation in Counseling and Development, 39*, 42–55.

Lerman, D., Maldonado, R., & Luna., D. (2009). A theory-based measure of acculturation: The shortened cultural life style inventory. *Journal of Business Research, 62*, 399–406.

Lessenger, L. H. (1997). Use of acculturation rating scale for Mexican Americans-II with substance abuse patients. *Hispanic Journal of Behavioral Sciences, 19*, 387–398.

Lopez, F. A. (2009). Developmental considerations and acculturation of children: Measures and issues. *Hispanic Journal of Behavioral Sciences, 31*, 57–72.

Lopez, I. R., & Contreras, J. M. (2005). The best of both worlds: Biculturality, acculturation, and adjustment among young mainland Puerto Rican mothers. *Journal of Cross-Cultural Psychology, 36*, 192–208.

Magana, J. R., Rocha, O. D., Amsel, J., Magana, H. A., Fernandez, M. I., & Rulnick, S. (1996). Revisiting the dimensions of acculturation: Cultural theory and psychometric practice. *Hispanic Journal of Behavioral Sciences, 18*, 444–468.

Martinez, C. R. (2006). Effects of differential family acculturation on Latino adolescent substance abuse. *Family Relations, 55*, 306–317.

McKee, M. D., Zayas, L. H., & Jankowski, K. R. B. (2004). Breastfeeding intention and practice in an urban minority population: Relationship to maternal depressive symptoms and mother-infant closeness. *Journal of Reproductive and Infant Psychology, 22*, 167–181.

Mendoza, R. (1994). *Cultural life styles inventory. Version 2.0*. Author.

Mezzich, J. E., Ruiperez, M. A., Yoon, G., Liu, J., & Zapata-Vega, M. I. (2009). Measuring cultural identity: Validation of a modified Cortez, Rogler, and Malgady bicultural scale in three ethnic groups in New York. *Culture, Medicine, & Psychiatry, 33*, 451–472.

Miglietta, A., & Tartaglia, S. (2008). The influence of length of stay, linguistic competence, and media exposure in immigrants' adaptation. *Cross-Cultural Research, 20*, 1–16.

Morandi, B., & Risco, C. (2006). Perceived discrimination experiences and mental health of Latina/o American persons. *Journal of Counseling Psychology, 53*, 411–421.

Norris, A. E., Ford, K., & Bova, C. A. (1996). Psychometrics of a brief acculturation scale for Hispanics in a probability sample of urban Hispanic adolescents and young adults. *Hispanic Journal of Behavioral Sciences, 18*, 29–38.

Perez, W., & Padilla, A. M. (2000). Cultural orientation across three generations of Hispanic adolescents. *Hispanic Journal of Behavioral Sciences, 22*, 390–398.

Phinney, J. S. (1992). The multigroup ethnic identity measure: A new scale for use with diverse groups. *Journal of Adolescent Research, 7*, 156–176.

Rivera-Sinclair, E. A. (1997). Acculturation/biculturalism and its relationship to adjustment in Cuban-Americans. *International Journal of Intercultural Relations, 21*, 379–391.

Rojas-Guyler, L., Ellis, N., & Sanders, S. (2005). Acculturation, health protective sexual communication, and HIV/AIDS risk behavior among Hispanic women in a large Midwestern city. *Health Education and Behavior, 32*, 767–779.

Ruiz, R. J., Dolbier, C. L., & Fleschler, R. (2006). The relationships among acculturation, biobehavioral risk, stress, corticotrophin-releasing hormone, and poor birth outcomes in Hispanic women. *Ethnicity and Disease, 16*, 926–931.

Ruiz, Y. (2009). Predictors of academic achievement for Latino middle schoolers. *Journal of Human Behavior in the Social Environment, 19*, 419–433.

Schaefer, S. E., Salazar, M., Bruhn, C., Saviano, D., Boushey, C., & Van Loan, M. D. (2009). Influence of race, acculturation, and socioeconomic status on tendency toward overweight in Asian-American and Mexican-American early adolescent females. *Journal of Immigrant and Minority Health, 11*, 188–197.

Schiffner, T., & Buki, L. (2006). Latina college students' sexual health beliefs about human Papillomavirus infection. *Cultural Diversity and Ethnic Minority Psychology, 12*, 687–696.

Schwartz, S. J., Pantin, H., Sullivan, S., Prado, G., & Szapocznik, J. (2006). Nativity and years in the receiving culture as markers of acculturation. *Journal of Cross-Cultural Psychology, 37*, 345–353.

Schwartz, S. J., Zamboanga, B. L., & Jarvis, L. H. (2007). Ethnic identify and acculturation in Hispanic early adolescents: Mediated relationships to academic grades, prosocial behaviors, and externalizing symptoms. *Cultural Diversity and Ethnic Minority Psychology, 13*, 364–373.

Serrano, E., & Anderson, J. (2003). Assessment of a refined short acculturation scale for Latino preteens in rural Colorado. *Hispanic Journal of Behavioral Sciences, 25*, 240–253.

Singelis, T. M., Yamada, A. M., Barrio, C., Laney, J. H., Her, P., Ruiz-Anaya, A., et al. (2006). Metric equivalence of the bidimensional acculturation scale, the satisfaction with life scale, and the self-construal scale across Spanish and English language versions. *Hispanic Journal of Behavioral Sciences, 28*, 231–244.

Suarez-Morales, L., Dillon, F. R., & Szapocznik, J. (2007). Validation of the acculturative stress inventory for children. *Cultural Diversity and Ethnic Minority Psychology, 13*, 216–224.

Unger, J. B., & Molina, G. B. (2000). Acculturation and attitudes about contraceptive use among Latina women. *Health Care for Women International, 21*, 235–249.

U.S. Census Bureau. (2008). *2006–2008 American Community Survey 3-year estimates.* http://factfinder.census.gov

Wallen, G. R., Feldman, R. H., & Anliker, J. (2002). Measuring acculturation among Central American women and the use of a brief language scale. *Journal of Immigrant Health, 4*, 95–102.

Weisskirch, R. S., & Alva, S. A. (2002). Language brokering and the acculturation of Latino children. *Hispanic Journal of Behavioral Sciences, 24*, 369–378.

Yoshioka, M. R., Gilbert, L., El-Bassel, N., & Baig-Amin, M. (2003). Social support and disclosure of abuse: Comparing south Asian, African American, and Hispanic battered women. *Journal of Family Violence, 18*, 171–180.

Zea, M. C., Reisen, C. A., Poppen, P. J., Echeverry, J. J., & Bianchi, F. T. (2004). Disclosure of HIV-positive status to Latino gay men's social networks. *American Journal of Community Psychology, 3*, 107–116.

Chapter 3
African Americans

Overview

African Americans, numbering about 39 million, are the second largest minority group in America (U.S. Census Bureau, 2008). While the term "African American" has been used to classify a single ethnic/racial group, it includes members from a number of ethnic groups from around the world including the Caribbean, various countries in South and Central America, and Africa. Some "African Americans" are recent arrivals while others have had ancestors who have been in America since before the Mayflower (Bennett, 1962).

There are significantly more African American women than men, so that African Americans are believed to have the greatest gender imbalance of any group in America. This fact is often important to those who conduct research on African Americans as it has potential implications for gender biases in sampling and for a variety of intra-group dynamics. As is true for most non-White populations, African Americans are younger and have higher birth rates than do Whites. For a more detailed discussion on the status of African Americans we refer the reader to Davis, Wallace, and Shanks (2008).

African Americans have been the most researched and studied minority group. Indeed, considerable attention has been paid to the study of their history, culture, education, family life, religiosity, health, wealth, and employment. Researchers have studied both between-group and within-group differences among African Americans. Most of the inter-group research focused on relationships between African Americans and Whites. More recent research has compared Africans Americans with other groups as these other racial/ethnic groups have grown in size and accessibility. However because of the increasing diversity among African Americans, researchers will need to pay greater attention to within group differences.

In this chapter we review a select group of intra-racial and inter-racial measures that focus on African Americans. The area of intra-racial identity has received perhaps more attention than most others we have elected to address. As a result we refer the reader to additional sources of intra-group measures of African American identity, some of which are extensive (Jones, 1996).

L.E. Davis, R.J. Engel, *Measuring Race and Ethnicity*,
DOI 10.1007/978-1-4419-6697-1_3, © Springer Science+Business Media, LLC 2011

Second, we have reviewed scales that assess the quality and/or extent of interracial interaction between African Americans and other ethnic/racial groups. We are aware that this area of research has a long history beginning most notably perhaps with such early measures as the Bogardus Scale. It is not our goal to do a historical survey of every such measure, but rather to provide the reader with scales presently in use. In particular, these measures assess racial prejudices/attitudes, cultural mistrust, and race-related stress among African Americans.

Citations

Bennett (1962)
U.S. Census Bureau (2008)
Davis, Wallace, and Shanks (2008)
Jones (1996)

A. *Measures of Racial Identity*

1. Multi-Construct African American Identity Questionnaire (MCAIQ) (Smith & Brookins, 1997)
2. Racial Identity Scale for Low-Income African Americans (Resnicow & Ross-Gaddy, 1997)
3. Racial/Ethnic Identity Scale (Adolescent Survey of Black Life) (Resnicow, Soler, Braithwaite, Selassie, & Smith, 1999)
4. Multidimensional Racial Identification Scaled-Revised (MRIS-R) (Sanders Thompson, 1995)
5. Black Ethnocentrism Scale (Chang & Ritter, 1976)

B. *Measures of Acculturation*

1. African American Acculturation Scale-Revised (AAAS-R) (Landrine & Klonoff, 2000)
2. African American Acculturation Scale (Snowden & Hines, 1999)

C. *Measure of Inter-racial Interaction*

1. Racism Reaction Scale (RRS) (Thompson, Neville, Weathers, Poston, & Atkinson, 1990).
2. Attitudes Toward Blacks Scales (ATB) (Brigham, 1993)
3. Attitudes Toward Whites Scale (ATW) (Brigham, 1993)
4. Prejudice Perception Assessment Scale (PPAS) (Gilbert, 1998)
5. Cultural Mistrust Inventory (CMI) (Terrell & Terrell, 1981)
6. Index of Race-Related Stress (IRRS) (Utsey & Ponterotto, 1996)
7. Race-based Rejection Sensitivity Questionnaire (RSR-Race) (Mendoza-Denton, Downey, Davis, Purdie, & Pietrzak, 2002)

Measures of Racial Identity

The Multi-Construct African American Identity Questionnaire (Smith & Brookins, 1997)

The Multi-Construct African American Identity Questionnaire (MCAIQ) measures racial orientation (attitudes toward African Americans) and cooperative–competitive values.

Description: The MCAIQ includes 21 items designed to assess social orientation, appearance orientation, and attitudes about African Americans. The social orientation subscale (items 7, 11, 13, 15, 17) measures socializing with other African Americans; the appearance subscale (items 4, 8, 9, 16, 20, 21) assesses attitudes about physical characteristics; and the stereotype subscale (items 1, 2, 3, 5, 6, 10, 12, 14, 18, 19) measures endorsement of African American stereotypes. Questions are answered using a 5-point Likert scale ranging from *strongly agree* (1) to *strongly disagree* (5). While not explicitly stated in the original source article, it appears that the total score is the average of the sum of the number of questions for which there are responses. The summed total score is calculated by first reverse coding negatively worded items, noted by (R) (3, 4, 5, 7, 8, 10, 11, 12, 13, 14, 17, 18, 20, 21). Higher total scores represent a stronger ethnic identify. The scale is self-administered. The authors also evaluated a brief version of the MCAIQ including eight items (5, 8, 9, 10, 12, 14, 18, 21). Note that the authors also provide five items for a scale to measure cooperation; we have not included these items.

Sample: The study sample included 159 African American youth. Most respondents (62%) were female; the average age of the participants was 13 with 75% of the sample between the ages of 11 and 13.

Reliability: The alpha coefficient for the entire scale was .87 and the subscale alphas were .66 for the social subscale, .63 for the appearance subscale, and .80 for the stereotype subscale. Coefficient alpha for the Brief MCAIQ was .82. The test–retest correlation over a 5 to 10-week period for the total MCAIQ was .65 and for the subscales the correlations were .50 for the social subscale, .60 for appearance, and .65 for stereotypical subscale. The test–retest reliability for the Brief MCAIQ was .57.

Validity: Convergent validity was assessed in relation to the Multigroup Ethnic Identify Measure (MEIM) a more general measure of ethnic identity. As hypothesized, the total score of the MCAIQ and the three subscales were statistically significantly correlated with the total score MEIM and with most of the MEIM subscales. The total scores correlation was .39; the total score of the Brief MCAIQ and the MEIM was .54. Construct validity was assessed by comparing the total score of the MCAIQ and Bronstein-Cruz Child/Adolescent Self-Concept and Adjustment Scale (BC-Scale); the correlation was .33 for the full MCAIQ and .45 for the Brief MCAIQ.

Comments: The MCAIQ as a measure of racial/ethnic identity exhibits a reasonable internal consistency, test–retest reliability, and construct validity. To our knowledge this instrument has not been tested with other ethnic populations and may not be suitable for other Black racial groups (Jamaicans, Haitians, and Caribbean). Belgrave et al. (2004) report similar alpha coefficients with a sample of adolescent African American girls. The MCAIQ avoids a response set by using positively and negatively worded questions.

Location: Smith, E. P., & Brookins, C. C. (1997). Toward the development of an ethnic identity measure for African American youth. *Journal of Black Psychology, 23*, 358–377.

Selected Publications

Belgrave, F. Z., Reed, M. C., Plybon, L. E., Butler, D. S., Allison, K. W., & Davis, T. (2004). An evaluation of sisters of Nia: A cultural program for African American girls. *Journal of Black Psychology, 30*, 329–343.

Multi-Construct African American Identity Questionnaire (MCAIQ)

This questionnaire looks at your feelings specifically toward Black people or African Americans. There are no right or wrong answers. Please respond to them as if you were talking to someone about what you think. Please be honest because your answers will be kept confidential. Please circle the number to indicate how much you agree or disagree with each statement.

Response categories: 1 = Strongly disagree; 2 = Disagree; 3 = Neither; 4 = Agree; 5 = Strongly agree

1. Black people should be proud of their race.
2. Black people can do anything if they try.
3. I think White people do better in school than Black people (R).
4. I believe White people look better than Black people (R).
5. Black people do not do well in business (R).
6. Black people are good at other things besides sports.
7. I prefer to go to a school with mostly White students (R).
8. I think most Black people have bad hair (R).
9. I think short hair is as nice as long hair.
10. Black people do not speak as well as White people (R).
11. I prefer to have mostly White friends (R).
12. Black people are not good at maths (R).
13. I do not like being around Black people (R).
14. I think that most Black people cannot be trusted (R).
15. I prefer to live in a Black neighborhood.
16. I believe that "Black is beautiful."
17. I prefer to live in a White neighborhood (R).
18. I believe White people speak better than Black people (R).
19. Black people are very smart.
20. I wish my skin was lighter (R).
21. I think people of other races look better than Black people (R).

Racial Identity Scale for Low-Income African Americans (Resnicow & Ross-Gaddy, 1997)

The Racial Identity Scale for Low-Income African Americans (RISLIAA) measures the racial identity of African American adults with low literacy skills.

Description: The Racial Identity Scale for Low-Income African Americans was designed to assess two dimensions of racial identity: recognition of racism (anti-White) and positive Afrocentric attitudes/behaviors (pro-Black). The original version of the scale includes 20 items and the scale developers recommend only using 18 items, dropping items 12 and 13. The response categories for items 1–18 are *agree a lot* (1) to *disagree a lot* (4); the response categories for items 19–20 are scored from *never* (1) to *more than three times* (5). To obtain a total scale score, nine items (1, 6, 7, 11, 13, 14, 18, 19, 20) are reverse coded and the items are summed. Lower values indicate a stronger racial identity. The scale was read to respondents and took approximately minutes to complete.

Sample: The instrument was administered as part of larger psychosocial evaluation protocol. The sample included 261 African American women who were parents or guardians of children participating in an after-school health program. The average age of respondents was 35 years and 71% of the women were not married. Most of the respondents (76%) earned less than $15,001 and 55% were unemployed. The majority of the sample (83%) did not complete college. A subsample of 40 respondents was re-interviewed 3–4 months later.

Reliability: Cronbach's alpha was .70. The test–retest correlation for a 3- to 4-month time lag was .62.

Validity: Contrary to expectation, an exploratory factor analysis produced five factors: Recognition of Racism, Afrocentric Attitudes, Afrocentric Involvement (in activities), Integrationism (attitudes toward integration), and Interpersonal Trust (positive trust and social relations). The last factor did not seem to fit with the other factors. Factor three was correlated with past experiences with racism.

Comments: While there is evidence of reliability, there is little evidence of validity. The authors suggest not using items 12 and 13. The authors recommend using factor scores; this makes using the scale quite difficult and may impact comparability across studies. The scale has only been evaluated with low-income African Americans: women in the original study and both genders in Nollen et al. (2007). Nollen et al. (2007) report a weaker internal consistency (alpha = .60). The RISLIAA avoids a response set by using positively and negatively worded questions.

Location: Resnicow, K. & Ross-Gaddy, D. (1997). Development of racial identity scale for low-income African Americans. *Journal of Black Studies, 28*, 239–254.

Selected Publications

Nollen, N., Ahluwalia, J. S., Mayo, M. S., Richter, K., Choi, W. S., Okuyemi, K. S., & Resnicow, L. (2007). A randomized trial of targeted educational materials for smoking cessation in African Americans using transdermal nicotine. *Health Education & Behavior, 34*, 911–927.

Racial Identity Scale for Low-Income African Americans

Response categories for items 1–18: 1 = Agree a lot; 2 = Agree; 3 = Disagree; 4 = Disagree a lot

Response categories for items 19–20: 1 = Never; 2 = Once; 3 = Twice; 5 = Three times or more

1. It is okay for a Black person to date or marry a White person (R).
2. It is important to learn more about African American history.
3. Most White people feel they are superior to (better than) Black people.
4. Black people should give their children African names.
5. White people still owe us something because of what they did to us in the past, like slavery.
6. I would like to have more White friends (R).
7. I do not really care what happens to Blacks in Africa (R).
8. Things in America are getting worse for Black people.
9. I am happy that I am Black.
10. In America it is hard for Black people to succeed.
11. I trust most White people (R).
12. I trust most Black people.
13. America is a good place for Black people to live (R).
14. I would like to live in a neighborhood that has White and Black people in it (R).
15. Most of my friends are Black.
16. The United States government does not care about Black people.
17. It is wrong for Blacks to move out of Black neighborhoods when they become successful.
18. I would rather people think of me as an American than a Black or African American (R).
19. How many times in the past month have you read a book, magazine, or article about African American history or culture? (R)
20. How many times in the past year did you attend an African American cultural activity such as a Kwanza club, discussion group, Black history lecture, or African American dance performance, play, or concert? (R)

Racial/Ethnic Identity Scale (Adolescent Survey of Black Life) (Resnicow et al., 1999)

The Racial/Ethnic Identity Scale Adolescent Survey of Black Life (ASBL) was developed to measure racial/ethnic identification of African American adolescents.

Description: We limit our discussion to the 16-item ASBL (see Comments section). The scale captures three constructs: (a) attitudes about being Black (Pro-Black; items 1–7); (b) attitudes toward Whites (anti-White; items 8–11); and (c) perceptions of racism (Perceived Racism or Racism Awareness; items 12–16). Responses are obtained on a 4-point scale with categories ranging from *agree a lot* (1) to *disagree a lot* (4). Subscale scores are calculated by reverse coding items within each subscale and summing the scores; higher scores indicate more pro-Black attitudes, more anti-White attitudes, and more perceived racism. There is no discussion of a total scale score. The scale is self-administered.

Sample: The psychometric properties of the ASBL were assessed using two samples of African American youth. Sample 1 was drawn from a public housing substance use prevention program and included 286 respondents; 52% of participants were females and their average age was 12.6 and 52% were female. Sample 2 included 60 youth not enrolled in prevention programs; 53% of the participants were female and their average age was 12.3 years.

Reliability: Sample 1/sample 2 alpha coefficients for each domain were .81/.69 (Pro-Black), .69/.55 (anti-White), and .53/.58 (Perceived Racism).

Validity: Using participants in sample 1, exploratory factor analysis produced the three hypothesized factors which were replicated in sample 2 using confirmatory factor analysis. Self-concept, school attitudes, problem behaviors, prosocial behaviors, drug-related attitudes, and substance use behaviors were used to establish evidence of construct validity. In both samples, the Pro-Black domain was statistically significantly related to anti-drug attitudes. In sample 1, Pro-Black attitudes were statistically significantly related to school attitudes ($r = .53$), positive school behaviors ($r = .19$), problem behaviors ($r = -.13$) and self-esteem ($r = -.17$). In sample 2, scores on the anti-White domain were statistically significantly related in the expected directions to school attitudes ($r = -.29$), positive school behaviors ($r = -.26$), prosocial behaviors ($r = -.30$), and lifetime drug use ($r = .39$). In Sample 1, awareness of racism was statistically significantly associated with problem behaviors ($r = .14$), school attitudes ($r = .12$), and lifetime drug use ($r = .18$).

Comments: The summary above is based on 16 items though the initial scale had 18 items. There is moderate evidence of reliability and inconsistent evidence of construct validity. Subsequent to this assessment, the authors added additional items; the psychometric properties for the more recent scale including the additional items has not been published but as noted in the article are available from the authors.

Location: Resnicow, K., Soler, R. E., Braithwaite, R. L. Selassie, M. B., & Smith, M. (1999). Development of a racial and ethnic identity scale for African American adolescents: The survey of black life. *Journal of Black Psychology, 25*, 171–188.

Selected Publications

None

Racial/Ethnic Identity Scale (Adolescent Survey of Black Life)

Subscale 1: Pro-Black

1. It is important to learn more about African American History (R).
2. I care what happens to Black people in Africa (R).

3. I am happy that I am Black (R).
4. Being Black is very important to me (R).
5. For my career, I would like to work on improving things in the Black community (R).
6. My parents are proud to be Black (R).
7. Most of my friends are Black (R).

Subscale 2: Anti-White

8. It is okay for Black people to date or marry White people.
9. I would like to have many more friends who are White.
10. I trust most White people.
11. I would like to live in a neighborhood that has White and Black people in it.

Subscale 3: Racism Awareness

12. Most White people feel they are better than Black people (R).
13. White people still owe us something because of slavery (R).
14. Things in America are getting worse for Black people (R).
15. In America, it is harder for Black people to succeed than White people (R).
16. There is still a lot of racism in this country (R).

Appendix – Additional Items Added to the ASBI, Since the Initial Testing

a. I trust Black people more than I trust White people.
b. I trust White people more than I trust Black people.
c. Most White people are prejudiced against Blacks.
d. Most White people are racist.
e. It is important to shop in Black-owned stores.
f. I would like to attend a historically Black college or university.
g. Earning a lot of money is important to me.
h. Getting in touch with my African ancestry is important to me.
i. Being Black makes it harder to succeed in America.
j. Blacks can be close friends with Whites.
k. Black people complain too much about racism.
l. It is important to learn about African culture.
m. I think police treat Blacks unfairly.
n. If I had a lot of money, I would donate some of it to African American causes.
o. Sometimes I wish I were White.

The Multidimensional Racial Identification Scale-Revised (Sanders Thompson, 1995)

The Multidimensional Racial Identification Scale-Revised (MRIS-R) assesses African American racial identification.

Description: The MRIS-R assesses four aspects of racial identification including physical identity (acceptance and comfort with physical attributes), sociopolitical identity (awareness and commitment to resolution of issues affecting African Americans), cultural identity (awareness of language, are, literature and social traditions), and psychological identity (pride in and commitment to the African American community). The number of scale items is not clear as the original article reports 30 items but displays the wording for 25 items and a subsequent study reports 29 items (Sanders Thompson, 2001). The scale utilizes a 5-point rating scale ranging from *strongly agree* (5) to *strongly disagree* (1). Negatively worded items are reverse scored to obtain a total score. The author suggests that subscale scores may be calculated (see Comments section). Higher scores indicate a stronger sense of racial identification while lower scores indicate a negative self-identification. The scale is self-administered.

Sample: To assess the properties of the MRIS-R, a sample of 425 African American residents residing in the St. Louis Metropolitan area was recruited. The sample was predominantly female (59.7%) and the average age was 33 years. The respondents' median income was $24,000. Six percent of the participants had less than a high-school education, 13.2% were high-school graduates, 43.3% had some college, 18.6% were college graduates, and 17.4% had some graduate education.

Reliability: Coefficient alpha for the total scale was .88. Subscale alphas were: physical identity, .75; cultural identity, .85; sociopolitical identity, .62; and psychological identity, .86. Test–retest reliability for total scale was .96; physical racial identity subscale, .89; cultural racial identity subscale, .92; sociopolitical racial identity subscale, .89; and psychological racial identity subscale, .90. Note that the time between administrations was not available though from the author's description it may have been within the context of the same sitting.

Validity: Factor analysis supported a 4-factor solution though the item distribution was not as hypothesized.

Comments: There is adequate evidence of reliability but little evidence of validity other than factorial validity. The number of items is not clear based on the two available studies. The items for each subscale are also not clearly defined; in the primary study the author notes that the positively worded items thought to be related to the sociopolitical factor did not load on that factor. The MRIS-R avoids a response set by using positively and negatively worded questions.

Location: Sanders Thompson, V. L. (1995). The multidimensional structure of racial identification. *Journal of Research in Personality, 29*, 208–222.

Selected Publications

Sanders Thompson, V. L. (2001). The complexity of African American racial identification. *Journal of Black Studies, 32,* 155–165.

The Multidimensional Racial Identification Scale-Revised (MRIS-R)

Note: Below are the 25 items organized by the factor to which they were identified in Sanders Thompson (1995).

1. Psychological Identity

    1. I am very concerned about the problems Black people have.
    2. I am committed to strength and cohesion in the Black family.
    3. African Americans need more political representation.
    4. I feel a commitment to the African American community.
    5. I am committed to increasing African American representation in all occupations.
    6. The contributions and role of African Americans should be documented and taught to everyone.
    7. Black actresses, actors, models are as attractive as those of other groups in film and on T.V.
    8. I am proud to be an African American.
    9. I have a strong attachment to other Black people.
    10. It is important to keep up with issues important to Black people.
    11. I am committed to changing discrimination African Americans experience.

2. Physical Identity

    1. I feel that it is inappropriate to wear natural hairstyles at formal or racially mixed social functions.
    2. I feel it is inappropriate to wear natural hairstyles at work.
    3. Blacks are less attractive when wearing natural hairstyles.
    4. I think that African-style clothing is unattractive.
    5. Blacks with lighter skin tones are generally better looking than those with darker skin tones.
    6. African Americans with a slender nose are more attractive than those with a broad nose.

3. Cultural Identity

    1. It is important to promote Black literature, music, art, etc.
    2. I enjoy and would purchase African art.
    3. I enjoy and would purchase African music.

4. Sociopolitical Identity

    1. Blacks contribute less to society than others.
    2. African Americans expect this country to do too much for them and need to work harder.
    3. African Americans often behave in a way I find offensive.
    4. There is enough opportunity in America but Blacks do not benefit because they are not motivated to do well.
    5. African Americans are hard to trust in business dealings.

The Black Ethnocentrism Scale (Chang & Ritter, 1976)

The Black Ethnocentric Scale (BES) measures Black ethnocentrism expressed through pro-Black and anti-White attitudes.

Description: The Black Ethnocentric Scale is a self-report 40-item Likert-type scale consisting of two dimensions: Pro-Black Subscale (PBS) and Anti-White Subscale (AWS). Each subscale includes 20 items (PBS are the odd items and AWS are the even items). The scale uses a 7-point Likert-response format ranging from *strongly disagree* (1) to *strongly agree* (7). A scale total score and subscale scores are computed by averaging the items (score divided by number of items with valid responses). Note that items 4, 12, and 31 are first reverse coded. Scores higher than 4 indicate agreement with the focus of the particular scale, and scores lower than 4 suggest disagreement. The scale is self-administered.

Sample: Reliability was assessed with 99 African American students enrolled in a psychology course at a predominantly Black southern university. Validity was assessed with a sample of 92 African American students enrolled in a general psychology course; 66 (71%) were females.

Reliability: Split-half reliability was .91 for the total scale score, .88 for the PBS, and .87 for the AWS. Test–retest reliability, assessed for a 4-week interval, was .87 for the total scale score, .82 for the PBS, and .80 for the AWS.

Validity: There is evidence of criterion validity. The AWS was statistically significantly related to Steckler's Anti-White Scale ($r = .72$). There is also evidence of construct validity: the PBS and AWS were statistically significantly related as hypothesized with an Ethnocentrism Scale ($r = .32$; $r = .31$) and an Authoritarianism scale ($r = .27$; $r = .26$).

Comments: There is evidence of reliability and validity. The evidence is dated and comes from a college sample. The scale may only be relevant for college students as it has not been evaluated with other populations. In general, the age of the scale suggests that revisions might be needed. The BES avoids a response set by using positively and negatively worded questions.

Location: Chang, E. C., & Ritter, E. H. (1976). Ethnocentrism in black college students. *The Journal of Social Psychology, 100,* 89–98.

The Black Ethnocentrism Scale

1. If a Black person and a White person were selling the same thing, I would go out of my way to buy it from the Black person.
2. Most Whites sympathize with the Ku Klux Klan.
3. Blacks should elect public officials of their own race regardless of the campaign issue.
4. You cannot condemn the entire White race because of the actions of some if its members (R).
5. The highest duty of a man is to fight for the glory and power of his own race.
6. White men are by nature prejudiced and bigoted.

7. A political party consisting of only Black members should be formed.
8. We will not have a true democracy in this country as long as Whites are in power.
9. Blacks should forget about integration and struggle for Black power.
10. Racial discrimination will not disappear until prejudiced Whites are severely punished.
11. I am in favor of creating a Black sovereign state within the United States.
12. Blacks and Whites are brothers (R).
13. I am for my own race, right or wrong.
14. Whites will remain oppressive even though integration is accomplished.
15. On the whole, Blacks have better qualities of character than Whites.
16. There is little hope for improving race relations because of deliberate attempts by Whites to suppress Black people.
17. We need more Black leaders who speak up for Black supremacy.
18. It is disgraceful for a Black girl to invite a White man to her home.
19. The use of force to overthrow the unjust law is always justified.
20. Most Whites who sympathize with the civil rights movement are primarily motivated by guilt or fear.
21. Blacks should focus on Black pride rather than integration.
22. Court decisions are most often unjust when Black are involved.
23. Blacks who lack "black pride" are abandoning their own people.
24. It is a shame for a Black to marry a person of the White race.
25. The Black race is better than any other.
26. Whites who are friendly with Blacks are only trying to use them.
27. The Black community should have the right to stop other racial groups from living in it.
28. Whites must pay their debt to Black people.
29. In general, Black people are more creative than Whites.
30. "A tooth for a tooth" is fair practice against the White man's injustice.
31. Blacks should give their first loyalty to America instead of to their own kind (R).
32. Blacks should give up trying to be on friendly terms with Whites.
33. Blacks, on the whole, are genetically superior to Whites
34. Blacks and Whites can never get along well.
35. The US Constitution should be amended to ensure that either the President or Vice-president of the United States would be Black.
36. Only fools believe that friendliness toward Whites can accomplish anything in the Black peoples' struggle.
37. There should be a national Black committee on education to see to it that schools teach children Black culture and history.
38. Individuals who are not members of the Black race should not be permitted to teach in predominantly Black schools and colleges.
39. Black children, from a very early age, should be taught to be loyal to their own race.
40. White people try to keep Black people down.

Acculturation

The African American Acculturation Scale-R (Landrine & Klonoff, 2000)

The African American Acculturation Scale-R (AAAS-R) was developed to measure levels of immersion in African American culture. It is a revision of the original 74-item AAAS (Landrine & Klonoff, 1994, 1995).

Description: The 47-item self-report African American Acculturation Scale-R consists of eight factors: religious beliefs and practices (items 1–10); preference for things African American (items 11–19); inter-racial attitudes (items 20–26); family practices (items 27–30); health beliefs and practices (items 31–35); cultural superstitions (items 26–29); racial segregation (items 40–43); and family values (items 44–47). Responses are provided on a Likert-type scale ranging from *totally disagree* (1) to *totally agree* (7). Subscale scores are the sum of scores on the items on that subscale; the authors recommend inserting the participant's mean score on the subscale for any missing items. The total scale score is the sum of the all the items and ranges from 49 to 329. Higher scores indicate a more traditional cultural orientation and lower scores correspond to a more acculturated orientation. The scale is self-administered.

Sample: Ten middle-and working-class census tracts from San Bernardino County, CA. Going door-to-door, all participants who self-identified as Black were asked to participate in the survey; all potential participants agreed. The sample included 520 African American adults: 53.2% were female; the average age of the participants was 28 years (18–79); their average level of education was 13 years; and the average income of participants was about $17,000.

Reliability: The internal consistency for the AAAS-R was very high ($r = .93$). The internal consistency reliabilities of the eight subscales ranged from .67 to .89, with all but one of the subscales having reliabilities of .70 or higher. The subscales with the lowest internal consistency also had the fewest items (four). The split-half reliability of the total scale was ($r = .79$).

Validity: There is evidence of construct validity. African Americans who live in Black neighborhoods scored higher on the scale than those living in mixed or predominantly White neighborhoods. African Americans score higher than other ethnic groups on the subscales and the total score. Drinking alcohol is related to subscale and total scores in the expected direction. Hypothesized gender differences were found on the total score and two subscale scores. There were no differences by income, education, or age.

Comments: This instrument assessed levels of African American acculturation with an adult community sample. The scale has not been assessed for Black subgroups such as from the Caribbean. There is evidence of validity and reliability; other studies have replicated the scale's validity (Guevarra et al., 2005) and reliability, though the reliability scores are mixed in their strength (Guevarra et al., 2005; Nasim, Corona, Belgrave, Utsey, & Fallah, 2007). The racial segregation subscale may not be a measure of acculturation rather a factor associated with discrimination (authors' comments) and therefore may confound the total scale score. There is also a short-form of this scale (Landrine & Klonoff, 1995) for which the authors have found similar psychometric characteristics, though with 10 subscales.

Location: Landrine, H. & Klonoff, E. A. (2000). Revising and improving the African American acculturation scale. *Journal of Black Psychology, 26*, 235–261.

Selected Publications

Guevarra, J. S., Kwate, N. O. A., Tang, T. S., Valdimarsdottir, H. B., Freeman, H. P., & Bovbjerg, D. H. (2005). Acculturation and its relationship to smoking and breast self-examination frequency in African American women. *Journal of Behavioral Medicine, 28*, 191–199.

Landrine, H., & Klonoff, E. A. (1994). The African American acculturation scale. *Journal of Black Psychology, 201*, 104–127.

Landrine, H., & Klonoff, E. A. (1995). The African American acculturation scale II: Cross-validation and short form. *Journal of Black Psychology, 21*, 124–152.

Nasim, A., Corona, R., Belgrave, F., Utsey, S. O., & Fallah, N. (2007). Cultural orientation as a protective factor against tobacco and marijuana smoking for African American young. *Journal of Youth and Adolescence, 36*, 503–516.

*African American Acculturation Scale – Revised**

* Asterisk items reflect short form.

Below are some beliefs and attitudes about religion, families, racism, Black people, White people, and health. Please tell us how much you personally agree or disagree with these beliefs and attitudes by circling a number. There are no right or wrong answers; we simply want to know your views and beliefs.

Note: Respondents are asked to circle 1 through 7 where: 1 = I totally disagree not true at all; 4 = Sort of agree, sort of true; 7 = I strongly agree, absolutely true. The items are:

1. I believe in the Holy Ghost.*
2. I like gospel music.*
3. I believe in heaven and hell.*
4. The church is the heart of the Black community.*
5. I have seen people "get the spirit" or speak in tongues.
6. I am currently a member of a Black church.*
7. When I was young, I was a member of a Black church.
8. Prayer can cure disease.*
9. What goes around, comes around.
10. I used to sing in the church choir.
11. Most of the music I listen to is by Black artists.*

12. I like Black music more than White music.*
13. I listen to Black radio stations.*
14. I try to watch all the Black shows on TV.*
15. The person I admire the most is Black.*
16. I feel more comfortable around Blacks than Whites.
17. When I pass a Black person (a stranger) on the street, I always say hello or nod at them.
18. Most of my friends are Black.*
19. I read (or used to read) *Essence* or *Ebony* magazine.
20. I don't trust most White people.
21. IQ tests were set up purposefully to discriminate against Black people.*
22. Most Whites are afraid of Blacks.
23. Deep in their hearts, most White people are racists.*
24. Whites don't understand Blacks.
25. Most tests (like the SATs and tests to get a job) are set up to make sure that Blacks don't get high scores on them.*
26. Some members of my family hate or distrust White people.
27. When I was young, I shared a bed at night with my sister, brother, or some other relative.
28. When I was young, my parent(s) sent me to stay with a relative (aunt, uncle, grandmother) for a few days or weeks, and then I went back home again.*
29. When I was young, my cousin, aunt, grandmother, or other relative lived with me and my family for awhile.
30. When I was young, I took a bath with my sister, brother, or some other relative.*
31. Some people in my family use Epsom salts.
32. Illnesses can be classified as natural types and unnatural types.
33. Some old Black women/ladies know how to cure diseases.
34. Some older Black women know a lot about pregnancy and childbirth.
35. I was taught that you shouldn't take a bath and then go outside.
36. I avoid splitting a pole.*
37. When the palm of your hand itches, you'll receive some money.*
38. There's some truth to many old superstitions.*
39. I eat Black-eyed peas on New Year's Eve.
40. I grew up in a mostly Black neighborhood.*
41. I went to (or go to) a mostly Black high school.*
42. I went to a mostly Black elementary school.*
43. I currently live in a mostly Black neighborhood.
44. It's better to try to move your whole family ahead in this world than it is to be out for only yourself.*
45. Old people are wise.*
46. I often lend money or give other types of support to members of my family.
47. A child should not be allowed to call a grown woman by her first name, "Alice." The child should be taught to call her "Miss Alice."

Additional short-form items not on the list above:

a. I know how to cook chit'lins.
b. I eat chit'lins once in a while.
c. Sometimes I cook ham hocks.
d. I know how long you are supposed to cook collard greens.
e. I have seen people "fall out."
f. I know what "falling out" means.
g. When I was a child, I used to play tonk.
h. I know how to play bid whist.

African American Acculturation Scale (Snowden & Hines, 1999)

African American Acculturation Scale (AAAS-SH) was developed to measure acculturation focusing on identification with aspects of African American life and culture.

Description: The African American Acculturation Scale is a 10-item scale to measure immersion in African American culture and life focusing on media preferences, social interactions, and race-related attitudes. The response options range from *most or all/strongly agree* (0) to *less than half/strongly disagree* (3). Total scores are calculated by summing the ten items and range from 0 to 27. The higher the score the less identification with African American life and culture and, therefore, the greater the acculturation. The scale is completed either by an interview or self-administration.

Sample: The AARS was first evaluated with 923 African Americans living in households in the 48 contiguous United States; multistage probability sampling was used to draw the sample. The response rate was 70%. There were 533 women and 390 men.

Reliability: The coefficient alpha for the scale was .75.

Validity: Factor analysis of the scale supported a unidimensional structure. Most of the hypothesized relationships drawn from theory and previous research were confirmed providing evidence for construct validity. Specifically for men, level of acculturation was related to age, income, likelihood of marriage, urban residence, and the importance of religion, while for women, acculturation was related to marital status, income, education, and urban residence.

Comment: Use of a national probability sample enhances the generalizability of the findings. The scale is short and easy to administer. There is moderate reliability and evidence of construct validity from the original article. A briefer version with seven items found weaker reliability (alpha = .61; Thompson, Valdimarsdottir, Winkel, Jandorf, & Redd, 2004). A subsequent confirmatory factor analysis found that a 3-factor, correlated model provided a better fit that a single-factor model (Reid, Brown, Peterson, Snowden, & Hines, 2009) but given the correlations, it appears that the scale measures a single higher order construct with three dimensions. Scale scores were not correlated with other related constructs calling into question construct validity (Reid et al., 2009).

Location: Snowden, L. R. & Hines, A. M. (1999). A scale to assess African American acculturation. *Journal of Black Psychology, 25*, 36–47.

Selected Publications

Reid, R. J., Brown, T. L., Peterson, N. A., Snowden, L., & Hines, A. (2009). Testing the factor structure of a scale to assess African American acculturation: A confirmatory factor analysis. *Journal of Community Psychology, 37*, 293–304.

Thompson, H. S., Valdimarsdottir, H. B., Winkel, G., Jandorf, L., & Redd, W. (2004). The group-based medical mistrust scale: Psychometric properties and association with breast cancer screening. *Preventive Medicine, 38*, 209–218.

African American Acculturation Scale

Note: Respondents use the following categories: 0 = Most or all/strongly agree; 1 = Agree; 2 = About half/disagree; 3 = Less than half/strongly disagree. The slash reflects different questions.

1. When you listen to music, you prefer Black rather than White music.
2. When you watch television, you prefer to watch Black rather than White shows.
3. When you listen to the radio, you prefer to listen to Black rather than White stations.
4. The greatest proportions of your friends that you usually see these days are Black.
5. The greatest proportions of the people in your church congregation these days are Black.
6. The greatest proportions of parties that you usually attend these days are Black.
7. The greatest proportions of people in your neighborhood these days are Black.
8. Socially, you feel less at ease with Whites than Blacks.
9. When you need help, you rely mainly on your relatives.
10. You believe that Blacks should only marry Blacks.

Measures of Inter-racial Identity

The Racism Reaction Scale (Thompson, Neville, Weathers, Poston, & Atkinson, 1990)

The Racism Reaction Scale (RRS) was developed to assess individual feelings of differential and inferior treatment, referred to as racism reaction.

Description: The RRS includes 19 items addressing racism reaction statements. A 7-point Likert-type scale is used with responses ranging from *strongly agree* (1) to *strongly disagree* (7). The total score for the RRS is obtained by summing the items. Higher scores reflect less agreement with the racism reaction statements while lower scores reflect more agreement with the racism reaction statements. The scale is self-administered.

Sample: Students were recruited from classes at a predominately White university in California. Eighty-seven students self-identified as African American (37 men and 49 women) and 70 self-identified as White (31 men and 39 women). The average age of this sample was 21. Thirty-five were freshman (23%), 41 were sophomores (26%), 38 were juniors (24%), and 43 were seniors (27%).

Reliability: The entire sample's Cronbach's alpha was .680 while .587 for African Americans and .689 for Whites.

Validity: To assess construct validity, scores on the RSS and scores from two subscales of the Cultural Mistrust Inventory (CMI; a measure of group cultural mistrust) were evaluated. Correlations were: Interpersonal Relations Subscale ($r = .217$), the CMI Education and Training Subscale ($r = .431$), and the CMI combined score ($r = .343$).

Comments: This instrument was developed with a specific focus on college students. The reliability score is moderate to low but a subsequent study (Wright & Littleford, 2002) with a sample of 115 college students reported much higher alpha coefficients (total: $r = .94$; African Americans: $r = .90$; Asian Americans: $r = .92$; Hispanics: $r = .95$; Multiracial students: $r = .95$; Whites: $r = .93$). There is minimal evidence of construct validity.

Location: Thompson, C. E., Neville, H., Weathers, P. L., Poston, W. C., & Atkinson, D. R. (1990). Cultural mistrust and racism reaction among African American students. *Journal of College Student Development, 31*, 162–168.

Selected Publications

Wright M. O., & Littleford, L. N. (2002). Experiences and beliefs as predictors of ethnic identify and intergroup relations. *Journal of Multicultural Counseling and Development, 30*, 2–20.

Racism Reaction Scale

1. People don't really want to accept me for who I am; they just want me to fit in and not be different even though I am different.
2. When I walk in the room, everyone stops talking.
3. I am tired of being accused of being paranoid.
4. People laugh at me behind my back.
5. People keep asking me about my manner of grooming.
6. I feel lonely and frightened on this campus.

7. The only reason I stay on this campus is because I have to prove to myself and everyone else that I can make it.
8. Professors act surprised when I raise my hand to contribute to class discussions.
9. People object to my taste in music because it is different from their own.
10. I have to be prepared to deal with a threatening environment.
11. People where I live always want me to turn down my music even though it is no louder than anyone else's.
12. Professors treat me differently from other students.
13. A lot of people look at me strangely.
14. Other students are surprised to learn that I have some of the same feelings and goals that they have.
15. I am tired of having to give out 120% to prove myself.
16. When I walk into class, everyone turns his or her head to look at me.
17. Professors don't expect me to perform as well as other students.
18. The other students expect me to do poorly in our classes.
19. People ridicule me for who I am.

Attitude Toward Whites and Attitude Toward Blacks Scales (Brigham, 1993)

The Attitude Toward Whites (ATW) and Attitude Toward Blacks (ATB) scales are designed to assess attitudes toward each population group given current (i.e., year 1993) social and political events.

Description: The two scales are designed to assess the attitudes of African Americans toward Whites (ATW) and the attitudes of Whites to African Americans (ATB). The ATW includes 20 items reflecting White interactions with African Americans, social distance items, policy issues, and reactions to inter-racial couples. There are six positively worded items (items 2, 4, 8, 10, 17, 20) and 14 negatively worded items (items 1, 3, 5, 6, 7, 9, 11, 12, 13, 14, 15, 16, 18, 19). The ATB includes 20 items reflecting social distance (comfort in interactions with African Americans), affective reactions, policy issues, and an affirmative action-related issue. There are 10 positively worded questions (items 2, 4, 7, 9, 11, 13, 14, 16, 18, 19) and 10 negatively worded questions (items 1, 3, 5, 6, 8, 10, 12, 15, 17, 20). Both scales use a 7-point response format ranging from *strongly disagree* (1) to *strongly agree* (7). The total score for each scale appears to be calculated by reverse coding the negatively worded items and summing the 20 items. The higher the score, the more favorable the attitude the respondent has toward the other racial group. The scales are self-administered.

Sample: The psychometric properties of the ATW were assessed with a sample of 81 African American undergraduates from a predominantly African American university in the south; the psychometric properties of the ATB were assessed with a sample of 260 White undergraduates from a predominantly White university in the south.

Reliability: Cronbach's alpha for the ATW was .75 and Cronbach's alpha for the ATB was .88.

Validity: The ATW scale scores were statistically significantly correlated with the Multifactor Racial Attitude Inventor (MRAI) ($r = .53$), an Affect/Social Distance Scale ($r = .84$) and to respondents own evaluation of their attitudes ($r = .56$) providing evidence of convergent validity. Construct validity was shown in that ATW scores were statistically significantly related to the amount of contact with Whites ($r = .41$). ATB scale scores were statistically significantly correlated with the MRAI ($r = .86$), the Modern Racism Scale ($r = .70$), the Affect/Social Distance scale ($r = .92$), the Symbolic Racism Scale ($r = .45$) and respondents own evaluation of their attitudes ($r = .64$). Positive attitudes were correlated with more contact ($r = .22$).

Comments: Both scales have demonstrated reliability and validity. High internal consistency has been found in other studies using the ATB (Plant, Devine, & Brazy, 2003, alpha = .91; Voils, Ashburn-Nardo, & Monteith, 2002, alpha = .84). The findings may be restricted to college students though Voils and colleagues had a broader sample. Given that the scale is designed to measure "current context," some questions may need to be updated. The ATW and ATB avoid a response set by using positively and negatively worded questions.

Location: Brigham, J. C. (1993). College students' racial attitudes. *Journal of Applied Social Psychology, 23*, 1933–1967.

Selected Publications

Plant, E. A., Devine, P., & Brazy, P. (2003). The Bogus pipeline motivations to respond without prejudice: revisiting the fading and faking of racial prejudice. *Group Process & Intergroup Relations*, *6*, 187–200.

Voils, C., Ashburn-Nardo, L., & Monteith, M. (2002). Evidence of prejudice-relates conflict associates affect beyond the college setting. *Group Process & Intergroup Relations*, *5*, 19–33.

The Attitude Toward Whites (ATW) and Attitude Toward Blacks (ATB) Scales

Attitude and Opinion Scale – Attitude Toward Whites (ATW)

This questionnaire contains 20 questions concerning your opinions about current social issues. Please respond to each question in terms of the 1-to-7 scale below, where 1 = *strong disagreement* with the statement and 7 = *strong agreement*. Write a number from 1 to 7 that best represents your opinion on the line to the left of each question. Please answer *every question*; do not leave any out. There are no "right" or "wrong" answers; please be as honest and straightforward as you can. All responses will be treated confidentially and analyzed as group data only.

Response categories: 1 = Strongly disagree; 2 = Disagree; 3 = Disagree somewhat; 4 = Neither agree or disagree; 5 = Agree somewhat; 6 = Agree; 7 = Strongly agree

1. Over the past few years, Blacks have gotten less economically than they deserve (R).
2. I would accept an invitation to a New Year's Eve party given by a White couple in their own home.
3. I have as much respect for Whites as I do for some Blacks, but the average White person and I share little in common (R).
4. Racial integration (of schools, businesses, residences, etc.) has benefited both Whites and Blacks.
5. Most Whites fear that Blacks will bring violence to neighborhoods when they move in (R).
6. I would rather not have Whites live in the same apartment building I live in (R).
7. Most Whites can't be trusted to deal honestly with Blacks (R).
8. If a White were put in charge of me, I would not mind taking advice and direction from him or her.
9. Most Whites feel that Blacks are getting too demanding in their push for equal rights (R).
10. Whites should support Blacks in their struggle against discrimination and segregation.
11. I feel that Black people's troubles in the past have built in them a stronger character than White people have (R).
12. By and large, I think Blacks tend to be better athletes than Whites (R).
13. Some Whites are so touchy about race that it is difficult to get along with them (R).
14. I think that White people look more similar to each other than Black people do (R).
15. It is not right to ask Americans to accept integration if they honestly don't believe in it (R).
16. Most Whites cannot understand what it's like to be Black (R).
17. I favor open housing laws that allow more racial integration of neighborhoods.
18. When I see an inter-racial couple I feel that they are making a mistake in dating each other (R).
19. Local city officials often pay less attention to a request or complaint from a Black person than from a White person (R).
20. It would not bother me if my new roommate was White.

Attitude and Opinion Scale – Attitude Toward Blacks (ATB)

This questionnaire contains 20 questions concerning your opinions about current social issues. Please respond to each question in terms of the 1-to-7 scale below, where 1 = *strong disagreement* with the statement and 7 = *strong agreement*. Write a number from 1 to 7 that best represents your opinion on the line to the left of each question. Please answer *every question*; do not leave any out. There are no "right" or "wrong" answers; please be as honest and straightforward as you can. All responses will be treated confidentially and analyzed as group data only.

Response categories: 1 = Strongly disagree; 2 = Disagree; 3 = Disagree somewhat; 4 = Neither agree or disagree; 5 = Agree somewhat; 6 = Agree; 7 = Strongly agree

1. I enjoy a funny racial joke, even if some people might find it offensive (R).
2. If I had a chance to introduce Black visitors to my friends and neighbors, I would be pleased to do so.
3. I would rather not have Blacks live in the same apartment building I live in (R).
4. Racial integration (of schools, businesses, residences, etc.) has benefited both Whites and Blacks.
5. I probably would feel somewhat self-conscious dancing with a Black in a public place (R).
6. I think that Black people look more similar to each other than White people do (R).
7. It would not bother me if my new roommate was Black.
8. Inter-racial marriage should be discouraged to avoid the "who-am-I?" confusion which the children feel (R).
9. If a Black were put in charge of me, I would not mind taking advice and direction from him or her.
10. Generally, Blacks are not as smart as Whites (R).
11. The federal government should take decisive steps to override the injustices Blacks suffer at the hands of local authorities.
12. It is likely that Blacks will bring violence to neighborhoods when they move in (R).
13. Black and White people are inherently equal.
14. I get very upset when I hear a White make a prejudicial remark about Blacks.
15. I worry that in the next few years I may be denied my application for a job or a promotion because of preferential treatment given to minority group members (R).
16. I favor open housing laws that allow more racial integration of neighborhoods.
17. Black people are demanding too much too fast in their push for equal rights (R).
18. I would not mind at all if a Black family with about the same income and education as me moved in next door.
19. Whites should support Blacks in their struggle against discrimination and segregation.
20. Some Blacks are so touchy about race that it is difficult to get along with them (R).

Prejudice Perception Assessment Scale (Gilbert, 1998)

The Prejudice Perception Assessment Scale was developed to assess the degree of stigma vulnerability or the extent to which a respondent attributes negative feedback to prejudice.

Description: The PPAS consists of five vignettes. Four vignettes are specific to cross-racial college-related situations including faculty-student, roommates, and peers; the fifth vignette deals with a typical college activity (shopping at a campus store). The PPAS is reversed scored and then summed with higher scores indicating a stronger orientation toward being vulnerable to stigma. The author notes that both extremely high and extremely low scores indicate a lack of objectivity with extremely low scores suggesting denial. The scale is self-administered.

Sample: This scale was tested with two samples. Study 1 included 66 African American college students enrolled in a predominantly White university; most (70%) participants were female and ranged in age from 17 to 28 years. Study 2 comprised 109 African American students on predominantly White campuses in the South; participants were primarily female (65%) and ranged in age from 17 to 48 years (average age was 24).

Reliability: In Study 2, coefficient alpha was .84.

Validity: In Study 1, convergent validity was established as the PPAS score was associated in the expected direction ($r = .38$) to a composite score of two subscales of the Cultural Mistrust Inventory. The PPAS was unrelated to a measure of social desirability providing evidence of discriminant validity. In Study 2, there is evidence from an exploratory factor analysis that the scale is unidimensional.

Comments: There is limited evidence of reliability and validity and no additional studies could be found to support the psychometric properties of the scale. We found no studies that adapted this scale to other American Americans.

Location: Gilbert, D. J. (1998). The prejudice perception assessment scale: Measuring stigma vulnerability among African American students at predominantly Euro-American universities. *Journal of Black Psychology, 24*, 305–321.

Selected Publications

None

The Prejudice Perception Assessment Scale (PPAS)

The following five situations are hypothetical. Each situation ends with a negative outcome for a hypothetical, African American student. Please read each scenario carefully and respond to each one by circling the number below the response that best fits your opinion about why the negative outcome occurred.

1. It is the first day of class for the spring semester and your first class is being held in a large auditorium. You arrive and take a seat in the front of the room next

to a student, who happens to be White. You notice the student is looking around and, right away, the student gets up and moves to another seat. You do not notice where the student sits, but you are wondering why the student decided to move to another seat. In your opinion, the likelihood that this event has happened because the White student is prejudiced against African American is

Extremely Very Somewhat Unable to Somewhat Very Extremely
Likely Likely Likely Determine Unlikely Unlikely Unlikely
(1) (2) (3) (4) (5) (6) (7)

2. You are enrolled in a small class in which you are the only African American student. Your professor happens to be White. You study hard for your first exam (essay questions only) and you expect to get an A or a high B. However, when you get your exam back, your grade is a C. You do not know what other students' grades are. However, you are wondering why your grade is so much lower than what you expected. In your opinion, the likelihood that this low grade is due to prejudice of the professor against African Americans.

   Extremely Very Somewhat Unable to Somewhat Very Extremely
   Likely Likely Likely Determine Unlikely Unlikely Unlikely
   (1) (2) (3) (4) (5) (6) (7)
3. You make a visit to a department store near the campus during the store's busy season. You notice that the store is crowded, and there are lots of salesclerks of various racial backgrounds. One particular salesperson, who is White, is casually following you as you wander through the store glancing at merchandise. In your opinion, the likelihood that this sales clerk's interest in you is due to prejudice against African Americans is

   Extremely Very Somewhat Unable to Somewhat Very Extremely
   Likely Likely Likely Determine Unlikely Unlikely Unlikely
   (1) (2) (3) (4) (5) (6) (7)
4. You answer an advertisement for a roommate. The advertisement states, "Two students living in three-bedroom house need third student," and goes on to list the price and a location in town where many students reside. When you arrive to check out the place, you discover that the two students are White. They let you know that many students contacted them about the advertisement, and they have scheduled three people to interview for the roommate position later that day. Two days later, you learn that they selected another person, who is also White, for their roommate. In your opinion, the likelihood that these two students did not choose you as their roommate because of prejudice against African Americans is

   Extremely Very Somewhat Unable to Somewhat Very Extremely
   Likely Likely Likely Determine Unlikely Unlikely Unlikely
   (1) (2) (3) (4) (5) (6) (7)
5. During the beginning of the semester, you decide to make a drop-in visit to your professor's office to discuss your plans for the term paper assignment. You have never had this professor for a class before. The time that you arrive is not a designated time for office hours, but you notice the professor is talking with another student (who is not in your class). Both the professor and student are White. The professor sees you but does not immediately acknowledge your presence or let

you know how long you may be waiting. After waiting about 10 minutes, you are starting to wonder if you should stay or leave. In your opinion, the likelihood that this professor's actions are due to prejudice against African Americans is

Extremely Likely	Very Likely	Somewhat Likely	Unable to Determine	Somewhat Unlikely	Very Unlikely	Extremely Unlikely
(1)	(2)	(3)	(4)	(5)	(6)	(7)

Revised Cultural Mistrust Inventory (Terrell, F. & Terrell, S., 1981)

The Revised Cultural Mistrust Inventory (CMI) was developed to measure the extent to which African Americans are distrustful of Whites and White-related organizations.

Description: The CMI is a 48-item self-report measure to assess cultural mistrust in four domains. These domains include: (1) Education and Training (7 items: 2, 3, 4, 7, 30, 32, 48); (2) Interpersonal Relations (14 items: 11, 12, 19, 20, 21, 22, 23, 24, 25, 26, 27, 28, 33, 42); (3) Business and Work (15 items: 1, 5, 13, 14, 15, 17, 35, 36, 37, 38, 39, 43, 44, 45, 46); and (4) Politics and Law (12 items: 6, 8, 9, 10, 16, 18, 29, 31, 34, 40, 41, 47). The scale has 27 positive and 21 negative worded statements (items 1, 6, 10, 12, 14, 17, 19, 23, 26, 27, 28, 31, 32, 33, 34, 35, 36, 41, 43, 44, 48). The score options range from *strongly disagree* (1) to *strongly agree* (7). The instrument is scored by reverse scoring the negative items and summing all items. Higher scores indicate more cultural mistrust. Subscale scores are calculated in a similar fashion. The scale is self-administered.

Sample: The initial evaluation sample consisted of 172 African American first and second-year college males. A second sample of 69 male college students was used to assess test–retest reliability.

Reliability: Two-week test–retest reliability was .86 for the entire scale.

Validity: There is convergent validity as the CMI was significantly related to racial discrimination; respondents reporting increased incidences of racial discrimination had higher mean scores on the CMI. The lack of relationship to a measure of social desirability demonstrated discriminant validity. The correlations between subscales were low suggesting each can be used as a separate subscale.

Comments: Additional studies have found acceptable internal consistency for the entire scale (.89, Nickerson, Helms, & Terrell, 1994; .89, Townes, Cunningham, & Chavez-Korell, 2009; .84, Whaley, 2002) and mixed results for the subscales (Poston, Craine, & Atkinson, 1991: Interpersonal Relations, .86; Whaley, 2002: Business and Work, .75, Education and Training, .65; Interpersonal Relations, .48; Politics and Law, .50). Nickerson et al. (1994; college students) found construct validity as the CMI was statistically significantly related to help seeking behavior. Whaley (2002; inpatient psychiatric patients) reported convergent validity with paranoia, and discriminant validity as the CMI was weakly related to self-esteem (though poor construct validity), and social desirability. There is some question about whether the subscales should be used (Whaley, 2002). The CMI avoids a response set by using positively and negatively worded questions.

Location: Terrell, F., & Terrell, S. (1981). An inventory to measure cultural mistrust among Blacks. *The Western Journal of Black Studies, 5*, 180–185.

Selected Publications

Nickerson, K. J., Helms, J. E., & Terrell, F. (1994). Cultural mistrust, opinions about mental illness, and Black students' attitudes toward seeking psychological help from White counselors. *Journal of Counseling Psychology, 41*, 378–385.
Poston, W. C, Craine, M., & Atkinson, D. R. (1991). Counselor dissimilarity confrontation, client cultural mistrust, and willingness to self-disclose. *Journal of Multicultural Counseling and Development, 19*, 65–73.
Townes, D. L., Cunningham, N. J., & Chavez-Korell, S. (2009). Reexaming the relationships between racial identify, cultural mistrust, help-seeking attitudes, and preference for a Black counselor. *Journal of Counseling Psychology, 56*, 330–336.
Whaley, A. (2002). Psychometric analysis of the cultural mistrust inventory with a Black psychiatric inpatient sample. *Journal of Clinical Psychology, 58*, 383–396.

Revised Cultural Mistrust Inventory (CMI)

Directions: Enclosed are some statements concerning beliefs, opinions, and attitudes about Blacks. Read each statement carefully and give your honest feelings about the beliefs and attitudes expressed. Indicate the extent to which you agree by using the following scale:

Response categories: 1 = Strongly disagree; 2 = Disagree; 3 = Slightly disagree; 4 = Neither disagree nor agree; 5 = Slightly agree; 6 = Agree; 7 = Strongly agree

The higher number you choose for the statement, the more you agree with that statement. For example, if you "moderately agree" with a statement, you would choose among the numbers 4 and 5 which appear above the label "Moderately agree." If you chose number 5, this means you agree more with the statement than if you had chosen the number 4. The same principle applies for the other labels. The higher the number you chose, the more you agree with the statement.

Finally, there are no right or wrong answers, only what is right for you. If in doubt, blacken the space which seems most nearly to express your present feelings about the statement. Please answer all items.

1. Whites are usually fair to all people regardless of race (R).
2. White teachers teach subjects so that they favor Whites.
3. White teachers are more likely to slant the subject matter to make Blacks look inferior.
4. White teachers deliberately ask Black students questions which are difficult so they will fail.
5. There is no need for a Black person to work hard to get ahead financially because Whites will take what you earn anyway.

6. Black citizens can rely on White lawyers to defend them to the best of his ability (R).
7. Black parents should teach their children not to trust White teachers.
8. White politicians will promise Blacks a lot but deliver little.
9. White policemen will slant a story to make Blacks appear guilty.
10. White politicians usually can be relied on to keep the promises they make to Blacks (R).
11. Blacks should be suspicious of a White person who tries to be friendly.
12. Whether you should trust a person or not is based on his race (R).
13. Probably the biggest reason Whites want to be friendly with Blacks is so that they can take advantage of them.
14. A Black person can usually trust his or her White co-workers (R).
15. If a White person is honest in dealing with Blacks, it is because of fear of being caught.
16. A Black person cannot trust a White judge to evaluate him or her fairly.
17. A Black person can feel comfortable making a deal with a White person simply by a handshake (R).
18. Whites deliberately pass laws designed to block the progress of Blacks.
19. There are some Whites who are trustworthy enough to have as close friends (R).
20. Blacks should not have anything to do with Whites since they cannot be trusted.
21. It is best for Blacks to be on their guard when among Whites.
22. Of all ethnic groups, Whites are really the Indian-givers.
23. White friends are least likely to break their promise (R).
24. Blacks should be cautious about what they say in the presence of Whites since Whites will try to use it against them.
25. Whites can rarely be counted on to do what they say.
26. Whites are usually honest with Blacks (R).
27. Whites are as trustworthy as members of any other ethnic group (R).
28. Whites will say one thing and do another (R).
29. White politicians will take advantage of Blacks every chance they get.
30. When a White teacher asks a Black student a question, it is usually to get information which can be used against him or her.
31. White policemen can be relied on to exert an effort to apprehend those who commit crimes against Blacks (R).
32. Black students can talk to a White teacher in confidence without fear that the teacher will use it against him or her later (R).
33. Whites will usually keep their word (R).
34. White policemen usually do not try to trick Blacks into admitting they committed a crime which they didn't (R).
35. There is no need for Blacks to be more cautious with White businessmen than with anyone else (R).
36. There are some White businessmen who are honest in business transactions with Blacks (R).
37. White store owners, salesmen, and other White businessmen tend to cheat Blacks whenever they can.

38. Since Whites can't be trusted in business, the old saying "one in the hand is worth two in the bush" is a good policy to follow.
39. Whites who establish businesses in Black communities do so only so that they can take advantage of Blacks.
40. Blacks have often been deceived by White politicians.
41. White politicians are equally honest with Blacks and Whites (R).
42. Blacks should not confide in Whites because they will use it against you.
43. A Black person can loan money to a White person and feel confident it will be repaid (R).
44. White businessmen usually will not try to cheat Blacks (R).
45. White business executives will steal the ideas of their Black employees.
46. A promise from a White is about as good as a three dollar bill.
47. Blacks should be suspicious of advice given by White politicians.
48. If a Black student tries, he will get the grade he deserves from a White teacher (R).

Index of Race-Related Stress (Utsey & Ponterotto, 1996) and Index of Race-Related Stress-Brief (Utsey, 1999)

The Index of Race-Related Stress (IRRS) is a multidimensional scale to measure stress associated with the experiences of racism and discrimination encountered by African Americans in their daily lives. There is both a long version and a brief version.

Description: The IRRS is a 46-item self-report questionnaire. The scale includes both a global measure and four subscales including: cultural racism (16 items: 2, 3, 8, 13, 15, 21, 23, 29, 31, 34, 35, 37, 40, 42, 43, 44) in which African American culture is disparaged; institutional racism (11 items: 12, 18, 19, 20, 26, 32, 38, 39, 41, 45, 46) consisting of practices and policies of organizations; individual racism (11 items: 1, 4, 5, 6, 9, 17, 22, 24, 27, 30, 33) measures personal experiences; and collective racism (8 items: 7, 10, 11, 14, 16, 25, 28, 36) measuring organized efforts at discrimination. Participants respond to items using a 5-point Likert-type scale ranging from *this never happened to me* (0) to *this event happened to me and I was extremely upset* (4). Both total and subscale scores can be used. Subscale scores are computed by summing the items. The total score is calculated by converting each total subscale score to a *z*-score and summing the *z*-scores. Higher scores reflect more stress associated with experiences of racism. The scale is self-administered.

The IRRS-Brief (IRRS-B) includes 22 items (2, 5, 8, 10, 13, 15, 22, 25, 24, 26, 27, 29, 32, 33, 35, 37, 40, 43, 41, 44, 6, 20) from the longer scale. The process by which the scale was developed resulted in three subscales: cultural racism (10 items: 2, 8, 13, 15, 29, 35, 37, 40, 43, 44), institutional racism (6 items: 26, 32, 41, 10, 25, 20), and individual racism (6 items: 5, 22, 24, 33, 27, 6).

Sample: Three separate studies were conducted in the initial report of the IRRS's psychometric properties. Study 1 included 302 participants ranging in age from 18 to 61 years (average age 26.77). Participants were mostly female (55%), single (76%), and enrolled in college (51%). Study 2 included 341 participants (31 not identified as African American). Of the 310 African American participants, two-thirds were female, most were single (85%) and college students (84%); participants ranged in age from 17 to 76 (average age 23.38). Study 3 involved 31 traditional college students and 19 students in adult education classes. The IRRS-B was evaluated using a sample of 239 African American participants and 25 White Americans who were included for comparative purposes. Participants came from a university, the community, and a substance abuse program. The average age of participants was 31, 58% were female, and averaged almost 14 years of education.

Reliability: *IRRS*: Cronbach's alpha coefficients were reported in Study 1 and Study 2 for the subscales: cultural racism ($\alpha = .87$, $\alpha = .89$), institutional racism ($\alpha = .85$, $\alpha = .82$), individual racism ($\alpha = .84$, $\alpha = .84$) and collective racism ($\alpha = .79$, $\alpha = .74$). Study 3 reported test–retest reliability for 3 weeks (college students) and 2 weeks (adult education students): cultural racism ($r = .77$, $r = .58$), institutional racism ($r = .69$, $r = .71$), individual ($r = .61$, $r = .54$), and collective ($r = .79$, $r = .75$).

IRRS-B: Cronbach's alphas for the subscales were: cultural racism ($\alpha = .78$), institutional racism ($\alpha = .69$), and individual racism ($\alpha = .78$). Subscales correlated with each other ranging from $r = .56$ to $r = .74$; the subscales were highly correlated with the total scale score ($r = .84$ to $r = .90$).

Validity: *IRRS*: Factorial validity was established in Study 1 (exploratory factor analysis provided four factor structure) and Study 2 (confirmatory factor analysis of the four factor model). To establish concurrent validity, the total score and the four subscales were correlated with the Racism and Life Experience Scales-Brief Version (RaLES-B) and the Perceived Stress Scale (PSS). Most of the subscales were statistically significantly related to the subscales of the RaLES-B; the total IRRS score and the total RaLES-B score were also statistically significantly related ($r = .39$). Relationships were weaker between the IRRS subscales and the PSS but the total scores were statistically significantly related ($r = .24$).

IRRS-B: The IRRS-B subscales were statistically significantly correlated with the RaLES-B global score, the Perceived Influences of Race subscale, and the Group Impact subscale. Mean ethnicity scores were lower for Whites than African Americans providing evidence that the scale discriminates between the two groups.

Comments: There is evidence of the reliability and validity of both versions of the IRRS. Additional studies have demonstrated the reliability of the full scale with elderly African Americans (Utsey, Payne, Jackson, & Jones, 2002) and with adolescents using a shorter version (32 items; Seaton, 2006). Additional studies of the IRRS-B have found consistently high Cronbach's alpha scores (Utsey, Chae, Brown, & Kelly, 2002; Utsey & Hook, 2007; Utsey, Lanier, Williams, Bolden, & Lee, 2006).

Location: Utsey, S., & Ponterotto, J. (1996). Development and validation of the index of race-related stress (IRRS). *Journal of Counseling Psychology, 43*, 490–501.

Utsey, S. (1999). Development and validation of a short form of the index of race-related stress (IRRS) – Brief version. *Measurement and Evaluation in Counseling and Development, 32*, 149–167.

Selected Publications

Seaton, E. K. (2006). An examination of the factor structure of the index of race-related stress among a sample of African American adolescents. *Journal of Applied Psychology, 36*, 1414–1429.

Utsey, S. O., Chae, M., Brown, C., & Kelly, D. (2002). Effect of ethnic group membership on ethnic identity, race-related stress, and quality of life. *Cultural Diversity and Ethnic Minority Psychology, 8*, 366–377.

Utsey, S. O., & Hook, J. N. (2007). Heart rate variability as a physiological moderator of the relationship between race-related stress and psychological distress in African Americans. *Cultural Diversity and Ethnic Minority Psychology, 13*, 250–253.

Utsey, S. O., Lanier, Y., Williams, O., Bolden, M., & Lee, A. (2006). Moderator effects of cognitive ability and social support on the relation between race-related stress and quality of life in a community sample of Black Americans. *Cultural Diversity and Ethnic Minority Psychology, 12*, 334–346.

Utsey, S. O., Payne, Y., Jackson, E., & Jones, A. (2002). Racism, quality of life indicators, and life satisfaction, and indicators of psychological and physical health among elderly African Americans. *Cultural Diversity and Ethnic Minority Psychology, 8*, 224–233.

Index of Race-Related Stress (IRRS)

This survey questionnaire is intended to sample some of the experiences that Black people have in this country because of their "blackness." There are many experiences that a Black person can have in this country because of his/her race. Some events happen just once, some more often, while others may happen frequently. Below you will find listed some of these experiences for which you are to indicate those that have happened to you or someone very close to you. *Please circle the number on the scale (from 0 to 4) that indicates the reaction you had to the event at the time it happened. Do not leave any items blank.* If an event has happened more than once, refer to the first time it happened. *If an event did not happen circle 0 and go on to the next item.*

Response categories: 0 = This has *never happened* to me; 1 = This event happened, but did not bother me; 2 = This event happened and I was slightly upset; 3 = This event happened and I was upset; 4 = This event happened and I was *extremely* upset.

1. You have been in a restaurant or other White/non-Black establishment where everyone was waited on before you.

2. You notice that crimes committed by White people tend to be romanticized, whereas the same crime committed by a Black person is portrayed as savagery, and the Black person who committed it, as an animal.
3. You notice that when a Black person is killed by a White mob or policeman no one is sent to jail.
4. You have been followed by security (or employees) while shopping in some stores.
5. Sales people/clerks did not say thank you or show other forms of courtesy and respect (i.e., put your things in a bag) when you shopped at some White/non-Black-owned business.
6. White people or other non-Blacks have treated you as if you were unintelligent and needed things explained to you slowly or numerous times.
7. You have been questioned about your presence in a White neighborhood for no apparent reason.
8. You notice that when Black people are killed by the police the media informs the public of the victim's criminal record or negative information in their background, suggesting they got what they deserved.
9. Whites/non-Blacks have failed to apologize for stepping on your foot or bumping into you.
10. You have been threatened with physical violence by an individual or group of White/non-Blacks.
11. You were physically attacked by an individual or group of White/non-Blacks.
12. You did not receive a promotion you deserved; you suspect it was because you are Black.
13. You have observed that White kids who commit violent crimes are portrayed as "boys being boys," while Black kids who commit similar crimes are wild animals.
14. You have had trouble getting a cab to go certain places or even stop for you.
15. You seldom hear or read anything positive about Black people on radio, TV, newspapers, or in history books.
16. While on public transportation or in public places White people/non-Blacks have opted to stand up rather than sit next to you.
17. Although waiting in line first, you were assisted after the White/non-Black person behind you.
18. White people have expected you to denounce or reject the views or remarks of controversial Black leaders.
19. You did not get the job you applied for although you were well qualified; you suspect because you are Black.
20. You were refused an apartment or other housing; you suspect it was because you are Black.
21. You have observed a double standard in the way the law or other systems of government (court, media, disciplinary committees, etc.) work (or don't work) when dealing with Blacks as opposed to Whites/non-Blacks.
22. While shopping at a store the sales clerk assumed that you couldn't afford certain items (i.e., you were directed toward the items on sale).

23. White/non-Black people have been apologetic about the Japanese internment, Jewish holocaust, and other violations of human rights, but would prefer to forget about slavery, Jim Crowism, and other abuses of Black people.
24. You were treated with less respect and courtesy than Whites and other non-Blacks while in a store, restaurant, or other business establishment.
25. You were the victim of a crime and the police treated you as if you should just accept it as part of being Black.
26. You were passed over for an important project although you were more qualified and competent than the White/non-Black person given the task.
27. Whites/non-Blacks have stared at you as if you didn't belong in the same place with them; whether it was a restaurant, theater, or other place of business.
28. You called the police for assistance and when they arrived they treated you like a criminal.
29. You have observed that the police treat White/non-Blacks with more respect and dignity than they do Blacks.
30. White/non-Black people have mistaken you for a sales person, waiter, or other service help when you were actually a customer.
31. You have noticed that the public services are inadequate or non-existent in Black communities (police, sanitation, street repairs, etc.).
32. You have been subjected to racist jokes by Whites/non-Blacks in positions of authority and you did not protest for fear they might have held it against you.
33. While shopping at a store, or when attempting to make a purchase you were ignored as if you were not a serious customer or didn't have any money.
34. You have heard Blacks constantly being compared to other immigrants and minorities in terms of what they have not achieved, in spite of having been in the United States for so much longer than the other groups.
35. You have observed situations where other Blacks were treated harshly or unfairly by Whites/non-Blacks due to their race.
36. You have attempted to hail a cab, but they refused to stop, you think because you are Black.
37. You have heard reports of White people/non-Blacks who have committed crimes, and in an effort to cover up their deeds falsely reported that a Black man responsible for the crime.
38. You have held back angry or hostile feelings in the presence of White/non-Black people for fear they would have accused you of having a "chip" on your shoulder.
39. You have been asked to pay in advance for goods/services that are usually paid for after a person receives them; you suspect it was because you are Black.
40. You notice that the media plays up those stores that cast Blacks in negative ways (child abusers, rapist, muggers, etc. [or as savages] Wild Man of 96th St., Wolf Pack, etc), usually accompanied by a large picture of a Black person looking angry or disturbed.
41. You have been given more work, or the most undesirable jobs at your place of employment while the White/non-Black of equal or less seniority and credentials is given less work, and more desirable tasks.

42. You have heard that Black men have an uncontrollable desire to possess a White woman.
43. You have heard racist remarks or comments about Black people spoken with impunity by White public officials or other influential White people.
44. You have heard or seen other Black people express the desire to be White or to have White physical characteristics because they disliked being Black or thought it was ugly.
45. When you have interacted with Whites/non-Blacks, you anticipated them saying or doing something racist either intentionally or unintentionally.
46. You have discovered that the White/non-Black person employed in the same capacity as you with equal or less qualifications is paid a higher salary.

The Race-based Rejection Sensitivity Questionnaire (Mendoza-Denton, Downey, Davis, Purdie, & Pietrzak, 2002)

The Race-based Rejection Sensitivity Questionnaire was developed to assess anxiety expectations of rejection in various social settings.

Description: The Race-based Rejection Sensitivity Questionnaire (RSQ-Race) is a self-report questionnaire consisting of 12 items to measure anticipatory anxiety of rejection due to race. Each question deals with situations in which there is the potential for rejection due to race. The questionnaire integrates both anxiety about rejection and degree of expectation of rejection. Anxiety or concern that there may be a negative outcome due to race is assessed using a 6-point scale ranging from *very unconcerned* (1) to *very concerned* (6). Expectation about the likelihood of rejection due to race in each social situation is assessed using a 6-point scale ranging from *very unlikely* (1) to *very likely* (6). Scores for the RSQ-Race are calculated by combining responses to each question by multiplying the two responses for each question. The overall score is calculated by taking the average of the anxiety-expectation scores. Higher scores indicate more concern about and expectations of rejection based on race. The scale is self-administered.

Sample: The study to assess the psychometric properties of the scale included 359 undergraduates attending a majority White university. The participants included 130 African Americans, 88 Asian Americans, and 141 White Americans. Their average age was 19.76 years and there were slightly more females (51%). Study 2 included 114 college students with a mean age of 20.82 years. This sample was equally divided among African Americans and Whites. Study 3 included 66 African Americans and had a mean age of 18.1 years; there were 19 males and 47 females.

Reliability: Cronbach's alpha was .90. The 2 to 3-week test–retest reliability for a subsample was .80.

Validity: Construct validity was assessed with the two sections of the Perceived Racism Scale (PRS; perceived race-based negativity and emotional reactivity to perceived race-based negativity) and the Ethnic Identity Scale (EIS; a general measure of ethnic identity). Relationships were statistically significant in the expected directions: PRS perceived race-based negativity, $r = .46$; PRS emotional reactivity, $r = .30$; and EIS, $r = .34$. African American respondents had higher average scores than Asian Americans and White Americans.

Comments: Initial findings suggest that the RQS-Race is a reliable and valid measure to assess concerns about and expectations of rejection based on race in certain situations among African Americans. This conclusion is limited to college students.

Location: Mendoza-Denton, R., Downey, G., Davis, A., Purdie, V. J., & Pietrzak, J. (2002). Sensitivity to status based rejection: Implications for African American students' college experience. *Journal of Personality and Social Psychology, 83,* 896–918.

Selected Publications

None

The Race-based Rejection Sensitivity Questionnaire

1. Imagine that you are in class one day, and the professor asks a particularly difficult question. A few people, including yourself, raise their hands to answer the question.
2. Imagine you are in a pharmacy, trying to pick out a few items. While you are looking at the different brands, you notice one of the clerks glancing your way.
3. Imagine you have just completed a job interview over the telephone. You are in good spirits because the interviewer seemed enthusiastic about your application. Several days later you complete a second interview in person. Your interviewer informs you that they will let you know about their decision soon.
4. It's late at night and you are driving down a country road you are not familiar with. Luckily, there is a 24-h 7–11 just ahead, so you stop there and head up to the counter to ask the young woman for directions.
5. Imagine that a new school counselor is selecting students for a summer scholarship fund that you really want. He has only one scholarship left and you are one of several students that are eligible for this scholarship.
6. Imagine you have just finished shopping, and you are leaving the store carrying several bags. It's closing time, and several people are filing out of the store at once. Suddenly, the alarm begins to sound, and a security guard comes over to investigate.
7. Imagine you are riding the bus one day. The bus is full except for two seats, one of which is next to you. As the bus comes to the next stop, you notice a women getting on the bus.
8. Imagine you are in a restaurant, trying to get the attention of your waitress. A lot of other people are trying to get her attention as well.
9. Imagine you are driving down the street, and there is a police barricade just ahead. The police officers are randomly pulling people over to check drivers' licenses and registrations.

10. Imagine that it's the second day of your new class. The teacher assigned a writing sample yesterday and today the teacher announces that she has finished correcting the papers. You wait for your paper to be returned.
11. Imagine you are standing in line for the ATM machine, and you notice a woman at the machine glances back while she's getting her money.
12. Imagine you are at a pay phone on a street corner. You have to make a call, but you don't have change. You decide to go into a store and ask for change for your bill.

Original Scale References

Brigham, J. C. (1993). College students' racial attitudes. *Journal of Applied Social Psychology, 23*, 1993–1967.
Chang, E. C., & Ritter, E. H. (1976). Ethnocentrism in black college students. *The Journal of Social Psychology, 100*, 89–98.
Gilbert, D. J. (1998). The prejudice perception assessment scale: Measuring stigma vulnerability among African American students at predominantly Euro-American universities. *Journal of Black Psychology, 24*, 305–321.
Landrine, H., & Klonoff, E. A. (2000). Revising and improving the African American acculturation scale. *Journal of Black Psychology, 26*, 235–261.
Mendoza-Denton, R., Downey, G., Davis, A., Purdie, V. J., & Pietrzak, J. (2002). Sensitivity to status based rejection: Implications for African American students' college experience. *Journal of Personality and Social Psychology, 83*, 896–918.
Resnicow, K., & Ross-Gaddy, D. (1997). Development of racial identity scale for low-income African Americans. *Journal of Black Studies, 28*, 239–254.
Resnicow, K., Soler, R. E., Braithwaite, R. L., Selassie, M. B., & Smith, M. (1999). Development of a racial and ethnic identity scale for African American adolescents: The survey of black life. *Journal of Black Psychology, 25*, 171–188.
Sanders Thompson, V. L. (1995). The multidimensional structure of racial identification. *Journal of Research in Personality, 29*, 208–222.
Smith, E. P., & Brookins, C. C. (1997). Toward the development of an ethnic identity measure for African American youth. *Journal of Black Psychology, 23*, 358–377.
Snowden, L. R., & Hines, A. M. (1999). A scale to assess African American acculturation. *Journal of Black Psychology, 25*, 36–47.
Terrell, F., & Terrell, S. (1981). An inventory to measure cultural mistrust among blacks. *The Western Journal of Black Studies, 5*, 180–185.
Thompson, C. E., Neville, H., Weathers, P. L., Poston, W. C., & Atkinson, D. R. (1990). Cultural mistrust and racism reaction among African American students. *Journal of College Student Development, 31*, 162–168.
Utsey, S. (1999). Development and validation of a short form of the index of race-related stress (IRRS) – brief version. *Measurement and Evaluation in Counseling and Development, 32*, 149–167.
Utsey, S., & Ponterotto, J. (1996). Development and validation of the index of race-related stress (IRRS). *Journal of Counseling Psychology, 43*, 490–501.

References

Belgrave, F. Z., Reed, M. C., Plybon, L. E., Butler, D. S., Allison, K. W., & Davis, T. (2004). An evaluation of sisters of Nia: A cultural program for African American girls. *Journal of Black Psychology, 30*, 329–343.

Bennett, L. (1962). *Before the Mayflower: A history of Black America*. Chicago: Johson Publishing Company.

Brigham, J. C. (1993). College students' racial attitudes. *Journal of Applied Social Psychology, 23*, 1933–1967.

Chang, E. C., & Ritter, E. H. (1976). Ethnocentrism in black college students. *The Journal of Social Psychology, 100*, 89–98.

Davis, L. E., Wallace, J., & Shanks, T. (2008). *Overview on African Americans, encyclopedia of social work* (20th ed., pp. 65–75). Washington, DC, and New York: NASW Press and Oxford University Press.

Gilbert, D. J. (1998). The prejudice perception assessment scale: Measuring stigma vulnerability among African American students at predominantly Euro-American universities. *Journal of Black Psychology, 24*, 305–321.

Guevarra, J. S., Kwate, N. O. A., Tang, T. S., Valdimarsdottir, H. B., Freeman, H. P., & Bovbjerg, D. H. (2005). Acculturation and its relationship to smoking and breast self-examination frequency in African American women. *Journal of Behavioral Medicine, 28*, 191–199.

Jones, R. L. (1996). *Handbook of tests and measurements for black populations*. Hampton, VA: Cobb & Henry Publishers.

Landrine, H., & Klonoff, E. A. (1994). The African American acculturation scale. *Journal of Black Psychology, 20I*, 104–127.

Landrine, H., & Klonoff, E. A. (1995). The African American acculturation scale II: Cross-validation and short form. *Journal of Black Psychology, 21*, 124–152.

Landrine, H., & Klonoff, E. A. (2000). Revising and improving the African American acculturation scale. *Journal of Black Psychology, 26*, 235–261.

Mendoza-Denton, R., Downey, G., Davis, A., Purdie, V. J., & Pietrzak, J. (2002). Sensitivity to status based rejection: Implications for African American students' college experience. *Journal of Personality and Social Psychology, 83*, 896–918.

Nasim, A., Corona, R., Belgrave, F., Utsey, S. O., & Fallah, N. (2007). Cultural orientation as a protective factor against tobacco and marijuana smoking for African American young. *Journal of Youth and Adolescence, 36*, 503–516.

Nickerson, K. J., Helms, J. E., & Terrell, F. (1994). Cultural mistrust, opinions about mental illness, and Black students' attitudes toward seeking psychological help from White counselors. *Journal of Counseling Psychology, 41*, 378–385.

Nollen, N., Ahluwalia, J. S., Mayo, M. S., Richter, K., Choi, W. S., Okuyemi, K. S., et al. (2007). A randomized trial of targeted educational materials for smoking cessation in African Americans using transdermal nicotine. *Health Education & Behavior, 34*, 911–927.

Plant, E. A., Devine, P., & Brazy, P. (2003). The Bogus pipeline motivations to respond without prejudice: Revisiting the fading and faking of racial prejudice. *Group Process & Intergroup Relations, 6*, 187–200.

Poston, W. C., Craine, M., & Atkinson, D. R. (1991). Counselor dissimilarity confrontation, client cultural mistrust, and willingness to self-disclose. *Journal of Multicultural Counseling and Development, 19*, 65–73.

Reid, R. J., Brown, T. L., Peterson, N. A., Snowden, L., & Hines, A. (2009). Testing the factor structure of a scale to assess African American acculturation: A confirmatory factor analysis. *Journal of Community Psychology, 37*, 293–304.

Resnicow, K., & Ross-Gaddy, D. (1997). Development of racial identity scale for low-income African Americans. *Journal of Black Studies, 28*, 239–254.

Resnicow, K., Soler, R. E., Braithwaite, R. L., Selassie, M. B., & Smith, M. (1999). Development of a racial and ethnic identity scale for African American adolescents: The survey of black life. *Journal of Black Psychology, 25*, 171–188.

Sanders Thompson, V. L. (1995). The multidimensional structure of racial identification. *Journal of Research in Personality, 29*, 208–222.

Sanders Thompson, V. L. (2001). The complexity of African American racial identification. *Journal of Black Studies, 32*, 155–165.

Seaton, E. K. (2006). An examination of the factor structure of the index of race-related stress among a sample of African American adolescents. *Journal of Applied Psychology, 36*, 1414–1429.

Smith, E. P., & Brookins, C. C. (1997). Toward the development of an ethnic identity measure for African American youth. *Journal of Black Psychology, 23*, 358–377.

Snowden, L. R., & Hines, A. M. (1999). A scale to assess African American acculturation. *Journal of Black Psychology, 25*, 36–47.

Terrell, F., & Terrell, S. (1981). An inventory to measure cultural mistrust among Blacks. *The Western Journal of Black Studies, 5*, 180–185.

Thompson, C. E., Neville, H., Weathers, P. L., Poston, W. C., & Atkinson, D. R. (1990). Cultural mistrust and racism reaction among African American students. *Journal of College Student Development, 31*, 162–168.

Thompson, H. S., Valdimarsdottir, H. B., Winkel, G., Jandorf, L., & Redd, W. (2004). The group-based medical mistrust scale: Psychometric properties and association with breast cancer screening. *Preventive Medicine, 38*, 209–218.

Townes, D. L., Cunningham, N. J., & Chavez-Korell, S. (2009). Reexaming the relationships between racial identify, cultural mistrust, help-seeking attitudes, and preference for a Black counselor. *Journal of Counseling Psychology, 56*, 330–336.

U.S. Census Bureau. (2008). *2006–2008 American Community Survey 3-year estimates.* http://factfinder.census.gov

Utsey, S. (1999). Development and validation of a short form of the index of race-related stress (IRRS) – Brief version. *Measurement and Evaluation in Counseling and Development, 32*, 149–167.

Utsey, S. O., Chae, M., Brown, C., & Kelly, D. (2002). Effect of ethnic group membership on ethnic identity, race-related stress, and quality of life. *Cultural Diversity and Ethnic Minority Psychology, 8*, 366–377.

Utsey, S. O., & Hook, J. N. (2007). Heart rate variability as a physiological moderator of the relationship between race-related stress and psychological distress in African Americans. *Cultural Diversity and Ethnic Minority Psychology, 13*, 250–253.

Utsey, S. O., Lanier, Y., Williams, O., Bolden, M., & Lee, A. (2006). Moderator effects of cognitive ability and social support on the relation between race-related stress and quality of life in a community sample of Black Americans. *Cultural Diversity and Ethnic Minority Psychology, 12*, 334–346.

Utsey, S. O., Payne, Y., Jackson, E., & Jones, A. (2002). Racism, quality of life indicators, and life satisfaction, and indicators of psychological and physical health among elderly African Americans. *Cultural Diversity and Ethnic Minority Psychology, 8*, 224–233.

Utsey, S., & Ponterotto, J. (1996). Development and validation of the index of race-related stress (IRRS). *Journal of Counseling Psychology, 43*, 490–501.

Chapter 4
Caucasians

Overview

White Americans are the largest racial group in the United States. At approximately 224 million they make up 74% of all Americans (U.S. Census Bureau, 2008). This number includes those that reported Caucasian only to the Census and those that reported Caucasian as well as some other race. The term "Caucasian" refers to people having ancestry in any of the original people of Europe, the Middle East, or North Africa in addition to individuals that identify as Irish, German, Italian, Lebanese, Near Easterner, Arab, or Polish. As is case for most racial/ethnic groups, women comprise a higher percentage of the Caucasian population than men. The median age of the White population is 39.1, slightly older than the median age off the general population at 36.7 (U.S. Census Bureau, 2008).

Most of the race-related research of any type conducted in America has been done so with White populations. Hence it is not surprising that the majority of social science research has focused on the perceptions and attitudes of Whites. Moreover, most of the race-related studies which have focused on White racism, discrimination practices, stereotyping, and prejudice have focused on their relationships with others. However, research is still rather limited on their relations with racial and ethnic groups other than Blacks. In this chapter, we review measures of inter-racial phenomena of racial prejudice/attitudes. A total of nine scales are reviewed for this chapter.

Reference

U.S. Census Bureau. (2008). *2006–2008 American Community Survey 3-year estimates*. Selected Population Profile in the United States, S0201. http://factfinder.census.gov

Inter-racial Measures

We reviewed nine measures of inter-group relationship among Caucasians:

1. Attitudes Toward Blacks Scales (ATB) (See Chapter 3)
2. Attitudes Toward Whites Scale (ATW) (See Chapter 3)

DOI 10.1007/978-1-4419-6697-1_4, © Springer Science+Business Media, LLC 2011

3. New Racism Scale (Jacobson, 1985)
4. Race and Politics Survey (Levine, Carmines, & Sniderman, 1999)
5. Psychosocial Cost of Racism to Whites (Spanierman & Heppner, 2004)
6. Pro-Black and Anti-Black Attitudes Questionnaire (Katz & Hass, 1988)
7. Modern Racism Scale (McConahay, Hardee, & Batts, 1981)
8. Being White in America Scale (Bahk & Jandt, 2004)

The New Racism Scale (Jacobson, 1985)

The New Racism Scale (NRS) is a self-report measure that assesses feelings and beliefs of symbolic racism toward African Americans. Symbolic racism reflects feelings that African Americans are unfairly getting ahead of Whites through government action.

Description: The NRS consists of 7 items. The response format for each item is based on a 3 to 4-point scale depending on the question. Scores for the NRS are calculated by summing the item responses and total scores range from 7 to 26. Higher scores indicate more symbolic racist attitudes and lower scores indicate less symbolic racist attitudes. The scale is self-administered.

Sample: Data came from a national survey sponsored by the National Conference of Christians and Jews in 1978 and included 1,584 respondents who were identified as White.

Reliability: Cronbach's alpha for the final 7-item NRS was .70.

Validity: The NRS was statistically significantly related to a measure of traditional racism ($r = .49$) providing evidence of construct validity.

Comments: There is moderate evidence of reliability and validity. Subsequent studies using college student samples report Cronbach's alpha scores of .62 (Carter, 1990), .60 Pope-Davis & Ottavi, (1994), and .70 (Silvestri & Richardson, 2001). Carter (1990) found that the scale correlated with White identity. However, Jacobson (1998), in a study of college students found that three items (1, 6, 7) did not load on a single factor and eliminated them from the analysis.

Location: Jacobson, C. K. (1985). Resistance to affirmative action: Self interest or racism. *The Journal of Conflict Resolution, 29,* 306–329.

Selected Publications

Carter, R. T. (1990). The relationship between racism and racial identity among White Americans: An exploratory investigation. *Journal of Counseling and Development, 69*, 46–50.

Jacobson, C. (1998). Religiosity and prejudice: An update and denominational analysis. *Review of Religious Research, 39,* 264–272.

Pope-Deavis, D. B., & Ottavi, T. M. (1994). The relationship between racism and racial identity among White Americans: A replication and extension. *Journal of Counseling and Development, 72*, 293–297.

Silvestri, T. J., & Richardson, T. Q. (2001). White racial identity statuses and NEO personality constructs: An exploratory analysis. *Journal of Counseling and Development, 79*, 68–79.

New Racism Scale

1. Do you feel Blacks in this country have tried to move (3) too fast (2) too slow, or (1) at about the right pace?
2. Would it upset you personally (4) a lot (3) some but not a lot (2) only a little, or (1) not at all if Blacks moved into their neighborhood?
3. It's been said that if Black children went to school with White children, the education of White children would suffer. The reason given is that the Black children would hold back the White children. Do you believe that or not? (1 = Don't believe, 2 = Not sure, 3 = Believe)
4. Blacks are more likely to make progress in the future by being patient and not pushing so hard for change. (1 = disagree, 2 = not sure, 3 = agree)
5. If a fully qualified Black whose views were acceptable to you were nominated to run for president, how likely do you think you would be to vote for that candidate? (1 = Very likely, 2 = Somewhat likely, 3 = Not likely, 4 = Not at all likely)
6. Whether you agree or not with the idea of affirmative action, do you think Blacks are given special consideration and hired before Whites for jobs? (4 = Frequently, 3 = Occasionally, 2 = Hardly ever, 1 = Never at all)
7. How about in higher education institutions – that is, colleges and universities? Do you think Blacks are given special consideration and admitted before Whites in higher education institutions? (4 = Frequently, 3 = Occasionally, 2 = Hardly ever, 1 = Never at all)

The 1991 Race and Politics Survey (Levine, Carmines, & Sniderman, 1999)

The 1991 Race and Politics Survey includes a set of questions to assess Caucasian beliefs about the personal attributes of African Americans.

Description: The 1991 Race and Politics Survey questions on race were designed to measure positive and negative racial stereotypes. The scale consists of 14 questions designed to measure positive traits (9 items: 5–13) and negative traits (5 items: 1, 2, 3, 4, 14). Responses range from a *very inaccurate description of most Blacks* (0) to a *very good description of most Blacks* (10). Though not discussed, it appears that the total score is obtained by reverse coding the negative items; the higher the score, the more positive the belief. The scale was administered using a telephone interview.

Sample: The sample for this study was taken from the 1991 National Race and Politics telephone survey (random-digit) conducted by the Survey Research Center of the University of California, Berkeley. The analysis included only the 1,841 White respondents.

Reliability: Not Reported.

Validity: Using confirmatory factor analysis, the authors conclude that a unidimensional model is appropriate and that the scale is measuring stereotypes on a positive–negative continuum.

Comments: Little psychometric work has been done on this scale. Federico (2006) found a more nuanced relationship that suggests that negative and positive attributions are independent from each other given political ideology; this suggests that the two subscales may be used.

Location: Levine, J., Carmines, E. G., & Sniderman, P. M. (1999). The empirical dimensionality of racial stereotypes. *Public Opinion Quarterly, 63*, 371–384.

Selected Publications

Federico, C. M. (2006). Ideology and the affective structure of Whites' racial perceptions. *Public Opinion Quarterly, 70,* 327–353.

The 1991 Race and Politics Survey

Now I'll read a few words that people sometimes use to describe Blacks. Of course, no word fits absolutely everybody, but as I read each one, please tell me using a number from 0 to 10 how well you think it describes Blacks as a group. If you think it's a *very good* description of most Blacks, give it a 10. If you feel a word is a *very inaccurate* description of most Blacks, give it a 0.

Item wording: On a scale from 0 to 10, how well do you think it describes most Blacks?

1. How about "aggressive or violent?"
2. (How about) "lazy?"
3. (How about) "irresponsible?"
4. (How about) "complaining?"
5. (How about) "dependable?"
6. (How about) "friendly?"
7. (How about) "keep up their property?"
8. (How about) "good neighbors?"
9. How about "intelligent at school?"
10. (How about) "smart with practical, everyday things?"
11. (How about) "law abiding?"
12. (How about) "determined to succeed?"
13. (How about) "hardworking?"
14. (How about) "boastful?"

Psychosocial Costs of Racism to Whites Scale (Spanierman & Heppner, 2004)

The Psychosocial Costs of Racism to Whites (PCRW) Scale is used to assess psychosocial costs Whites experience as members of the dominant group in a society marked by racism.

Description: The PCRW is a self-report measure consisting of 16 items. The PCRW assesses three domains derived from factor analytic work on the scale: White Empathetic Reactions Toward Racism reflecting affective costs of racism (WERTR; 6 items: 1, 3, 6, 20, 14, 16); White Guilt measuring feelings of shame (WG; 5 items: 4, 7, 8, 12, 15); and White Fear of Others assessing fears about other racial groups (WFO; 5 items: 2, 5, 9, 11, 13). Responses are offered on a 6-point scale ranging from *strongly disagree* (1) to *strongly agree* (6). Subscale scores are calculated by reverse coding 3 items (2, 8, 12) and summing the responses. The authors recommend against using a total scale score. Higher scores reflect more experiences with the psychosocial costs of racism. The scale is self-administered.

Sample: The initial scale development and assessment involved three studies. The sample for Study 1 included 361 White participants recruited from undergraduate classes at a mid-size Midwestern university. The sample for Study 2 included 366 White participants recruited from undergraduate classes at a mid-size Midwestern university and undergraduate education classes at a large Midwestern university. The final sample (Study 3) included 35 students chosen from the sample of Study 2.

Reliability: Cronbach's alpha coefficients for the PCRW subscales for each sample were: WERTR (α = .78; .79; .85), WG (α = .73; .70; .81) and WFO (α = .63; .69; .78). The PCRW had satisfactory test–retest reliability statistics, accept for White Guilt (.69). Two week test–retest scores were: WERTR, r = .84; WG, r = .69; and WFO, r = .95.

Validity: To assess the subscales' convergent validity, the authors used the Color Blind Racial Attitude Scale (CoBRAS), the Quick Discrimination Index (QDI), Scale of Ethnocultural Empathy (SEE), and Oklahoma Racial Attitude Scale (ORAS). As hypothesized, the subscales were related to the CoBRAS. The WERTR subscale and the WG subscale were significantly negatively correlated with CoBRAS scores (r = –.19; r = –.29) and the White Fear of Others factor was significantly and positively correlated with CoBRAS scores (r = .19). Relationships with the SEE subscales were more mixed. The WERTR and WFO subscales were statistically significantly related in the expected directions with the SEE subscales but the WG subscale was not related in the expected directions. The PSRW subscales were related as predicted to various subscales of the QDI and ORAS. The PRSW subscales were not statistically significantly related to the Marlowe–Crowne Social Desirability Scale, providing evidence for discriminant validity. The subscale structure derived from an exploratory factor analysis was reproduced with a confirmatory factor analysis providing support for factorial validity.

Comments: There is evidence of reliability and validity for the subscales of the PCRW. Subsequent studies with college students, graduate students, counselors, and employed adults have produced similar reliability measures (Poteat & Spanierman, 2008; Spanierman, Poteat, Beer, & Armstrong, 2006; Spanierman, Poteat, Wang, & Oh, 2008; Spanierman, Todd, & Anderson, 2009). The convergent validity of the scale has been demonstrated with a mixed gender employed group of adults (Poteat & Spanierman, 2008); the three subscales were statistically significantly related to color-blind racial beliefs (measured by the CoBRAS) and White Empathy and White Fear of Others were associated with two of the three subscales measuring universal diverse orientation (Milville-Guzman Universality Scale-Short; Poteat & Spanierman, 2008). Discriminant validity was demonstrated as each subscale was unrelated to social desirability (Poteat & Spanierman, 2008). The PCRW avoids a response set by using positively and negatively worded questions.

Location: Spanierman, L. B., & Heppner, M. J. (2004). Psychosocial costs of racism to Whites scale (PCRW): Construction and initial validation. *Journal of Counseling Psychology, 51,* 249–262.

Selected Publications

Poteat, V. P., & Spanierman, L. B. (2008). Further validation of the psychosocial costs of racism to Whites scale among employed adults. *Counseling Psychologist, 36,* 871–894.

Spanierman, L. B., Poteat, V. P., Beer, A. M., & Armstrong, P. I. (2006). Psychosocial costs of racism to Whites: Exploring patterns through cluster analysis. *Journal of Counseling Psychology, 53*, 434–441.

Spanierman, L. B., Poteat, V. P., Wang, Y.-F., & Oh, E. (2008). Psychosocial costs of racism to White counselors: Predicting various dimensions of multicultural counseling competence. *Journal of Counseling Psychology, 55*, 75–88.

Spanierman, L. B., Todd, N. R., & Anderson, C. J. (2009). Psychosocial costs of racism to Whites: Understanding patterns among university students. *Journal of Counseling Psychology, 56*, 239–252.

Psychosocial Costs of Racism to Whites Scale

Please respond to the following statements by inserting only one number next to the item from the chart below. *Your possible choices range from 1 to 6. Please answer honestly, as there are no right answers or wrong answers.* Avoid answering as you think you "should" feel or as how you would expect others to answer. All responses are completely anonymous.

Response categories: 1 = Strongly disagree; 2 = Moderately disagree; 3 = Slightly disagree; 4 = Slightly agree; 5 = Moderately agree; 6 = Strongly agree

1. When I hear about acts of racial violence, I become angry or depressed.
2. I feel safe in most neighborhoods, regardless of the racial composition (R).
3. I feel helpless about not being able to eliminate racism.
4. Sometimes I feel guilty about being White.

5. I have very few friends of other races.
6. I become sad when I think about racial injustice.
7. Being White makes me feel personally responsible for racism.
8. I never feel ashamed about being White (R).
9. I am fearful that racial minority populations are rapidly increasing in the United States, and my group will no longer be the numerical majority.
10. I am angry that racism exists.
11. I am distrustful of people of other races.
12. I feel good about being White (R).
13. I often find myself fearful of people of other races.
14. Racism is dehumanizing to people of all races, including Whites.
15. I am afraid that I abuse my power and privilege as a White person.
16. It disturbs me when people express racist views.

Pro-Black and Anti-Black Questionnaire (Katz & Hass, 1988)

The Pro-Black and Anti-Black Attitudes Questionnaire (PAAQ) measures favorable and unfavorable attitudes of Caucasians to African Americans.

Description: The PAAQ is designed to measure two conceptually different constructs: pro-Black attitudes, or sympathetic beliefs and feelings toward African Americans, and anti-Black attitudes, or beliefs about deviant characteristics and associated negative affective feelings. Each scale consists of 10 statements designed to reflect Caucasians' impressions about African Americans in various domains such as work, education, family roles, and civil rights. Participants respond to items using a 6-point Likert-type scale ranging from *strongly agree* (0) to *strongly disagree* (5) with no neutral point. Each scale includes two items (Pro-Black scale: 4 and 5; Anti-Black scale: 6 and 10) that are worded using negative language; these items are reversed when scored. It appears that the items for each scale are summed though this is not explicitly discussed by the authors. For the Pro-Black scale, the lower the score, the more positive the attitude; for the Anti-Black scale, the lower the score, the more negative the attitude. The scales are self-administered.

Sample: The Pro-Black and Anti-Black scales were assessed with various samples of White undergraduate students at a Northeastern university; sample sizes ranged from 59 to 115. The results were then compared to samples from other Northern and Southern universities.

Reliability: Cronbach's alphas for the scales were .73 for the Pro-Black scale and .80 for the Anti-Black scale.

Validity: Two subscales, Derogatory Beliefs and Ease in Inter-racial Contacts of the Multifactor Racial Attitude Inventory (MRAI) were used to test convergent and discriminant validity for the Anti-Black scale. The statistically significant relationship for the Anti-Black and Derogatory Beliefs ($r = .64$ and lack of relationship to the Ease scale ($r = -.02$) were as expected. The Pro-Black scale and the Ease scale were statistically significantly related ($r = .55$). Unexpectedly, the Pro-Black scale and the Derogatory Beliefs Scale were correlated until similar items were deleted.

Comments: The instruments have some evidence of reliability and validity. Subsequent studies with college students have found similar evidence of reliability (Heider & Skowronski, 2007; Jackson & Poulson, 2005; Wittenbrink, Judd, & Park, 1997), mixed results about the independence of the two scales (Heider & Skowronski, 2007) and predictive validity of the Pro-Black scale (Heider & Skowronski, 2007). However, the instruments have been assessed with college students and should be evaluated using other samples. In a subsequent article (Hass, Katz, Rizzo, Bailey, & Eisenstadt, 1991) the authors develop a construct, ambivalence, to summarize the two scores; they suggest that ambivalence reflects the degree to which there are strongly held and competing attitudes to African Americans. This score is calculated using normalized scores for each scale and then the product of the normal scores is calculated. The PAAQ avoids a response set by using positively and negatively worded questions.

Location: Katz, I., & Hass, R. G. (1988). Racial ambivalence and American value conflict: Correlational and priming studies of dual cognitive structures. *Journal of Personality and Social Psychology, 55*, 893–905.

Selected Publications

Hass, R. G., Katz, I., Rizzo, N., Bailey, J., & Eisenstadt, D. (1991). Cross-racial appraisal as related to attitude ambivalence and cognitive complexity. *Personality and Social Psychology Bulletin, 17,* 83–92.

Heider, J. D., & Skowronski, J. J. (2007). Improving the predictive validity of the implicit association test. *North American Journal of Psychology, 9,* 53–76.

Jackson, J. W., & Poulsen, J. R. (2005). Contact experiences mediate the relationship between five-factor model personality traits and ethnic prejudice. *Journal of Applied Social Psychology, 35,* 667–685.

Wittenbrink, B., Judd, C. M., & Park, B. (1997). Evidence for racial prejudice at the implicit level and its relationship with questionnaire measures. *Journal of Personality and Social Psychology, 72,* 262–274.

Pro-Black Scale

1. Black people do not have the same employment opportunities that Whites do.
2. It's surprising that Black people do as well as they do, considering all the obstacles they face.
3. Too many Blacks still lose out on jobs and promotions because of their skin color.
4. Most big corporations in America are really interested in treating their Black and White employees equally (R).
5. Most Blacks are no longer discriminated against (R).
6. Blacks have more to offer that they have been allowed to show.
7. The typical urban ghetto public school is not as good as it should be to provide equal opportunities for Blacks.

8. This country would be better off if it were more willing to assimilate the good things in Black culture.
9. Sometimes Black job seekers should be given special consideration in hiring.
10. Many Whites show a real lack of understanding of the problems that Blacks face.

Anti-Black Scale

1. The root cause of most of the social and economic ills of Blacks is the weakness and instability of the Black family.
2. Although there are exceptions, Black urban neighborhoods don't seem to have strong community organization or leadership.
3. On the whole, Black people don't stress education and training.
4. Many Black teenagers don't respect themselves or anyone else.
5. Blacks don't seem to use opportunities to own and operate little shops and business.
6. Very few Black people are just looking for a free ride (R).
7. Black children would do better in school if their parents had better attitudes about learning.
8. Blacks should take the jobs that are available and then work their way up to better jobs.
9. One of the biggest problems for a lot of Blacks is their lack of self-respect.
10. Most Blacks have the drive and determination to get ahead (R).

Modern Racism Scale (McConahay, Hardee, & Batts, 1981)

The Modern Racism Scale (MRS) was developed to assess White racial attitudes toward African Americans that are considered to be less overtly racist.

Description: The MRS is a 7-item measure that attempts to explain racial attitudes. Respondents indicate their agreement with each of the items on a 5-point ratings scale ranging from *agree strongly* (2) to *disagree strongly* (–2). The scale is scored by recoding the items from 0 to 4 or 1 to 5 and a total score is calculated by reverse coding items, all the items but item 1. The higher the score, the more negative the respondent's attitude is toward Blacks. The scale has been both used in interviews and self-administered.

Sample: We summarize several studies and experiments completed by McConahay and colleagues. McConahay et al. (1981) and McConahay (1983) are based on undergraduate samples while McConahay (1982) includes 739 White respondents, 18 years and older.

Reliability: McConahay et al. (1981) report high 6-week test–retest correlations ($r = .93$ with White experimenter; $r = .87$ with African American experimenter).

McConahay (1982) reports Cronbach's alpha = .75; McConahay (1983) reports Cronbach's alpha = .86.

Validity: McConahay (1982) reports construct validity as the scale correlates with the Sympathetic Identification with a Black Underdog scale ($r = -.30$) and a feeling toward Blacks thermometer ($r = -.38$) and predictive validity regarding voting for a Black versus White candidate. The scale scores predicted hiring preferences (McConahay, 1983).

Comments: Similar psychometric results have been found in other studies using the MRS (Lambert, Cronen, Chasteen, & Lickel, 1996 alpha = .88; Awad, Cokley, & Ravitch, 2005; alpha = .82; Monteith, 1996 alpha = .76). George and Martinez (2002) reported Cronbach's alpha equal to .82 using six items while deleting the school desegregation item (item 2). Predictive validity has been found in other studies (Lambert et al., 1996 judgement about people; Awad et al., 2005 affirmative action support); and construct validity (Monteith-scale related to other distinctly different measures of prejudice). The scale has been adapted by other researchers by substituting "minority" for "Black" in each statement (Aosved & Long, 2006). Rather than the –2 to +2 scoring of the scale, some studies use a 1–5 scoring. The scale appears to be non-reactive to race of researcher (McConahay et al., 1981).

Location: McConahay, J. B., Hardee, B., & Batts, V. (1981). Has racism declined in America? It depends on who is asking and what is asked. *The Journal of Conflict Resolution, 25*, 563–579.

Selected Publications

Aosved, A. C., & Long, P. (2006). Co-occurrence of rape myth acceptance, sexism, racism, homophobia, ageism, classism, and religious intolerance. *Sex Roles, 55,* 481–492.

Awad, G. H., Cokley, K., & Ravitch, J. (2005). Attitudes toward affirmative action: A comparison of color-blind versus modern racist attitudes. *Journal of Applied Social Psychology, 35,* 1384–1399.

George, W. H., & Martinez, L. J. (2002). Victim blaming in rape: Effects of victim and perpetrator race, type of rape, and participant racism. *Psychology of Women Quarterly, 26,* 110–119.

Lambert, A. J., Cronen, S., Chasteen, A. L., & Lickel, B. (1996). Private vs. public expressions of racial prejudice. *Journal of Experimental Social Psychology, 32,* 437–459.

McConahay, J. B. (1982). Self-interest versus racial attitudes as correlates of anti-busing attitudes in Louisville: Is it the buses or the Blacks? *Journal of Politics, 44,* 692–720.

McConahay, J. B. (1983). Modern racism and modern discrimination: The effects of face, racial attitudes, and context on simulated hiring decisions. *Personality and Social Psychology Bulletin, 9,* 551–558.

Monteith, M. J. (1996). Contemporary forms of prejudice-related conflict: In search of a nutshell. *Personality and Social Psychology Bulletin, 22,* 461–473.

Modern Racism Scale

1. It is easy to understand the anger of Black people in America.
2. Blacks have more influence upon school desegregation plans than they ought to have.
3. Blacks are getting too demanding in their push for equal rights.
4. Over the past few years Blacks have gotten more economically than they deserve.
5. Over the past few years the government and news media have shown more respect to Blacks than they deserve.
6. Blacks should not push themselves where they are not wanted.
7. Discrimination against Blacks is no longer a problem in the United States.

Being White in America Scale (Bahk & Jandt, 2004)

The Being White in America Scale (BWAS) measures the extent to which a person perceives White people to be privileged compared with other racial groups in the United States.

Description: The BWAS consists of 25 items to assess perceptions of "Whiteness." Whiteness is defined as "having distinctness, dominance, normalcy, privilege, superiority, and unsociability in US society (Bahk & Jandt, 2004, p. 60)." Responses are offered on a 5-point scale ranging from *strongly disagree* (1) to *strongly agree* (5). There are five reversed scored items in the BWAS (items: 2, 8, 16, 21, 22). Scores for the BWAS are obtained by summing the item scores and then attaining an average score, with higher scores reflecting a stronger belief that White people are more privileged than other racial groups. The scale is self-administered.

Sample: Seven hundred (700) undergraduate and graduate students were recruited from a mid-size university on the West Coast. Most respondents were female (70.1%), and the group had an average age of 29.9 years (SD = 10.2). The racial distribution among respondents included 355 Whites, 153 Hispanics, 52 African Americans, 52 Asian Americans, and 13 Native Americans.

Reliability: Cronbach's alpha for the 25 items was .90. Excluding five items (items 2, 15, 16, 21, 23) based on Principal Components Factor analysis (see validity) resulted in a Cronbach's alpha of .95 for the entire sample, .95 for Whites, and .93 for non-Whites.

Validity: While principal components factor analysis produced multiple factors, 21 of the 25 items loaded on the primary factor for Whites and 22 of the 25 items loaded on the primary factor for non-Whites. As predicted, non-Whites scored higher than Whites and there were no gender differences.

Comments: There is evidence of internal consistency however little evidence of validity. No other studies could be located. The findings are not generalizable beyond the sample. The BWAS avoids a response set by using positively and negatively worded questions.

Location: Bahk, C. M., & Jandt, F. E. (2004). Being white in America: Development of a scale. *The Howard Journal of Communications, 15*, 57–68.

Selected Publications

None

Being White in America Scale

Response categories: 1 = Strongly Disagree; 2 = Disagree; 3 = Not Sure; 4 = Agree; 5 = Strongly Agree

1. White people have privilege in the United States.
2. White people are not much different from the people of other racial groups in the United States (R).
3. White people tend to distance themselves from other racial groups in the United States.
4. Many rules and laws in this society have been formulated according to the standard of White people.
5. When people refer to "American," it is usually White people that they have in mind.
6. In the United States, being White determines how a person is treated in everyday life.
7. The US society is largely permeated by the values and norms of White Americans.
8. Being White doesn't mean much in the United States (R).
9. White people are the most powerful racial group in the United States.
10. Whites can achieve the most success economically in the United States.
11. The politics in the United States are dominated by Whites.
12. The current social status of Whites in the United States is almost impenetrable.
13. In the United States, Whites are considered more intelligent than people of other races.
14. White people are regarded as superior to people of other racial groups in the United States.
15. It is quite easy for me to distinguish Whites from non-Whites.
16. Attempting to label Caucasians separately is simply nonsense (R).
17. US Media assume that readers and users are Whites.
18. Whites tend to be over-presented in US television shows and movies.
19. Whites draw more positive attention from news media in the United States.
20. Whites tend to mingle much better with Whites than non-Whites.
21. Whites do not get along with non-Whites (R).
22. Whites feel comfortable with the presence of non-Whites at social gatherings (R).
23. There are always some irreconcilable differences between Whites and non-Whites in the United States.
24. Whites tend to choose to interact with other Whites rather than with non-Whites in social situations.
25. There is a wall between Whites and non-Whites in the United States.

Original Scale References

Bahk, C. M., & Jandt, F. E. (2004). Being white in America: Development of a scale. *The Howard Journal of Communications*, *15*, 57–68.

Jacobson, C. K. (1985). Resistance to affirmative action: Self-interest or racism. *The Journal of Conflict Resolution*, *29*, 306–329.

Katz, I., & Hass, R. G. (1988). Racial ambivalence and American value conflict: Correlational and priming studies of dual cognitive structures. *Journal of Personality and Social Psychology*, *55*, 893–905.

Levine, J., Carmines, E. G., & Sniderman, P. M. (1999). The empirical dimensionality of racial stereotypes. *Public Opinion Quarterly*, *63*, 371–384.

McConahay, J. B., Hardee, B., & Batts, V. (1981). Has racism declined in America? It depends on who is asking and what is asked. *The Journal of Conflict Resolution*, *25*, 563–579.

Spanierman, L. B., & Heppner, M. J. (2004). Psychosocial costs of racism to Whites scale (PCRW): Construction and initial validation. *Journal of Counseling Psychology*, *51*, 249–262.

References

Aosved, A. C., & Long, P. (2006). Co-occurrence of rape myth acceptance, sexism, racism, homophobia, ageism, classism, and religious intolerance. *Sex Roles*, *55*, 481–492.

Awad, G. H., Cokley, K., & Ravitch, J. (2005). Attitudes toward affirmative action: A comparison of color-blind versus modern racist attitudes. *Journal of Applied Social Psychology*, *35*, 1384–1399.

Carter, R. T. (1990). The relationship between racism and racial identity among White Americans: An exploratory investigation. *Journal of Counseling and Development*, *69*, 46–50.

Federico, C. M. (2006). Ideology and the affective structure of Whites' racial perceptions. *Public Opinion Quarterly*, *70*, 327–353.

George, W. H., & Martinez, L. J. (2002). Victim blaming in rape: Effects of victim and perpetrator race, type of rape, and participant racism. *Psychology of Women Quarterly*, *26*, 110–119.

Hass, R., G. , Katz, I., Rizzo, N., Bailey, J., & Eisenstadt, D. (1991). Cross-racial appraisal as related to attitude ambivalence and cognitive complexity. *Personality and Social Psychology Bulletin*, *17*, 83–92.

Heider, J. D., & Skowronski, J. J. (2007). Improving the predictive validity of the implicit association test. *North American Journal of Psychology*, *9*, 53–76.

Jackson, J. W., & Poulsen, J. R. (2005). Contact experiences mediate the relationship between five-factor model personality traits and ethnic prejudice. *Journal of Applied Social Psychology*, *35*, 667–685.

Jacobson, C. (1998). Religiosity and prejudice: An update and denominational analysis. *Review of Religious Research*, *39*, 264–272.

Lambert, A. J., Cronen, S., Chasteen, A. L., & Lickel, B. (1996). Private vs. public expressions of racial prejudice. *Journal of Experimental Social Psychology*, *32*, 437–459.

McConahay, J. B. (1982). Self-interest versus racial attitudes as correlates of anti-busing attitudes in Louisville: Is it the buses or the blacks? *Journal of Politics*, *44*, 692–720.

McConahay, J. B. (1983). Modern racism and modern discrimination: The effects of face, racial attitudes, and context on simulated hiring decisions. *Personality and Social Psychology Bulletin*, *9*, 551–558.

Monteith, M. J. (1996). Contemporary forms of prejudice-related conflict: In search of a nutshell. *Personality and Social Psychology Bulletin*, *22*, 461–473.

Pope-Deavis, D. B., & Ottavi, T. M. (1994). The relationship between racism and racial identity among White Americans: A replication and extension. *Journal of Counseling and Development*, *72*, 293–297.

Poteat, V. P., & Spanierman, L. B. (2008). Further validation of the psychosocial costs of racism to Whites scale among employed adults. *Counseling Psychologist*, *36*, 871–894.

Silvestri, T. J., & Richardson, T. Q. (2001). White racial identity statuses and NEO personality constructs: An exploratory analysis. *Journal of Counseling and Development*, *79*, 68–79.

Spanierman, L. B., Poteat, V. P., Beer, A. M., & Armstrong, P. I. (2006). Psychosocial costs of racism to Whites: Exploring patterns through cluster analysis. *Journal of Counseling Psychology*, *53*, 434–441.

Spanierman, L. B., Poteat, V. P., Wang, Y.-F., & Oh, E. (2008). Psychosocial costs of racism to White counselors: Predicting various dimensions of multicultural counseling competence. *Journal of Counseling Psychology*, *55*, 75–88.

Spanierman, L. B., Todd, N. R., & Anderson, C. J. (2009). Psychosocial costs of racism to Whites: Understanding patterns among university students. *Journal of Counseling Psychology*, *56*, 239–252.

U.S. Census Bureau. (2008). *2006–2008 American Community Survey 3-year estimates*. Selected Population Profile in the United States, S0201. http://factfinder.census.gov

Wittenbrink, B., Judd, C. M., & Park, B. (1997). Evidence for racial prejudice at the implicit level and its relationship with questionnaire measures. *Journal of Personality and Social Psychology*, *72*, 262–274.

Chapter 5
Generic Measures

Overview

America is increasingly a racially and ethnically diverse country. It is host to people from every country in the world. In fact it has been said that American probably is the only country in the world which could send a native of every country in the world back to their country of origin as an ambassador. The point being that there are people from all over the world who are now living in America. The most numerous Americans are presently Whites, Hispanics, African Americans, Asians, and Native Americans. But noteworthy is the fact that the major groups of color: Asians, Hispanics, and African Americans are growing at rates faster than the White population. For example in 1960 these three groups made up roughly 20% of the population. By the year 2000, they were 30% of the population and by the middle of this century they are projected to make up half of the populace (U.S. Census Bureau, 2008). And despite the fact that significant racial segregation continues to exist, it is now common for different racial/ethnic group members to be neighbors.

Historically most of the inter-group relations research has focused on interactions between Blacks and Whites. This paradigm is rapidly changing. Even now it is not African Americans, but Hispanics who are the country's largest minority group. It is also true that Asian Americans are growing more rapidly than African American, or Whites. These facts suggest that as both the absolute as well as proportions of these groups grow we will witness more interactions between a variety of racial groups. As we noted in the African American section of this volume, in the past, most of the inter-group relations scales were designed to assess Black–White attitudes or interactions. Scales which might instead access attitudes or perceptions of interactions between Hispanics and Asians, or African Americans and Asians are still comparatively rare. Consequently researchers attempting to inspect intra- or inter-group dynamics may need to rely on scales that are racially or ethnically generic in their construction. This fact is particularly true for those research efforts which have as their goal the assessment of smaller ethnic groups, e.g., Mong or Dominicans.

Therefore unlike the measures reviewed in the first three sections of this volume which focus on specific racial groups, those in this chapter are more generic. In particular, we have elected to review measures that assess multi-cultural ethnic

L.E. Davis, R.J. Engel, *Measuring Race and Ethnicity*,
DOI 10.1007/978-1-4419-6697-1_5, © Springer Science+Business Media, LLC 2011

identity, acculturation, ethno-cultural empathy, and inter-racial attitudes, and aspects of social distance. Specifically, the intra-racial scales tap into the ethnic identity and acculturation differences among various ethnic/racial groups. Of course the notion of social distance was originally conceived by Park (1924), but the measurement scale itself was created by Bogardus (1925). In many respects both the idea and creation of a social distance measure laid the groundings for a volume such as this. In fact, we considered including the original Bogardus scale in this volume. However like many scales we reviewed, it seemed simply too outdated. Still scholars and students may want to review this measure as it provides some perspective on how the measurement of relations between groups has progressed from assessing solely the majority group's views to now also including the perspectives of minority groups.

Sixteen scales are reviewed in this section. These measures assess both intra-racial and inter-racial aspects of attitudes and social distance. We have elected to review 12 scales, which assess inter-racial attitudes, two scales of intra-racial identity; two scales focus on acculturation among various ethnic groups, three scales of inter-group phenomenon which focus on social distance and discrimination, and a final scale that focuses on ethno-cultural empathy. This final scale is designed to measure empathy toward people from racial and ethnic backgrounds different than one's own.

Measures of Racial Attitude/Prejudice

1. Attitude Toward Diversity Scale (Montei, Adams, & Eggers, 1996)
2. Color-Blind Racial Attitudes Scale (Neville, Lilly, Lee, Duran, & Browne, 2000)
3. Modified Godfrey-Richman ISM Scale (Godfrey, Richman, & Withers, 2000)
4. Suppression of Prejudice Scale (Crandall, Eshleman, & O'Brien, 2002)
5. The Organizational Diversity Inventory (Hegarty & Dalton, 1995)
6. The Motivation to Control Prejudiced Reactions Scale (Dunton & Fazio, 1997)
7. Self-Evaluation of Biases and Prejudices Scale (Paniagua, 1998)
8. Internal and External Motivation to Respond without Prejudice Scale (Plant & Devine, 1998)

Measures of Social Distance/Discrimination

1. Reverse Social Distance Scale (Lee, Sapp, & Ray, 1996)
2. Experiences of Discrimination Scale (Krieger, Smith, Naishadham, Hartman, & Barbeau, 2005)
3. Quick Discrimination Index (Ponterotto et al., 1995)

Measures of Racial Identity

1. Multi-group Ethnic Identity Measure (Phinney, 1992; Roberts et al., 1999)
2. Ethnic Identity Scale (Umaña-Taylor, Yazedijan, & Bamaca-Gomez, 2004)

Measures of Identity Development and Acculturation

1. Acculturation, Habits, and Interest Multi-scale for Adolescents (Unger et al., 2002)
2. Stephenson Multi-group Acculturation Scale (Stephenson, 2000)
3. Orthogonal Cultural Identification Scale (Oetting, Swaim, & Chiarella, 1998)

Measure of Ethnocultural Empathy

1. Scale of Ethnocultural Empathy (Wang et al., 2003)

Citations

Bogardus (1925)
U.S. Census Bureau (2008)
Park (1924)

Measures of Racial Attitude/Prejudice

The Attitudes Toward Diversity Scale (Montei, Adams, & Eggers, 1996)

The Attitudes Toward Diversity Scale (ATDS) measures attitudes toward diversity in the workplace.

Description: The ATDS is a 30-item self-report measure and includes three subscales: Coworker subscale or attitude toward having coworkers who are a minority (items 1–10); Supervisor subscale or attitude toward having a supervisor who is a minority (items 11–20); and Hiring subscale or attitude toward the hiring and promoting of minorities in the organization (items 21–30). Responses are offered on a 5-point Likert-type scale ranging from *strongly agree* (1) to *strongly disagree* (5). Total scale scores are obtained by reverse coding 12 items (items 1, 7, 9, 10, 12, 14, 15, 19, 22, 23, 26, 29) and then summing scores. Higher scores indicate more positive attitudes toward diversity in the workplace and lower scores indicate more negative attitudes toward diversity in the workplace. Subscale scores are calculated in a similar fashion. The scale is self-administered.

Sample: Two studies were described in the initial scale assessment. Study 1: The sample included 67 full-time employees. Respondents were predominantly White (92.5%), single (52.2%), and female (65.7%); age was bimodal with the largest percentages either under 26 (43.3%) or between 35 and 50 years (40.3%). Study 2: The sample included 70 civil service workers and 279 full-time workers. The majority of respondents were male (52.4%), White (82.2%), single (53.7%), and under age 26 (42.7%).

Reliability: Study 1 and Study 2 total scale Cronbach's alphas were .91 and .90. Subscale Cronbach's alphas were: Coworker subscale, .78 and .79; Supervisor subscale, .71 and .81; and Hiring subscale, .83 and .76.

Validity: The correlation between the ATDS and the Marlowe–Crowne Social Desirability Scale was low ($r = -.09$ suggesting discriminant validity). A confirmatory factor analysis of the 3-factor model provided evidence of factorial validity.

Comments: There is evidence of internal consistency which has also been found in a subsequent study (Strauss, Connerley, & Ammermann, 2003). While there is less evidence of validity, Strauss et al. (2003) found that authoritarianism and agreeableness were related to the ATDS but contrary to expectation openness was not related to the ATDS. Based on the findings of the confirmatory factor analysis, it may be appropriate to use subscale scores. The samples used suggest little generalizability and have been predominantly White. The ATDS avoids a response set by using positively and negatively worded questions.

Location: Montei, M. S., Adams, G. A., & Eggers, L. M. (1996). Validity of scores on the attitudes toward diversity scale (ATDS). *Educational and Psychological Measurement, 56*, 293–303.

Selected Publications

Strauss, J. P., Connerley, M. L., & Ammermann, P. A. (2003). The "threat hypothesis" personality and attitudes towards diversity. *The Journal of Applied Behavioral Science, 39*, 32–52.

Attitudes Toward Diversity Scale

Coworker Subscale

1. All in all, I would say that minority workers are just as productive as other workers (R).
2. I often pick up the slack for some of my female coworkers who are less productive.
3. Sometimes I have to compensate for the lack of productivity of minority workers.
4. The most qualified workers in my job seem to be male.
5. I find that minority workers seem to be less productive on average.
6. The minorities in this organization have a greater degree of difficulty getting along with others.
7. If a member of my workgroup were prejudiced, he or she would be less likely to fit in (R).
8. If one of my coworkers were racist, I would confront that person and let him or her know of my disapproval (R).

9. Workers who are prejudiced have no place in this organization (R).
10. I do not feel comfortable with coworkers who are racist (R).

Supervisor Subscale

11. I feel that women have a more difficult time handling positions of authority relative to men.
12. I would feel just as comfortable with a Black or Hispanic supervisor as I do with a White supervisor (R).
13. It seems that those minorities in supervisory positions are ineffective relative to other supervisors.
14. Most of the women in management positions do an outstanding job (R).
15. I feel that diversity is good for this organization even if it means I will have a supervisor who is a minority (R).
16. Relative to male supervisors, female supervisors seem to be less effective.
17. Under most circumstances, I would prefer a male supervisor.
18. I would feel less comfortable with a female supervisor than I would with a male supervisor.
19. Most of the minority supervisors in this organization possess the same leadership qualities as those supervisors who are White (R).
20. It seems as if some of the women I work with need to be more assertive to be effective supervisors.

Hiring Subscale

21. I know some workers who would be fired if they were not minorities.
22. It does not bother me that some preferential hiring goes on because we need more of a mix in this organization (R).
23. Because some tests are known to be biased toward minorities, I feel it is right to adjust test scores to even things out (R).
24. I am against hiring by quotas even when done out of necessity.
25. I know many more qualified White males who should have been hired instead of some minorities that have been hired lately.
26. We would have a more creative work environment if more women and minorities were hired (R).
27. I feel it is wrong for an organization to have two sets of test scores for minorities and non-minorities, even when the test is somewhat biased.
28. Some of the members of this organization were hired just because they are women.
29. I feel that increasing the hiring of women and minorities can only help this organization (R).
30. Some of the members of this organization were only hired because they are minorities.

Color-Blind Racial Attitudes Scale (Neville, Lilly, Lee, Duran, & Browne, 2000)

The Color-Blind Racial Attitudes Scale (CoBRAS) assesses the cognitive aspects of color-blind racial attitudes, that is, denial or belief that race does not "matter."

Description: The CoBRAS is a 20-item self-report instrument. Responses are offered on a 6-point scale ranging from *strongly disagree* (1) to *strongly agree* (6). There are three subscales: (1) Unawareness of Racial Privilege (RP; seven items: 1, 2, 6, 8, 12, 15, 20), Institutional Discrimination (ID; seven items: 3, 4, 9, 13, 14, 16, 18), and Blatant Racial Issues (BRI; six items: 5, 7, 10, 11, 17, 19). Ten items are reverse coded (items 2, 4, 5, 6, 8, 11, 12, 15, 17, 20). The total scale score is the sum of the items as are subscale scores. Higher scores on each subscale and total scale reflect higher denial or sense of justice. The scale is self-administered.

Sample: Five separate studies were reported in the initial scale assessment. Study 1: The sample included 302 college students and community members. Most (71%) were female, 81% were White, 8% were African American, and 11% were members of other ethnic groups. Study 2: The sample included 594 college students or community participants. Slightly more than half of the participants (51.3%) were female and 67% were White, 19% were African American, 6% were Latino, 2% were Asian American, and 1% were American Indian. Respondents' average age was 22.8 years and ranged from 14 to 88. Study 3. The sample included 102 college students, who were mostly female (72.4%) and White (90%). Study 4: The sample size was 145 college students and community members. The sample was mostly female (61.8%), had an average age of 31.4 (range was 18–85), and the most were White (70%), while 19% were Latino, with the rest African American, American Indian, Asian American or "other." Study 5: Participants included 21 college students enrolled in a multi-cultural training course. Most were female (66.7%) and students of color or multi-racial (85.7%).

Reliability: The coefficient alphas for the three factors and the total score were: Total score, .91; RP, .83; ID, 81; and BRI, .76 (Study 1). Satisfactory Cronbach's alphas were reported in Studies 2 and 4: Total score alphas were .86 and .84; RP alphas were .80 and .71; ID alphas were .76 and .73; and BRI alphas were .86 and .84. Guttman split-half reliability was .72 (Study 2). 2 week test retest coefficients (Study 3) were .68 for the total scale score, .80 for both RP and ID subscales, and .34 for the BRI subscale.

Validity: Exploratory factor analysis (Study 1) produced a 3-factor solution including 20 items; the three factors were moderately related. This structure was reproduced using confirmatory factor analysis (Study 2) offering support for factorial validity. Concurrent validity (Study 2) was demonstrated by correlations of the total score with two beliefs in the world scales, the Global Belief in a Just World Scale ($r = .53$) and the Multi-dimensional Belief in a Just World Scale ($r = .61$); statistically significant correlations were also found for the CoBRAS subscales. Discriminant validity (Study 2) was reported as the CoBRAS total scale score and the RP and ID scales were unrelated to social desirability whereas the relationship of the BRI and social desirability while statistically significant was weak.

There were mixed findings regarding racial and gender differences (Studies 2, 3, and 4) so there is no conclusion regarding criterion validity. There is evidence of construct validity (Study 4) as the total scale score and subscales were related as predicted to the Quick Discrimination Index (total scale score $r = .71$) and Modern Racism Scale (total scale score $r = .52$). As hypothesized, CoBRAS total scale score and the RP subscale scores declined after multi-cultural training instruction (Study 5).

Comments: The initial report provides evidence of reliability and validity. Subsequent studies have found other evidence of reliability (Gushue, 2004; Neville, Coleman, Falconer, & Holmes, 2005; Neville, Spanierman, & Doan, 2006; Spanierman, Poteat, Beer, & Armstrong, 2006), validity (Gushue, 2004; Neville et al., 2005, 2006; Spanierrman, Poteat, Beer, & Armstrong, 2006), and independence from social desirability (Neville et al., 2006). There is a need to broaden the assessment of the scale to a broader population. The CoBRAS avoids a response set by using positively and negatively worded questions.

Location: Neville, H. A., Lilly, R. L., Duran, G., Lee, R. M., & Browne, L. (2000). Construction and initial validation of the color-blind racial attitudes scale (CoBRAS). *Journal of Counseling Psychology, 47*, 59–70.

Selected Publications

Gushue, G. V. (2004). Race, color-blind racial attitudes, and judgments about mental health: A shifting standards perspective. *Journal of Counseling Psychology, 51*, 398–407.

Neville, H. A, Coleman, M. N., Falconer, J. W., & Holmes, D. (2005). Color-blind racial attitudes and false consciousness among African Americans. *Journal of Black Psychology, 31*, 27–45.

Neville, H., Spanierman, L., & Doan, B.-T. (2006). Exploring the association between color-blind racial ideology and multi-cultural counseling competencies. *Cultural Diversity and Ethnic Minority Psychology, 12*, 275–290.

Spanierman, L. B., Poteat, V. P., Beer, A. M., & Armstrong, P. I. (2006). Psychosocial costs of racism to Whites: Exploring patterns through cluster analysis. *Journal of Counseling Psychology, 53*, 434–441.

Color-Blind Racial Attitudes Scale

Below is a set of questions that deal with social issues *in the United States*. Using the 6-point scale, please give your honest rating about the degree to which you *personally* agree or disagree with each statement. Please be as open and honest as you can; there are no right or wrong answers. Record your responses to the left of each item.

Response categories: 1 = Strongly disagree; 6 = Strongly agree

1. Everyone who works hard, no matter what race they are, has an equal chance to become rich.
2. Race plays a major role in the type of social services (such as type of health care or day care) that people receive in the United States (R).
3. It is important that people think of themselves as American and not African-American, Mexican-American, or Italian-American.
4. Due to racial discrimination, programs such as affirmative action are necessary to help create equality (R).
5. Racism is a major problem in the United States (R).
6. Race is very important in determining who is successful and who is not (R).
7. Racism may have been a problem in the past, but it is not an important problem today (R).
8. Ethnic minorities do not have the same opportunities as White people in the US.
9. White people in the United States are discriminated against because of the color of their skin.
10. Talking about racial issues causes unnecessary tensions.
11. It is important for political leaders to talk about racism to help work through or solve society's problems (R).
12. White people in the United States have certain advantages because of the color of their skin (R).
13. Immigrants should try to fit into the culture and adopt the values of the United States.
14. English should be the only official language in the United States.
15. White people are more to blame for racial discrimination in the United States than racial and ethnic minorities (R).
16. Social policies, such as affirmative action, discriminate unfairly against White people.
17. It is important for public schools to teach about the history and contributions of racial and ethnic minorities (R).
18. Racial and ethnic minorities in the United States have certain advantages because of the color of their skin.
19. Racial problems in the United States are rare, isolated situations.
20. Race plays an important role in who gets sent to prison (R).

Modified Godfrey-Richman ISM More Perfect Scale (Godfrey, Richman, & Withers, 2000)

The Modified Godfrey-Richman ISM Scale simultaneously assesses stereotypes, prejudicial attitudes, religious group and ethnic discrimination, and sexist and heterosexist attitudes.

Description: The M-GRISMS-M is a revised version of the Godfrey-Richman ISM scale developed in 1995 and the M-GRISMS. The M-GRISMS is a 50-item self-report questionnaire while the M-GRISMS-M is a 33-item scale based on the best items of the longer scale. The first four items enable the user to exclude some items based on the responses to these demographic questions. In addition to the total scale score, the authors suggest there are four subscales: racism, heterosexism, sexism, and religion. The M-GRISMS-M scale includes items with different response categories including yes/no, agree/disagree, and yes/no/same. Scoring information is neither provided nor is score interpretation. The scale is self-administered.

Sample: The M-GRISMS-M was evaluated using 131 students enrolled in an introductory psychology class: 54% of the sample was female and 93% were White, 5% Black, and 2% Asian or Native American. Participants ranged in age from 18 to 23 years.

Reliability: Cronbach's alphas for each subscale were: religion = .40; sexism = .52; heterosexism = .72; and racism = .64. Test–retest reliabilities over an 8-week period for the subscales were: religion = .75; sexism = .77; heterosexism = .81; and racism = .80. The total scale score Cronbach's alpha was .82 and test–retest reliability was .89.

Validity: Construct validity was assessed by comparing the M-GRISMS-M to the Modern and Old Fashioned Racism Scale (MOFRS), a short version of the Attitudes Toward Women Scale (AWS), and a combination of the Heterosexual Attitudes Toward Homosexuality and the Index of Homophobia (HATH/IHP). The correlation between M-GRISMS-M racism subscale and the MOFRS was .75, M-GRISMS-M heterosexism subscale and the HATH/IHP was .77, and the M-GRISMS-M sexism subscale and the AWS was .55.

Comments: This is a difficult scale to use. It is not clear from the authors' description which of the 33 items are to be included in the M-GRISMS-M; the article notes items to exclude but there remain more than 33 items. Scoring information is not provided. The subscale alphas are fairly low, though this may reflect the number of items. There is evidence of construct validity.

Location: Godfrey, S., Richman, C. L., & Withers, T. N. (2000). Reliability and validity of a new scale to measure prejudice: The GRISMS. *Current Psychology, 19*, 3–20.

Selected Publications

None

Modified Godfrey-Richman ISM Scale

Note: We have included the entire 50-item scale. Asterisks indicate the items noted by the authors to exclude when creating the M-GRISMS-M scale. We have used different spacing to conserve space.

1. Gender:

    _____ a. Male
    _____ b. Female

2. Religion:

_____ a. Christian
_____ b. Jewish
_____ c. Islam
_____ d. Agnostic
_____ e. Atheist
_____ f. Other (please specify ________________________)

3. Race:

_____ a. African American
_____ b. Latin American
_____ c. Asian American
_____ d. Native American
_____ e. Euro-American
_____ f. Other (please specify ________________________)

4. Sexual Orientation:

_____ a. Heterosexual
_____ b. Homosexual
_____ c. Bisexual

*5. Rate each of these on a scale of 1–5: *very common* (5) *not very common* (1) in the United States. (Please give a score (1, 2, 3, 4, or 5) for each category.)

_____ a. Anti-Semitism
_____ b. Homophobia
_____ c. Racism
_____ d. Sexism

*6. Rate each of these on a scale of 1–5: *very serious* (5) *not very serious* (1) in the United States. (Please give a score (1, 2, 3, 4, or 5) for each category.)

_____ a. Anti-Semitism
_____ b. Homophobia
_____ c. Racism
_____ d. Sexism

*7. Rank order these groups from 1 to 5: *most victimized* (1) to *the least victimized* (5) in the United States.

_____ a. African American
_____ b. Latin American
_____ c. Asian American
_____ d. Native American
_____ e. Euro-American

*8. Rank order these groups from 1 to 5: *most victimized* (1) to *the least victimized* (5) in the United States.

_____ a. Christian
_____ b. Jewish

_____ c. Islam
_____ d. Agnostic
_____ e. Atheist

*9. Rank these in order of "isms" from 1 to 4: *has decreased the most* (1) to *has decreased the least* (4) in the past 10 years.

_____ a. Anti-Semitism
_____ b. Homophobia
_____ c. Racism
_____ d. Sexism

10. Native American men are more aggressive and brutal than other men. Agree/Disagree

*11. With which person would you least prefer to work? Check one in each group: A, B, C, or D.

A. _____ 1. African American
_____ 2. Latin American
_____ 3. Asian American
_____ 4. Native American
_____ 5. Euro-American

B. _____ 1. Christian
_____ 2. Jewish
_____ 3. Islam
_____ 4. Agnostic
_____ 5. Atheist

C. _____ 1. Heterosexual
_____ 2. Homosexual

D. _____ 1. Male
_____ 2. Female

*12. Heterosexual men have a strong desire to dominate and take advantage of women. Agree/Disagree

13. African Americans are more prone to commit crime than European Americans. Agree/Disagree

14. Moslems are more treacherous than other religious group people. Agree/Disagree

15. Homosexuals should be blamed for the AIDS epidemic. Agree/Disagree

16. Gay men attract more attention to themselves than heterosexual men. Agree/Disagree

17. Do you feel that homosexuals are more flamboyant as a response to prejudices held against them? Yes/No

18. Hispanic/Latino men tend to show more of a "macho" attitude than other men. Agree/Disagree

19. Men are more intellectually competent than women. Agree/Disagree

20. Sexism was created by women as an excuse for their lower-level success in the business world. Agree/Disagree
21. Women use their sexuality to gain advantages over men. Agree/Disagree
22. Atheist/Agnostic people are more self-centered than people from other religious groups. Agree/Disagree
23. Would you seriously consider marrying someone of a different race than you? Yes/No
24. Would you seriously consider marrying someone of a different religion than you? Yes/No
*25. Men use their sexuality to gain advantages over women. Yes/No
26. Asian-American business owners are greedier than other business owners. Agree/Disagree
27. Homosexuals should be permitted to teach children in schools. Agree/Disagree
28. Catholics have a "holier than thou" attitude. Agree/Disagree
*29. European Americans, compared to other groups, are spoiled and self-serving. Agree/Disagree
30. Do you believe that open discrimination against African Americans promotes crime and/or violence? Yes/No
31. Homosexual partners should be allowed to legally marry each other. Agree/Disagree
32. Do you feel that African American's intelligence level is lower than that of other racial groups? Yes/No
33. Do you feel that Hispanics' intelligence level is lower than that of other racial groups? Yes/No
34. Christians are tolerant of people with other religious beliefs. Agree/Disagree
35. Lesbian women have strong negative attitudes towards men. Agree/Disagree
36. Considering the Holocaust, do you feel Hitler had some justification persecuting Jews? Yes/No
37. AIDS came into being to punish homosexual lifestyle. Agree/Disagree
38. Considering the affirmative action issues, do you feel African Americans should have advantages over European Americans in situations such as job quotas, scholarships, etc. when all other things are equal? Yes/No
39. Do you believe that people of the same religious beliefs as you are morally better people than those of religious beliefs different than yours? Yes/No/Same
40. Do you believe that people of the same race as you are morally better people than those of races different than yours? Yes/No/Same
41. Do you believe that people of the same sexual orientation as you are morally better people than those of sexual orientation different than yours? Yes/No/Same
42. Do you believe that people of the same gender as you are morally better people than those of the other gender? Yes/No/Same
43. Jewish people are deceitful and money hungry. Agree/Disagree

44. Two women were jogging around the neighborhood in their sports bras and running shorts. It was about 10:00 pm. All of a sudden, two men appeared and raped them both. Do you feel these women provoked the rape? Yes/No
*45. A man and a woman decide to go to the mountains for the weekend. They rent a tent and camping gear and spend the weekend hiking, fishing, and talking by the campfire. On Saturday night, the man rapes the woman. Do you feel she invited this rape? Yes/No
46. A male homosexual couple decides to go downtown for the afternoon. They stroll down the streets holding hands and while waiting for the light to change, they share a quick kiss. Do you feel this couple was displaying too much affection in public? Yes/No
47. A European-American woman is walking in the mall prior to closing. She sees two African-American males walking toward her. She immediately clutches her purse. Do you feel her behavior was justified? Yes/No
48. Two women were jogging around their neighborhood in their sport bras and running shorts. It was about 10:00 pm. Do you feel these women were acting in a rape-proving manner? Yes/No
49. A man and a woman decide to go to the mountains for the weekend. They rent a tent and camping gear and spend the weekend hiking, fishing, and talking by the campfire. They pack up on Sunday and go home. Do you feel this woman was inviting rape by going away for the weekend with the man? Yes/No
50. A heterosexual couple decides to go downtown for the afternoon. They stroll down the streets holding hands and while waiting for the light to change, they share a quick kiss. Do you feel this couple was displaying too much affection in public? Yes/No

Suppression of Prejudice Scale (Crandall, Eshleman, & O'Brien, 2002)

The Suppression of Prejudice Scale (SPS) assesses individual differences on internal and external motivations to suppress prejudicial comments.

Description: The SPS is a self-report measure consisting of seven items. Responses are offered on a 10-point scale ranging from *strongly disagree* (0) to *strongly agree* (9). When scoring the scale, item 3 is reverse coded. Scores are obtained by summing the 7 item responses; higher scores indicate attitudes more consistent with suppression of prejudice.

Sample: There were two studies done to address reliability and/or validity. Study 1: The sample included 455 introductory psychology students; 52% of the participants were female and 88% were White. Study 2: The sample included 113 psychology students, half were female and 80% were White.

Reliability: Cronbach's alpha coefficient was .64 (Study 1).

Validity: The SPS correlated as hypothesized with the Modern Racism Scale ($r = -.35$). Gender differences in MRS scores were explained by willingness to suppress prejudicial expressions. In Study 2, the SPS was strongly related to a similar measure, the Concern Subscale of the Motivation to Control Prejudiced Reactions ($r = .62$).

Comments: The SPS has low internal consistency and does demonstrate construct validity. We found no additional studies assessing the scale's psychometric properties. The assessment was done only with psychology students and therefore, there is a need for additional scale assessment with a broader population.

Location: Crandall, C. S., Eshleman, A., & O'Brien, L. (2002). Social norms and the expression of prejudice: The struggle for internalization. *Journal of Personality and Social Psychology, 82*, 359–378.

Selected Publications

None

The Suppression of Prejudice Scale (SPS)

Response categories: 1 = Strongly disagree; 9 = Strongly agree

1. When I meet a person of another race or ethnicity, I try to avoid thinking about their race.
2. When describing someone I know, I might mention his or her race.
3. When other people are telling funny ethnic or sexist jokes, I might laugh and join in.
4. I do not want to appear sexist or racist, even to myself.
5. I won't use an ethnic slur, even if it's the word that pops into my head.
6. If someone was ugly, overweight, or had bad skin, I wouldn't mention this fact to anyone.
7. I do not laugh at jokes that are cruel toward some groups of people, even if they are funny.

The Organizational Diversity Inventory (Hegarty & Dalton, 1995)

The Organizational Diversity Inventory (ODI) examines attitudes towards diversity in the work place and, specifically, on the extent to which there is gender, racial, and lifestyle discrimination and the extent to which the organization perceives and addresses discrimination.

Description: The ODI includes 20 items. Factor analyses have produced five subscales including: (1) Existence of Discrimination (ED; six items: 1, 7, 9, 11, 18, 20); (2) Discrimination against Specific Groups (DSG; five items: 2, 8, 13, 16, 19); (3)

Managing Diversity (MD; three items: 14, 15, 17); Actions Regarding Minorities (ARM; three items: 3, 5, 10); and (5) Attitudes Toward Religion (ATR: three items: 4, 6, 12). Responses are offered on a 5-point Likert-type scale ranging from *strongly agree* (1) to *strongly disagree* (5). The scale is self-administered. Scoring as well as the use of subscales is not clear. It appears that five items are reverse coded (items 4, 14, 15, 17, 20) and that higher scores indicate a more positive view to issues of diversity.

Sample: The sample included 450 managers from 27 Midwestern organizations. Fifty-four percent of participants were male and respondents ranged in age from 24 to 65 with an average age of 35 years. Respondents had been employed in their current jobs for an average of 5.5 years and averaged 9 years of work experience.

Reliability: Coefficient alphas for the five subscales were .75 for ED, .80 for DSG, .65 for MD, .64 for ARM, and .65 for ATR.

Validity: Using a split sample, the 5-factor structure was validated using confirmatory factor analysis providing evidence of factorial validity.

Comments: There is little evidence of reliability and validity and none for a total scale score. It is not clear that a second-order factor model was used to determine whether a total scale score might be appropriate. One study used only two items and reported a reasonable internal consistency (Slaughter, Sinar, & Bachiochi, 2002). Scoring instructions are not clearly specified and were surmised by our review of the questions. We assume that the phrase, alternative life styles, is a euphemism for gay–lesbian relationships but that is not clear. There is a need for psychometric assessments with a broader population. The ODI avoids a response set by using positively and negatively worded questions.

Location: Hegarty, W. H., & Dalton, D. R. (1995). Development and psychometric properties of the organizational diversity inventory (ODI). *Educational and Psychological Measurement, 55*, 1047–1052.

Selected Publications

Slaughter, J. E., Sinar, E. F., & Bachiochi, P. D. (2002). Black applicants' reactions to affirmative action plans: Effects of plan content and previous experience with discrimination. *Journal of Applied Psychology, 87*, 333–344.

Organizational Diversity Inventory

Instructions: America's workforce is becoming more diverse. During the past decade more women, minorities, and immigrants have become wage earners. There are also more single parents than ever before. Additionally, there is now a greater awareness of persons who choose lifestyles different from what our country historically has considered to be traditional.

The statements in this survey are concerned with many aspects of diversity. There are no right or wrong answers. Respond to each statement from your own point of view.

You are being asked to respond honestly and your response will remain anonymous.

Response categories: 1 = Strongly disagree; 2 = Disagree; 3 = Not sure; 4 = Agree; 5 = Strongly agree

1. I have experienced the discomfort of discrimination.
2. Some people in my organization are not comfortable with women in managerial positions.
3. Sometimes I feel my organization hires minorities to fill unstated quotas.
4. I would be comfortable having a mentor who was not at all like me (R).
5. Our company actively recruits minorities.
6. Sometimes I feel people's religion affects how they are viewed in my organization.
7. Not everyone at my level in the organization is treated fairly.
8. Many people in my organization are biased against people who are gay.
9. Sexual discrimination exists in my organization.
10. Sometimes I feel people get assignments because they are a minority person.
11. Our company sometimes does not follow our policies against discrimination.
12. People of certain religious faiths are often not well integrated into the organization.
13. I have heard sexist remarks about women at work.
14. My organization has sponsored classes, workshops, and seminars on managing the diverse work force (R).
15. Managing diversity has helped my organization to be more effective (R).
16. I have heard racist remarks at work.
17. My company accommodates the needs of disabled person (R).
18. I have heard people at work make negative comments about gays.
19. Management talks about diversity, but does not really do anything about it.
20. My spouse (significant other) would say that they treat me fairly here (R).

The Motivation to Control Prejudiced Reactions Scale (Dunton & Fazio, 1997)

The Motivation to Control Prejudiced Reactions Scale (MCPRS) assesses differences in the extent to which individuals seek to control prejudicial reactions.

Description: The MCPRS is a self-report measure and consists of 17 items. The response format for each item is based on a 7-point Likert-type scale ranging from *strongly disagree* (–3) to *strongly agree* (3). Some scale items (2, 5, 8, 9, and 17) are reverse-scored. After reverse-coding, the item responses are summed. Higher scores reflect a stronger motivation to control expressions of prejudice. Factor analysis of the items suggests that there are two factors comprising a subset of the items. These factors are: Concern with Acting Prejudiced (nine items: 1, 3, 6, 10, 11, 12, 13, 14, and 15) and Restraint to Avoid Dispute (four items: 2, 4, 9, and 16). The authors use both the total scale score and factor scores (based on factor weights) for each of the two factors.

Sample: The scale was evaluated with four different samples. Samples 1, 2, and 3 comprised undergraduate students and included 55, 418, and 429 participants respectively. The fourth sample included 207 individuals who responded to advertisements in campus or town newspapers.

Reliability: Based on the 17 items, Cronbach's alpha for the four samples ranged from .74 to .81.

Validity: Predictive validity is suggested. Higher scores on the MCPRS were statistically significantly related to lowers scores on the Modern Racism Scale and to self-reported feelings toward African Americans. The two subscales moderated response to the Modern Racism Scale and the restraint factor moderated responses toward African Americans.

Comments: Other studies using the MCPRS tend to use the subscales identified by the factor analysis. This factor structure was found in other studies (Olson & Fazio, 2004; Towles-Schwen & Fazio, 2003). Using factor weights may be a challenge for some research. There is adequate evidence of reliability. Plant and Devine (1998) report a similar total scale score Cronbach's alpha (.73) and subscale alphas (Concern = .73; Avoidance = .68). Additional psychometric evidence, particularly validity, is needed; such work should also be completed with other population groups. The MCPRS avoids a response set by using positively and negatively worded questions.

Location: Dunton, B. C., & Fazio, R. H. (1997). An individual difference measure of motivation to control prejudiced reactions. *Personality & Social Psychology Bulletin, 23*, 316–32.

Selected Publications

Olson, M. A., & Fazio, R. H. (2004). Trait inferences as a function of automatically activated racial attitudes and motivation to control prejudiced reactions. *Basic and Applied Social Psychology, 26*, 1–11.

Plant, E. A., & Devine, P. G. (1998). Internal and external motivation to respond without prejudice. *Journal of Personality and Social Psychology, 75*, 811–832.

Towles-Schwen, T., & Fazio, R. H. (2003). Choosing social situations: The relation between automatically activated racial attitudes and anticipated comfort interacting with African Americans. *Personality and Social Psychology Bulletin, 29*, 170–182.

The Motivation to Control Prejudiced Reactions Scale

Response categories: –3 = Strongly disagree; +3 = Strongly agree

1. In today's society, it is important that one should not be perceived as prejudiced in any manner.
2. I always express my thoughts and feelings, regardless of how controversial they might be (R).
3. I get angry with myself when I have a thought or feeling that might be considered prejudiced.
4. If I were participating in a class discussion and a Black student expressed an opinion with which I disagreed, I would be hesitant to express my own viewpoint.
5. Going through life worrying about whether you might offend someone is just more trouble than it's worth (R).
6. It's important to me that other people not think I am prejudiced.
7. I feel it's important to behave according to society's standards.
8. I am careful not to offend my friends, but I do not worry about offending people I do not know or do not like (R).
9. I think that it is important to speak one's mind rather than to worry about offending someone (R).
10. It's never acceptable to express one's prejudices.
11. I feel guilty when I have a negative thought or feeling about a Black person.
12. When speaking to a Black person, it's important to me that he/she not think I am prejudiced.
13. It bothers me a great deal when I think I have offended someone, so I am always careful to consider other people's feelings.
14. If I have a prejudiced thought or feeling, I keep it to myself.
15. I would never tell jokes that might offend others.
16. I am not afraid to tell others what I think even when I know they disagree with me (R).
17. If someone who made me uncomfortable sat next to me on a bus, I would not hesitate to move to another seat (R).

Self-Evaluation of Biases and Prejudices Scale (Paniagua, 1998)

The Self-Evaluation of Biases and Prejudices Scale (SEBPS) provides clinicians with a self-evaluation of unintended biases and prejudices against culturally diverse groups.

Description: The SEBPS has 10 items. Each item is rated on a 3-point scale ranging from *very much* (1) to *not at all* (3). Respondents are expected to provide their responses with a specific ethnic group in mind. Responses for the particular group are summed and then divided by the number of questions answered. The total score ranges from 1 to 3. The higher the score, the greater the probability of unintended biases and prejudices.

Sample: The sample size was 39. The majority of the sample was female (56.4%) and ranged in age from 20 to over 50, though most respondents (54.4%) fell in the age range of 30–49 years. Most respondents identified as White (56.4%) followed by African American (30.8%) and Hispanic (12.8%). The majority of the sample (64.1%) included counselors, teachers, social workers, and psychologists while the remaining were school principals and related school staff.

Reliability: Coefficient alpha was .87.

Validity: There is no report for validity.

Comments: The sample is small and limited to one setting. There is minimal evidence for reliability. Separate scores for each ethnic/racial group are not provided. There is no evidence of validity. We could find no additional studies detailing the scale's psychometric properties. The assessment was completed with a small and site-specific sample.

Location: Paniagua, F. A. (1998). *Assessing and treating culturally diverse clients: A practical guide* (2nd ed.). Newbury Park, CA: Sage.

Selected Publications

None

Self-Evaluation of Biases and Prejudices Scale

Circle the number that you believe corresponds with the answer to each of the ten questions listed below across five culturally diverse groups you are likely to serve in your clinical practice.

Response categories: 1 = Very much; 2 = Somewhat; 3 = Not at all

1. Have you had formal training with?
   a. African Americans
   b. American Indians
   c. Asians
   d. Hispanics
   e. Whites
2. Do you have cultural knowledge of
   a. African Americans
   b. American Indians
   c. Asians
   d. Hispanics
   e. Whites

3. As a parent, would you approve your son or daughter dating

   a. African Americans
   b. American Indians
   c. Asians
   d. Hispanics
   e. Whites

4. Would you date or marry a member from the following groups?

   a. African Americans
   b. American Indians
   c. Asians
   d. Hispanics
   e. Whites

5. Would you feel comfortable providing clinical services to

   a. African Americans
   b. American Indians
   c. Asians
   d. Hispanics
   e. Whites

6. Have you been exposed to the professional views of

   a. African Americans
   b. American Indians
   c. Asians
   d. Hispanics
   e. Whites

7. Are you familiar with the current literature (journals, books, periodicals) on

   a. African Americans
   b. American Indians
   c. Asians
   d. Hispanics
   e. Whites

8. Would you feel comfortable if you have a problem understanding

   a. African Americans
   b. American Indians
   c. Asians
   d. Hispanics
   e. Whites

9. Would you expect a favorable therapy outcome with
   a. African Americans
   b. American Indians
   c. Asians
   d. Hispanics
   e. Whites
10. Would you expect a favorable therapeutic relationship with
   a. African Americans
   b. American Indians
   c. Asians
   d. Hispanics
   e. Whites

Internal and External Motivation to Respond Without Prejudice Scale (Plant & Devine, 1998)

The Internal (IMS) and External (EMS) Motivation to Respond without Prejudice Scale assesses what motivates individuals to respond to African Americans without prejudice.

Description: The IMS, measuring internal motivations, and EMS, measuring external motivations, each consist of five items. IMS includes items 6–10 and EMS includes items 1–5. Responses are offered on a 9-point Likert-type scale ranging from *strongly disagree* (1) to *strongly agree* (9). When scoring, item 7 is reverse coded. Scores for each domain are obtained by summing the item responses. Higher scores reflect higher levels of that type of motivation. The scale is self-administered.

Sample: Three studies with multiple samples were conducted to develop items for the IMS and EMS and to examine the scale's psychometric properties. Study 1: Three samples taken from introductory psychology classes were used to develop the scale. The three samples included respectively 135 participants (78% female; 84% White), 245 participants (74% female; 84% White), and 1,363 participants (60% female; 85% White); 159 respondents in Sample 3, retook the instrument 9 weeks later. Study 2: Two samples were used to assess convergent and discriminant validity. The samples came from introductory psychology classes and included 247 students (78% female; 88% White) and 119 students (62% female; 90% White). Study 3: Two samples were used to assess predictive validity. The first sample consisted of 246 students. They were split into two groups: 152 into a personal standard group (how they should respond personally) and 144 into a campus standard group (how they should respond according to university standards). The second sample included 80 students from an introductory psychology class and were divided into four groups depending on their IMS and EMS scores.

Reliability: Cronbach's alphas for the IMS ranged from .81 to .85 and the EMS ranged from .76 to .80 (Study 1). The 9-week IMS test–retest reliability coefficient was .77 and the EMS test–retest reliability coefficient was .60 (Study 1).

Validity: Factorial validity was tested in Study 1: The 2-factor structure was replicated across samples and provided a better fit than a single-factor model; the two factors were weakly related to each other (< –.15). Convergent validity was examined in Study 2: As expected, the IMS was correlated with four measures of racial attitudes (Modern Racism Scale, $r = -.57$; Anti-Black Scale, $r = -.48$; Attitude Toward Blacks Scale, $r = .79$; and the Pro-Black Scale, $r = .24$) and three measures of more general prejudicial attitudes (Right-Wing Authoritarianism Scale, $r = -.24$; the Protestant Work Ethic Scale, $r = -.18$; and the Humanitarianism-Egalitarianism Scale, $r = .45$). As expected, the relationships between the EMS and the above measures were weak (Modern Racism Scale, $r = .22$; Attitude Toward Blacks Scale, $r = -.27$; and Right-Wing Authoritarianism Scale, $r = .13$) and the rest were not statistically significant. Discriminant validity was also assessed in Study 2: Both scales were unrelated to social desirability and the tendency and ability to strategically adjust one's behavior (Marlowe-Crowne Social Desirability Scale and Self-Monitoring Scale) while the IMS was not related to participant self-monitoring scores (Fear of Negative Evaluation Scale and Interaction Anxiousness Scale) while the EMS was weakly related to these scales. Predictive validity was assessed in Study 3: Responses to affect variables were predicted by IMS status. Participant agreement regarding stereotypes of Blacks was related to their IMS-EMS status.

Comments: There is evidence of reliability and validity. Other studies have found similar internal consistency coefficients (Hausmann & Ryan, 2004; Plant & Devine, 2001; Plant & Devine, 2009). Additional studies have found that the IMS and EMS predict other constructs and measurement of prejudice (Amodio, Harmon-Jones, & Devine, 2003; Crandall et al., 2002; Hausmann & Ryan, 2004; Plant & Devine, 2009; Schlauch, Lang, Plant, Christensen, & Donohue, 2009). The relative independence of the two constructs has enabled researchers to create four groups for their studies: High IMS/High EMS, High IMS/Low EMS, Low IMS/High EMS, and Low IMS/Low EMS. Note that all of these studies have involved college students and the scales should be assessed with broader populations. The studies typically deal with prejudicial attitudes toward African Americans.

Location: Plant, E. A., & Devine, P. G. (1998). Internal and external motivation to respond without prejudice. *Journal of Personality and Social Psychology, 75*, 811–832.

Selected Publications

Amodio, D. M., Harmon-Jones, E., & Devine, P. G. (2003). Individual differences in the activation and control of affective race bias as assessed by startle eyeblink response and self-report. *Journal of Personality and Social Psychology, 84*, 738–753.

Crandall, C. S., Eshleman, A., & O'Brien, L. (2002). Social norms and the expression and suppression of prejudice: The struggle for internalization. *Journal of Personality and Social Psychology, 82*, 359–378.

Hausmann, L. R. M., & Ryan, C. S. (2004). Effects of external and internal motivation to control prejudice on implicit prejudice: The mediating role of efforts to control prejudiced responses. *Basic and Applied Social Psychology, 26*, 215–225.

Plant, E. A., & Devine, P. G. (2001). Responses to other-imposed pro-Black pressure: Acceptance or backlash? *Journal of Experimental Social Psychology, 37*, 486–501.

Plant, E. A., & Devine, P. G. (2009). The active control of prejudice: Unpacking the intentions guiding control efforts. *Journal of Personality and Social Psychology, 96*, 64–652.

Schlauch, R. C., Lang, A. R., Plant, E. A., Christensen, R., & Donohue, K. F. (2009). Effect of alcohol on race-based responding: The moderating role of internal and external motivations to respond without prejudice. *Journal of Studies on Alcohol and Drugs, 70*, 328–336.

Internal Motivation to Respond Without Prejudice Scale and External Motivation to Respond Without Prejudice Scale

Instructions: The following questions concern various reasons or motivations people might have for trying to respond in non-prejudiced ways toward Black people. Some of the reasons reflect internal-personal motivations whereas others reflect more external-social motivations. Of course, people may be motivated for both internal and external reasons, we want to emphasize that neither type of motivation is by definition better than the other. In addition, we want to be clear that we are not evaluating you or your individual responses. All your responses will be completely confidential. We are simply trying to get an idea of the types of motivations that students in general have for responding in non-prejudiced ways. If we are to learn anything useful, it is important that you respond to each of the questions openly and honestly. Please give your response according to the scale below. 1 = Strongly disagree to 9 = Strongly agree

1. Because of today's PC (politically correct) standards, I try to appear non-prejudiced toward Black people.
2. I try to hide any negative thoughts about Black people in order to avoid negative reactions from others.
3. If I acted prejudicial toward Black people, I would be concerned that others would be angry with me.
4. I attempt to appear non-prejudiced toward Black people in order to avoid disapproval from others.

5. I try to act non-prejudiced toward Black people because of pressure from others.
6. I attempt to act in non-prejudiced ways toward Black people because it is personally important to me.
7. According to my values, using stereotypes about Black people is OK (R).
8. I am personally motivated by my beliefs to be non-prejudiced toward Black people.
9. Because of my personal values, I believe that using stereotypes about Black people is wrong.
10. Being non-prejudiced toward Black people is important to my self-concept.

Measures of Social Distance and Discrimination

The Reverse Social Distance Scale (Lee, Sapp, & Ray, 1996)

The Reverse Social Distance Scale (RSDS) is designed to measure minority groups' perceptions of how other groups accept them in various roles.

Description: The RSDS consists of five items rated with a Yes/No response. The scores range from 1 (all items are marked "N," indicating "no they do not mind") to 6 (all items are marked "Y," indicating "yes, they mind"). A low-scale score indicates closer distance. The scale is self-administered.

Sample: The sample included 108 minority university students. The sample's racial composition was: 44.4% were African American, 23.2% were Hispanic, and 32.4% were "other" (Japanese, Chinese, Native American, Indonesian, Vietnamese, Laotian, and Sri Lankan).

Reliability: Guttman coefficient of reproducibility for this scale was .99.

Validity: None reported, though it appears that scale score might be related to identifying one's ethnicity from the Twenty Statement's Test.

Comments: This scale was developed by modifying Bogardus's Social Distance Scale. The sample represented only 10% of the mailed surveys and therefore it is not generalizable. There is a lack of psychometric evidence in support of this modification of the Bogardus scale.

Location: Lee, M. Y., Sapp, S. G., & Ray, M. C. (1996). The reverse social distance scale. *The Journal of Social Psychology*, *136*, 17–24.

Selected Publications

None

Reverse Social Distance Scale

Considering *typical* Caucasian Americans you have known, not any specific person nor the worst or the best, circle Y or N to express your opinion.

Y N 1. Do they mind your being a citizen in this country?
Y N 2. Do they mind your living in the same neighborhood?
Y N 3. Would they mind your living next to them?
Y N 4. Would they mind your becoming a close friend to them?
Y N 5. Would they mind your becoming their kin in marriage?

Experiences of Discrimination Scale (Krieger, Smith, Naishadham, Hartman, & Barbeau, 2005)

The Experiences of Discrimination (EOD) Scale assesses exposure to racial discrimination.

Description: The EOD is a self-report measure consisting of nine items reflecting situations in which individuals may have experienced some form of racial discrimination. The EOD can be used to both measure the number of situations and the frequency of exposure to these situations. The number of situations is calculated by the number of yes/no responses to the nine questions; scores may range from 0 to 9. Higher scores reflect more situations in which racial discrimination had occurred. The response categories for the frequency of each situation are: *never* (0), *one time* (1), *two to three times* (2.5), *four or more times* (5). Responses are summed providing a range from 0 to 45. Higher scores reflect a greater frequency of exposure to discrimination. The scale is self-administered.

Sample: Potential participants were recruited from union lists at nine work-sites. There were 616 participants with complete racial data in the main study and included 159 African Americans, 249 Latin Americans, and 208 White Americans. The group was 50% male, 42% had incomes below the poverty line, and most were between age 25 and 44 years. The validation sample taken from the above participants included 98 African Americans and 100 Latinos.

Reliability: Cronbach's alphas for the situation/frequency scales were: African Americans = .81/.86, Latinos = .81/.79, and Whites = .77/.74. Test–retest reliabilities were .70 for frequency and .69 for situation. Test–retest reliability scores were .69 or higher for all racial groups.

Validity: Based on confirmatory factor analysis, the scale is unidimensional; further the scale is not influenced by ethnicity, age, gender, educational attainment, or social desirability. Both the frequency and situation measures were strongly correlated with the Williams Major and Everyday discrimination survey providing evidence of criterion validity. As hypothesized, there were differences in the actual experiences of discrimination by race; African Americans (8.92) tended to have more experiences with discrimination than Latinos (5.72) and Whites (4.94). There is evidence of construct validity as scale scores were related to psychological distress.

Comments: This scale is a revised version of the 7-item EOD proposed by Krieger and Sidney (1996). There is good psychometric evidence with a working class sample; however, this instrument should be tested with other populations such as professionals with the same ethnic backgrounds. There are both English and Spanish versions.

Location: Krieger, N., Smith, K., Naishadham, D., Hartman, C., & Barbeau, E. M. (2005). Experiences of discrimination: Validity and reliability of a self-report measure for population health research on racism and health. *Social Science and Medicine, 61*, 1576–596.

Original scale: Krieger, N., & Sidney, S. (1996). Racial discrimination and blood pressure: The CARDIA study of young black and white adults. *American Journal of Public Health, 86*, 1370–1378.

Selected Publications

None

Experiences of Discrimination (EOD) [English Version]

Have you ever experienced discrimination, been prevented from doing something, or been hassled or made to feel inferior in any of the following situations because of your race, ethnicity, or color?

For each situation to which the participant replied "yes" (vs. "no"), the follow-up question is: How many times did this happen? Response categories: 1 = Once; 2 = Two or three times; 3 = Four or more times

Situation

1. At school?
2. Getting hired or getting a job?
3. At work?
4. Getting housing?
5. Getting medical care?
6. Getting services in a store or restaurant?
7. Getting credit, bank loans, or a mortgage?
8. On the street or in a public setting?
9. From the police or in the courts?

Quick Discrimination Index (Ponterotto et al., 1995)

The Quick Discrimination Index (QDI) measures cognitive and affective attitudes toward racial diversity and general attitudes toward women's equality.

Description: The QDI consists of 30 items. The scale has three subscales: (1) cognitive attitudes about racial diversity (Cognitive Racial Attitudes or Factor 1; nine items: 3, 9, 13, 18, 19, 22, 23, 26, 27); (2) affective attitudes about racial contact (Affective Racial Attitudes or Factor 2; seven items: 4, 8, 11, 15, 17, 24, 29); and

(3) general attitudes toward women's equality (Cognitive Gender Attitudes or Factor 3; seven items: 1, 6, 7, 14, 16, 20, 30). The response format for each item is a 5-point Likert-type scale ranging from *strongly disagree* (1) to *strongly agree* (5). The scores for the QDI are obtained by reverse coding 15 items (1, 2, 3, 7, 9, 10, 13, 15, 16, 18, 19, 23, 25, 29, 30) and summing all the item responses. The total score ranges from 30 to 150 with higher scores indicating more positive attitudes toward multi-culturalism and women's equality. In lieu of the 30 item total score, a 23-item total score can be used by just including those items that form the three subscales. Subscale scores may also be calculated. The scale is self-administered.

Sample: Three studies were conducted to develop and evaluate the scale; the first study dealt with scale item identification primarily and tested only 25 items; we report the remaining two studies (2 and 3). Study 2: Sample 1 included 220 participants recruited from a variety of sites by the researcher. The sample included 104 adolescents and 116 adults ranging in age from 16 to 58 years with an average of 22 years. The majority of participants were female (59%) and 60% were White, 23% Hispanic/Latino, 10% African American, 4% Asian American, and 4% "other." Sample 2 included 37 undergraduate students ranging in age from 17 to 50; this sample was used for test–retest reliability. Study 3: The sample included 333 participants recruited from schools, college classes, and the general adult population. Participants had an average age of 27 and ranged in age from 16 to 63; 79% were females; and participants' racial identification included White (76%), African American (5%), Asian American (5%), Hispanic/Latino (8%), and "other" (6%).

Reliability: Cronbach's alpha for the total scale was .88; Cronbach's alphas for the three factors were .80, .83, and .76 (Study 2). 15-week test–retest reliability for each factor was: .90, .82, and .81 (Study 2). Cronbach's alpha for the total scale score was .88; for the three factors alphas were .85, .83, and .65 (Study 3).

Validity: In Study 2, three meaningful factors were identified; these three factors accounted for 23 items; four items did not load highly on any factor and three items (12, 26, 28) had high loadings on more than one factor. Construct validity showed a relationship between political affiliation and scores for each of the three factors. There were also differences in race and gender with factor scores. Study 3 focused on various forms of validity. There is evidence of construct validity as the three factors were correlated with the New Racism Scale and had stronger correlations with the two race-related factors (1 and 2) than with the gender factor (3). Further, convergent validity was evident as there were four correlations (of a possible six) between the three factors of the QDI and the two factors of the Multicultural Counseling Awareness Scale. The three QDI factors did not correlate with the Social Desirability Scale providing evidence of discriminant validity. The three factor structure was supported by a confirmatory factor analysis.

Comments: At least one item is dated (item 12) and one item is a double-barrelled question (item 21). The reading level is appropriate for Grade 9 adolescents (Utsey & Ponterotto, 1999). There is satisfactory evidence of internal consistency; this finding has been reported in other studies representing different geographic regions

(Neville, Lilly, Duran, Lee, & Browne, 2000; Utsey & Ponterotto, 1999) and diverse population subgroups such as White social workers for the race-related subscales (Green, Kiernan-Stern, & Basking, 2005), Asian American university students on the total scale score (Liu, Pope-Davis, Nevitt, & Toporek, 1999), and Vietnamese American university students (Lam, 2008). The 3-factor structure has been replicated (Utsey & Ponterotto, 1999). A 4-factor model with Whites only was reported by Burkhard, Jones, and Johill (2002). Support for a total scale score is evident in these various studies. There is evidence of validity from the initial studies as well as from additional studies. Liu and colleagues (1999) reported that higher total QDI scale scores were related to higher levels of acculturation, greater Asian identification, and exposure to multi-cultural education. Lam (2008) found that female Vietnamese American students had higher QDI scores and more acculturated scores were correlated with higher QDI scores. A summary of other validation studies is reported in Ponterotto, Potere, and Johansen (2002). Samples have cut across different population groups. The QDI avoids a response set by using positively and negatively worded questions.

Location: Ponterotto, J. G., Grieger, I., Burkard, A., Rieger, B. P., D'Onofrio, A., Dubuisson, A., et al. (1995). Development and validation of the Quick Discrimination Index (QDI). *Educational and Psychological Measurement, 55*, 1016–1031.

Selected Publications

Burkhard, A. W., Jones, J. A., & Johll, M. P. (2002). Hierarchical factor analysis of the Quick Discrimination Index. *Educational and Psychological Measurement, 62*, 64–78.

Green, R. G., Kiernan-Stern, M., & Basking, F. R. (2005). White social workers' attitudes about people of color. *Journal of Ethnic and Cultural Diversity in Social Work, 14*, 47–67.

Lam, B. T. (2008). The function of acculturation and collective self-esteem on prejudicial attitudes among Vietnamese American young adults. *Journal of Human Behavior in the Social Environment, 18*, 350–363.

Liu, W. M., Pope-Davis, D. B., Nevitt, J., & Toporek, R. L. (1999). Understanding the function of acculturation and prejudicial attitudes among Asian Americans. *Cultural Diversity and Ethnic Minority Psychology, 5*, 317–328.

Neville, H. A., Lilly, R. L., Duran, G., Lee, R. M., & Browne, L. (2000). Construction and initial validation of the Color-Blind Racial Attitudes Scale (CoBRAS). *Journal of Counseling Psychology, 47*, 59–70.

Ponterotto, J. G., Potere, J. C., & Johansen, S. A. (2002). The Quick Discrimination Index: Normative data and user guidelines for counseling researchers. *Journal of Multicultural Counseling and Development, 30*, 192–207.

Utsey, S. O., & Ponterotto, J. G. (1999). Further factorial validity assessment of scores on the Quick Discrimination Index (QDI). *Educational and Psychological Measurement, 59*, 325–335.

Quick Discrimination Scale

Social Attitude Scale (*Note*: This is the actual name of the scale used with respondents to avoid social desirability). (R) represents items that that are reverse coded.

Please respond to all items in the survey. Remember there are no right or wrong answers. The survey is completely anonymous; do not put your name on the survey. Please circle the appropriate number to the right. Response categories include: 1 = Strongly disagree; 2 = Disagree; 3 = Not sure; 4 = Agree; 5 = Strongly agree.

1. I do think it is more appropriate for the mother of a newborn baby, rather than the father, to stay home with the baby (not work) during the first year (R).
2. It is as easy for women to succeed in business as it is for men (R).
3. I really think affirmative action programs on college campuses constitute reverse discrimination (R).
4. I feel I could develop an intimate relationship with someone from a different race.
5. All Americans should learn to speak two languages.
6. I look forward to the day when a woman is President of the United States. (Or it upsets or angers me that a woman has never been President of the United States).
7. Generally speaking, men work harder than women (R).
8. My friendship network is very racially mixed.
9. I am against affirmative action programs in business (R).
10. Generally, men seem less concerned with building relationships than do women (R).
11. I would feel OK about my son or daughter dating someone from another race.
12. I look forward to the day when a racial minority person is President of the United States. (Or it upsets or angers me that a racial minority person has never been President of the United States).
13. In the past few years there has been too much attention directed toward multicultural issues in education (R).
14. I think feminist perspectives should be an integral part of the higher education curriculum.
15. Most of my friends are from my own racial group (R).
16. I feel somewhat more secure that a man rather than a woman is currently the President of the United States (R).
17. I think that it is (or would be) important for my children to attend schools that are racially mixed.
18. In the past few years there has been too much attention directed toward multicultural issues in business (R).
19. Overall, I think racial minorities in America complain too much about racial discrimination (R).
20. I feel (or would feel) very comfortable having a woman as my primary physician.

21. I think the President of the United States should make a concerted effort to appoint more women and racial minorities to the country's Supreme Court.
22. I think White people's racism toward racial minority groups still constitutes a major problem in America.
23. I think the school system, from elementary school through college, should encourage minority and immigrant children to learn and fully adopt traditional American values (R).
24. If I were to adopt a child, I would be happy to adopt a child of any race.
25. I think there is as much female physical violence toward men as there is male physical violence toward women (R).
26. I think the school system, from elementary school through college, should promote values representative of diverse cultures.
27. I believe that reading the autobiography of Malcolm X would be a value.
28. I would enjoy living in a neighborhood consisting of a racially diverse population (e.g., Asians, Blacks, Hispanics, and Whites).
29. I think it is better if people marry within their own race (R).
30. Women make too big of a deal out of sexual harassment issues in the workplace (R).

Measures of Racial Identity

Multigroup Ethnic Identity Measure (Phinney, 1992; Roberts et al., 1999)

The Multigroup Ethnic Identity Measure (MEIM) assesses ethnic identity for diverse groups.

Description: The revised form of the MEIM consists of 12 items (two items being deleted from the original 1992 version of the MEIM). The MEIM assesses two domains: Affirmation/Belonging/Commitment reflecting a sense of and pride in group membership (seven items: 3, 5, 6, 7, 9, 11, 12) and Exploration or behaviors reflecting involvement in ethnic activities (five items: 1, 2, 4, 8, 10). Responses are offered on a 4-point scale ranging from *strongly disagree* (1) to *strongly agree* (4). The total score, calculated as the average of the item responses, ranges from 1 to 4, with higher scores reflecting a stronger global ethnic identity. Subscale scores are calculated in a similar fashion with higher scores reflecting a stronger ethnic identity. The scale is self-administered. *Note*: We have included the deleted two items as studies still use these items.

Sample: The sample included 5,423 sixth- to eigth-grade students recruited from five middle schools in the Houston metropolitan area. Participants had an average age of 12.9 years and 49% were female. The sample included more than 20 distinctive ethnic groups.

Reliability: The 12-item Cronbach's alpha for the entire sample was .85; for the 11 largest ethnic groups the alphas ranged from .81 to .89. The Commitment subscale Cronbach's alpha was .84 for the entire sample and ranged from .81 to .86 for the 11 largest ethnic groups. The Exploration subscale Cronbach's alpha was .70 for the entire sample and ranged from .55 to .73 for the 11 largest ethnic groups.

Validity: There is evidence of construct validity. The entire sample and separately, three ethnic groups (European Americans, African Americans, and Mexican Americans) were included in the assessment. The MEIM was associated in the predicted directions with various measures of psychological well being including coping, mastery, self-esteem, optimism, loneliness, and depression. MEIM scores were also associated with salience of identify (the importance of one's ethnic background). Factorial validity was ascertained as the factor structure, though not individual item loadings, was equivalent across European Americans, African Americans, and Mexican Americans. One item loaded on two factors.

Comments: The samples for these studies tend to be adolescents and college students, therefore the scale may be appropriate only for younger respondents. Scores can be obtained for a global measure of identity and or two aspects of identity. There is some concern about the factor structure as the findings are mixed and they may be related to age of sample or ethnicity. There is general support for the 2-factor model (Pegg & Plybon (12 items), 2005; Spencer, Icard, Harachi, Catalano, & Oxford (14 items), 2000) or a modified version dropping four items (Yancy, Aneshensel, & Driscoll (14 items), 2001). Using the 14-item version, a 3-factor structure was found with a sample of Asian-American college students. There is evidence of reliability and validity though the exploration subscale reliability coefficients are low. For the 14- item version, Ponterotto and his colleagues, (Ponterotto, Gretchen, Utsey, Stracuzzi, & Saya, 2003) review of 12 studies found consistent reports of internal consistency with college and high-school samples as well as associations with a variety of related constructs. For the 12-item measure, similar findings have been reported for the Commitment subscale and Exploration subscale (Pegg & Plybon, 2005).

Location: Phinney, J. S. (1992). The multi-group ethnic identity measure: A new scale for use with adolescents and young adults. *Journal of Adolescent Research, 7*, 156–176.

Roberts, R. E., Phinney, J. S., Masse, L. C., Chen, Y. R., Roberts, C. R., & Romero, A. (1999). The structure of ethnic identity of young adolescents from diverse ethnocultural groups. *Journal of Early Adolescence, 19*, 301–322.

Selected Publications

Pegg, P. O., & Plybon, L. E. (2005). Toward the theoretical measurement of ethnic identity. *Journal of Early Adolescence, 25*, 250–264.

Ponterotto, J., Gretchen, D., Utsey, S., Stracuzzi, T., & Saya, R. (2003). The multigroup Ethnic Identity Measure (MEIM): Psychometric reviews and further validity testing. *Educational and Psychological Measurement, 63*, 502–525.

Spenser, M. S., Icard, L. D., Harachi, T. W., Catalano, R. F., & Oxford, M. (2000). Ethnic identity among monoracial and multiracial adolescents. *Journal of Early Adolescence, 20*, 365–387.

Yancey, A. K., Aneshensel, C. S., & Driscoll, A. K. (2001). The assessment of ethnic identity in a diverse urban youth population. *Journal of Black Psychology, 27*, 190–208.

Multigroup Ethnic Identity Measure

In this country, people come from many different countries and cultures, and there are many different words to describe the different backgrounds or *ethnic groups* that people come from. Some examples of ethnic groups are Latino, African American, Mexican, Asian American, Chinese, and many others. These questions are about your ethnicity or your ethnic group and how you feel about it or react to it.

Please fill in: In terms of ethnic group, I consider myself to be ______________________

Use the numbers below to indicate how much you agree or disagree with each statement.

1 = Strongly disagree; 2 = Disagree; 3 = Neutral; 4 = Agree; 5 = Strongly agree

Note: The items marked with an asterisk come from the original 14-item scale.

1. I have spent time trying to find out more about my ethnic group, such as its history, traditions, and customs.
2. I am active in organizations or social groups that include mostly members of my own ethnic group.
3. I have a clear sense of my ethnic background and what it means for me.
4. I think a lot about how my life will be affected by my ethnic group membership.
5. I am happy that I am a member of the group I belong to.
6. I have a strong sense of belonging to my own ethnic group.
7. I understand pretty well what my ethnic group membership means to me.
8. In order to learn more about my ethnic background, I have often talked to other people about my ethnic group
9. I have a lot of pride in my ethnic group.
10. I participate in cultural practices of my own group, such as special food, music, or customs.
11. I feel a strong attachment toward my own ethnic group.
12. I feel good about my cultural or ethnic background.

*13. I am not very clear about the role of my ethnicity in my life.

*14. I really have not spent much time trying to learn more about the culture and history of my ethnic group.

15. My ethnicity is:

    (1) Asian or Asian American, including Chinese, Japanese, and others
    (2) Black or African American

(3) Hispanic or Latino, including Mexican American, Central American, and others
(4) White, Caucasian, Anglo, European American; not Hispanic
(5) American Indian/Native American
(6) Mixed; parents are from two different groups
(7) Other (write in):

16. My father's ethnicity is (use numbers above)
17. My mother's ethnicity is (use numbers above)

The Ethnic Identity Scale (Umaña-Taylor, Yazedijan, & Bamaca-Gomez, 2004)

The Ethnic Identity Scale (EIS) assesses three domains of ethnic identity formation: exploration, resolution, and affirmation.

Description: The EIS consists of 17 items and assesses three domains of ethnic identity formation. These domains are: (1) Exploration or the degree to which individuals have explored aspects related to their ethnicity (seven items: 2, 4, 5, 6, 8, 11, 15); (2) Resolution or the degree to which individuals have resolved issues related to their ethnicity (four items: 3, 12, 14, 17); and (3) Affirmation or the degree to which individuals feel positively/negatively about their ethnicity (six items: 1, 7, 9, 10, 13, 16). Respondents rate each item on a 4-point scale ranging from *does not describe me at all* (1) to *describes me very well* (4). The scale has 10 positive and 7 negative questions (items 1, 2, 7, 9, 10, 13, 16). Reverse scoring is used for the negatively worded items. Subscale scores are created by summing the items; higher scores on each subscale indicate greater exploration, resolution, and affirmation. The scale is self-administered.

Sample: Two studies were conducted to examine the psychometric properties of the measure. Study 1: The sample included 615 undergraduate students enrolled in a Midwest university and a West Coast university. The sample was predominantly female (72%), had an average age of 21.8 (18–56) years, represented 193 ethnic backgrounds and were classified by the authors as White (45%), Latino (12%), Asian including Middle-Eastern (20%), African American (8%), multi-racial (7%), and other (4%). Study 2: The sample included 231 11th-grade high-school students. The majority (54.5%) were female and the average age of the participants was 16.6 years. The reported ethnic breakdown was White 28%, Latino 21%, African American 20%, Asian 11%, Native American 1%, multi-racial 8%, and other 3%.

Reliability: Study 1 and Study 2 coefficient alphas for the exploration, affirmation, and resolution subscales were .91/.89, .86/.84, and .92/.89 respectively.

Validity: Exploratory factor analysis (Study 1) reduced the scale to 22 items in three domains; subsequent confirmatory factor analysis replicated the 3-factor structure with the deletion of an additional five items. There is evidence of construct validity. For minority group members, the exploration and resolution subscales were positively associated with self-esteem and familial ethnic socialization and for Whites these two subscales were related to familial ethnic socialization but not to self-esteem. The authors classified persons as high/low in each category and found expected relationships with the eight possible combinations (Study 1). In Study 2, the relationship of the three subscales to familial ethnic socialization mirrored the findings in Study 1: For all ethnic groups, affirmation and resolution were related to self-esteem while for African Americans and Latino respondents, exploration was related to self-esteem.

Comments: There are no findings to support using a total scale score which is consistent with the authors' interpretation of ethnic identity. From the original studies, there is evidence of reliability for each of the subscales for college and high-school students across ethnic groups. Subsequent findings are mixed. Satisfactory internal consistency has been reported for the three subscales (Supple, Ghazarian, Frabutt, Plunkett, & Sands, 2006) or in studies just using the exploration and resolution factors (Umaña-Taylor & Updegraff, 2007). But, while Umaña-Taylor and Shin (2007) report satisfactory internal consistency for the exploration and resolution factors, they found poor internal consistency scores for the affirmation subscale for African American and Latino undergraduates in contrast to White and Asian American students. The factor structure for different ethnic groups has been confirmed by other studies (Supple et al., 2006; Umaña-Taylor & Shin, 2007). The findings vary for construct validity. Supple and colleagues report similar findings between the relationship of the three subscales and familial ethnic socialization and Umaña-Taylor and Updegraff (2007) report similar findings between exploration and resolution with self-esteem. Umaña-Taylor and Shin (2007) did find that the association between the three subscales and self-esteem varied for different ethnic groups and may be impacted by geographical location. Much of the research is based on high-school and college students. Efforts have been made to assess the scale with at least four categories of respondents: Whites, Latinos, African Americans, and Asian Americans. The EIS avoids a response set by using positively and negatively worded questions.

Location: Umaña-Taylor, A. J., Yazedijan, A., & Bamaca-Gomez, M. (2004). Developing the ethnic identity scale using Eriksonian and social identity perspectives. *Identity: An International Journal of Theory and Research, 4*, 9–38.

Selected Publications

Supple, A. J., Ghazarian, S. R., Frabutt, J. M., Plunkett, S. W., & Sands, T. (2006). Contextual influences on Latino adolescent ethnic identity and academic outcomes. *Child Development, 77*, 1427–1433.

Umaña-Taylor, A. J., & Shin, N. (2007). An examination of ethnic identity and self-esteem with diverse populations: Exploring variation by ethnicity and geography. *Cultural Diversity and Ethnic Minority Psychology, 13*, 178–186.

Umaña-Taylor, A. J., & Updegraff, K. A. (2007). Latino adolescents' mental health: Exploring the interrelations among discrimination, ethnic identity, cultural orientation, self-esteem, and depressive symptoms. *Journal of Adolescence, 30*, 549–567.

Ethnic Identity Scale

1. My feelings about my ethnicity are mostly negative (R).
2. I have not participated in any activities that would teach me about my ethnicity (R).
3. I am clear about what my ethnicity means to me.
4. I have experienced things that reflect my ethnicity, such as eating food, listening to music, and watching movies.
5. I have attended events that have helped me learn more about my culture.
6. I have read books, magazines, newspapers, or other materials that have taught me about my ethnicity.
7. I feel negatively about my ethnicity (R).
8. I have participated in activities that have exposed me to my ethnicity.
9. I am not happy with my ethnicity (R).
10. I wish I were a different ethnicity (R).
11. I have learned about my ethnicity by doing things such as reading books, magazines, newspapers, searching the internet, or keeping up with current events.
12. I understand how I feel about my ethnicity.
13. If I could choose, I would prefer to be of a different ethnicity (R).
14. I know what my ethnicity means to me.
15. I have participated in activities that have taught me about my ethnicity.
16. I dislike my ethnicity (R).
17. I have some clear sense of what my ethnicity means to me.

Measures of Identity Development and Acculturation

The Acculturation, Habits, and Interests Multicultural Scale for Adolescents (Unger et al., 2002)

The Acculturation, Habits, and Interests Multicultural Scale for Adolescents (AHIMSA) is designed to assess acculturation among adolescents.

Description: The AHIMSA consists of eight items. For each item, the response options are: (a) The United States, (b) The country my family is from, (c) Both, and (d) Neither. The AHIMSA scale can generate four scores with separate orientations to the dominant and ethnic culture: (1) Assimilation (USO) is the total number of US responses; (2) Separation (OCO) is the total number of country my family is from responses; (3) Integration (BCO) is the total number of both responses; and (4) Marginalization (NCO) is the total number of neither responses. The score for each orientation can range from 0 to 8. Any one of the orientations might be used but no more than three for any analysis. The scale is self-administered.

Sample: The sample included 317 sixth-graders recruited from 13 ethnically diverse middle schools in Los Angeles, CA. The sample was nearly equally split by gender (females were 50.2%) and had an average age of 11.5 years. Among the sample, 8.5% were White, 2.2% were African American, 19.2% Asian/Pacific Islander, 53% Hispanic/Latino, 14.2% Filipino, 1.3% Other, and 1.6% had no responses.

Reliability: Cronbach's alphas for the four scales were: USO/Assimilation was .79; OCO/Separation was .68; BCO/Integration was .79; and NCO/Marginalization was .50.

Validity: Three measures were used to test construct validity: English language use, generational status, and the US Orientation, Other Country Orientation and Integration scales of the Acculturation Rating Scale for Mexican-Americans – II (the scale language was adapted to be general in tone). The USO and OCO were associated with each in the expected directions; the BCO was only associated with the Integration scale, generation and English language, and the NCO was not related to any measure.

Comments: The authors note that the USO and OCO have evidence of reliability and validity, the BCO has mixed results, and the NCO is not a good measure. The evidence was for the total sample and not for specific population subgroups. Similar reliability results have been found in other studies of college students (Schwartz, Zamboanga, Rodriguez, & Wang, 2007) and Hispanic youth (Unger, Ritt-Olson, Wagner, Soto, & Baezconde-Garbanati, 2007). Schwartz and Zamboanga (2008) did find a higher internal consistency for the NCO with Hispanic college students. Concern about the NCO and the concept of marginalization has been reinforced by findings reported by Schwartz and Zamboanga (2008). USO and OCO scales were found to be associated in the expected directions with other acculturation measures (Unger et al., 2007).

Location: Unger, J. B., Gallaher, P., Shakib, S., Ritt-Olson, A., Palmer, P. H., Johnson, A. A. (2002). The AHIMSA acculturation scale: A new measure of acculturation for adolescents in a multicultural society. *Journal of Early Adolescence, 22*, 225–251.

Selected Publications

Schwartz, S. J., & Zamboanga, B. L. (2008). Testing Berry's model of acculturation: A confirmatory latent class approach. *Cultural Diversity and Ethnic Minority Psychology, 14*, 275–285.

Schwartz, S. J., Zamboanga, B. L., Rodriguez, L., & Wang, S. C. (2007). The structure of cultural identify in an ethnically diverse sample of emerging adults. *Basic and Applied Social Psychology, 29*, 159–173.

Unger, J. B., Ritt-Olson, A., Wagner, K., Soto, D., & Baezconde-Garbanati, L. (2007). A comparison of acculturation measures among Hispanic/Latino adolescents. *Journal of Youth Adolescence, 36*, 555–565.

AHIMSA Scale

Many people in the United States have ancestors who came from another country. Families come to the United States at different times. Maybe you and your parents moved to the United States Maybe your parents came to the United States when they were kids. Maybe your grandparents' grandparents were the ones who came to the United States.

Write the name(s) of the country (or countries) that your family came from:________________

When you think about this country...

Response categories: The United States; The country my family is from; Both; Neither

1. I am most comfortable being with people from ...
2. My best friends are from ...
3. The people I fit in with best are from ...
4. My favorite music is from ...
5. My favorite TV shows are from ...
6. The holidays I celebrate are from ...
7. The food I eat at home is from ...
8. The way I do things and the way I think about things are from ...

Stephenson Multigroup Acculturation Scale (Stephenson, 2000)

The Stephenson Multigroup Acculturation Scale (SMAS) assesses the degree to which individuals are immersed in dominant and ethnic cultural behaviors including language, interactions food, and media.

Description: The SMAS includes 32-item tapping into two domains. These domains are: Ethnic Society Immersion (ESI; 17 items: 1–17) and Dominant Society Immersion (DSI; 15 items: 18–32). Participants respond to items based on a Likert-type scale ranging from *false* (1) to *true* (4). Lower scores suggest more identification with the particular group. The scale is self-administered.

Sample: We describe Study 2 and Study 3 from the initial scale development. Study 2: The sample included 436 participants recruited from three cities in the Northeast. The sample was primarily female (70%), single (62%), and had an average age of nearly 30. Slightly more than three-fifths of the participants (62%) were community adults while the remaining participants were college students. Participants represented a range of ethnic groups (African Americans 8%, Asian Americans 8%, Whites 29%, Hispanics 19%, and African decent 36%) and generational status (47.3% were first generation; 19% were second generation; 13.73% were third generation; and 20.4% were fourth generation). Study 3: There were 208 undergraduate student participants. The sample was primarily female (79%) and had an average age of 22.8 years. The majority, 51%, were fourth generation or more while the remaining sample was distributed by generation as 14% first generation, 17% second generation, and 18% third generation. The majority of participants were White (73%) followed by Hispanics (15%), Asian Americans (7%), African descent (3%), and African Americans (2%).

Reliability: The total scale score coefficient alpha was .86; the ESI coefficient alpha was .87 and the DSI coefficient alpha was .90 (Study 2).

Validity: The 2-factor structure found in Study 2 was replicated in Study 3, though the factor loadings for some items were weaker and below the set criterion level. Indices of fit obtained from a confirmatory factor analysis (Study 3) were inconsistent and rather than being independent factors, the two domains were correlated. Construct validity was reported as ESI and DSI scores were related to generational status and DSI-mediated the relationship of ethnic status and the Global Severity Index of the SCL-90-R (Study 2). Criterion validity was ascertained using other measures of acculturation (Study 3); ESI scores were correlated with the Mexican Orientation and Anglo Orientation subscales of the Acculturation Rating Scale for Mexican Americans II and Hispanic Domain and Non-Hispanic Domain scales of the Bidimensional Acculturation Scale. Similarly, DSI scores were correlated as predicted for the AOS and MOS, though the latter was not statistically significant, and were correlated as predicted with the Non-Hispanic Doman and Hispanic Domain scales, though again the latter was not statistically significant. Note that the Acculturation Rating Scale for Mexican Americans II and Bidimensional Acculturation Scale language were modified to be more general in language rather than referenced to Hispanics.

Comments: The SMAS was developed for use across ethnic groups. There is evidence of reliability and validity. Findings of adequate internal consistency are reported in most studies though the ESI was low for Mexican Americans (.66) in one study and mainland Asian Americans (.67) in another study (Abad & Sheldon, 2008; Hall & Allard, 2009; Hall, Teten, Stanley, DeGarmo, & Stephens, 2005; Miville & Constantine, 2006; Schwartz & Zamboanga, 2008). The scales behaved as hypothesized with other constructs (Abad & Sheldon, 2008; Miville & Constantine, 2006). Other than the original study, all of these studies have been conducted with university students and there is a need to test this scale with broader population groups.

Location: Stephenson, M. (2000). Development and validation of the Stephenson multigroup acculturation scale (SMAS). *Psychological Assessment, 12*, 77–88.

Selected Publications

Abad, N. S., & Sheldon, K. M. (2008). Parental autonomy and ethnic cultural identification among second-generation immigrants. *Journal of Family Psychology, 22*, 652–657.

Hall, G. C. N., & Allard, C. B. (2009). Application to graduate psychology programs by undergraduate students of color: The impact of a research training program. *Cultural Diversity and Ethnic Minority Psychology, 15*, 223–229.
Hall, G. C., Teten, A. L., Stanley, S., DeGarmo, D. S., & Stephens, K. A. (2005). Ethnicity, culture, and sexual aggression: Risk and protective factors. *Journal of Consulting and Clinical Psychology, 73*, 830–840.
Miville, M. L., & Constantine, M. G. (2006). Sociocultural predictors of psychological help-seeking attitudes and behavior among Mexican American college students. *Cultural Diversity and Ethnic Minority Psychology, 12*, 420–432.
Schwartz, S. J., & Zamboana, B. L. (2008). Testing Berry's model of acculturation: A confirmatory latent class approach. *Cultural Diversity and Ethnic Minority Psychology, 14*, 275–285.

Stephenson Multigroup Acculturation Scale (SMAS)

Below are a number of statements that evaluate changes that occur when people interact with others of different cultures or ethnic groups. For questions that refer to *country of origin* or *native country*, please refer to the country from which your family originally came. For questions referring to *native language*, please refer to the language spoken where your family originally came.

Circle the answer that best matches your response to each statement: 1 = False, 2 = Partly false, 3 = Partly true, 4 = True.

1. I understand English, but I am not fluent in English.
2. I am uniformed about current affairs in the United States.
3. I speak my native language with my friends and acquaintances from my country of origin.
4. I have never learned to speak the language of my native country.
5. I feel totally comfortable with (Anglo) American people.
6. I eat traditional foods from my native culture.
7. I have many (Anglo) American acquaintances.
8. I feel comfortable speaking my native language.
9. I am informed on current affairs in my native country.
10. I know how to read and write in my native language.
11. I feel at home in the United States.
12. I attend social functions with the people from my native country.
13. I feel accepted by (Anglo) Americans.
14. I speak my native language at home.
15. I regularly read magazines of my ethnic group.
16. I like to speak my native language.
17. I know how to prepare (Anglo) American foods.
18. I am familiar with the history of my native country.
19. I regularly read a American newspaper.
20. I attend social functions with (Anglo) American people.

21. I think in my native language.
22. I stay in close contact with my family members and relatives in my native country.
23. I speak English at home.
24. I speak my native language with my spouse or partner.
25. When I pray, I use my native language.
26. I attend social functions with (Anglo) American people.
27. I think in my native language.
28. I stay in close contact with family members and relatives in my native country.
29. I am familiar with important people in American history.
30. I think in English.
31. I speak English with my spouse or partner.
32. I like to eat American foods.

Orthogonal Cultural Identification Scale (Oetting, Swaim, & Chiarella, 1998)

The Orthogonal Cultural Identification Scale (OCIS) measures identification with five different ethnic groups with the assumption that one might have high identification with more than one group.

Description: The OCIS consists of six questions and question ratings are made for each ethnic group (African Americans, American Indians, Asian Americans, Hispanics, and Whites). Items consist of statements about how closely an individual identifies with different cultures. Items reflect identification with the way of life, perceived and expected success in that culture, and involvement in cultural activities. Responses are offered on a 4-point scale ranging from *a lot* (4) to *not at all* (1). The scores for the OCIS are calculated separately for each ethnic group and then averaged from the six base questions. High identification with a particular group is indicated by a score of 3 or more, medium identification by a score of 2, and low identification with a score of 1 or lower. The scale is self-administered.

Note: The original article (Oetting & Beauvais, 1990–1991) describing the scale used a 4-item version with a sample of Native American and Mexican-American adolescents that is not described in the article. The authors report Cronbach's alphas that range from .80 to .89 for several of the scales. The scale items related to Indian Cultural Identify relate to other items related to Native-American culture and the scale adequately discriminates between Anglo and Hispanic Identification and other cultural variables. Since these findings are based on the 4-item scale, we describe findings using the 6 scale items. Also, we provide more detailed information in the Comments section of other studies.

Sample: The sample included 2,048 students in 7th through 12th grades. There were 450 Mexican-American 7th–9th graders (56% female), 458 Mexican-American 10th–12th graders (52.8% female), 567 American-Indian 7th–9th graders (53.3% female), and 577 American-Indian 10th–12th graders (56.8% female).

Reliability: None reported.

Validity: Factorial validity was assessed. The best fitting model was a hierarchical model (second order) with two first-order factors and was consistent with the theoretical perspective of the authors. The model fit across all groups and for both males and females. Factor loadings were also invariant across grade and gender and differed by ethnicity.

Comments: Given the lack of information available, we provide more detail. Venner, Wall, Lau, and Ehlers (2006) report for a sample of Mission Native-American adults' Cronbach's alphas ranging from .76 to .91 for each of the scales, concurrent validity correlated (though weak) with a variety of items specific to Mission Indian culture, and confirmed the 2-factor structure. Johnson, Wall, Guanipa, Terry-Guyer, and Velasquez (2002) examined the scale with a group of university students and found inadequate internal consistency (from .55 to .65) for the Hispanic, Native American, and African-American scales, better internal consistency for the Asian (.77) and Anglo (.75) scales; test–retest reliabilities for an average of 84 days ranged from .66 to .75. Using just the Asian and Anglo scales, an EFA identified two factors independent of each other. Johnson and colleagues (2002) also report construct validity as scores are related to another acculturation scale and length of residence in the United States. Overall, there is evidence of reliability that is strongest when using the study group ethnicity scale and the Anglo scale. The scale should be evaluated with broader number of population groups.

Location: Oetting, E. R., & Beauvais, F. (1990–1991). Orthogonal cultural identification theory: The cultural identification of minority adolescents. *The International Journal of the Addictions, 25*, 655–685.

Oetting, E. R., Swaim, R. C., & Chiarella, M. C. (1998). Factor structure and invariance of the orthogonal cultural identification scale among American Indian and Mexican American youth. *Hispanic Journal of Behavioral Sciences, 20*, 131–154.

Selected Publications

Johnson, M. L., Wall, T. L., Guanipa, C., Terry-Guyer, L., & Velasquez, R. J. (2002). The psychometric properties of the orthogonal cultural identification scale in Asian Americans. *Journal of Multicultural Counseling and Development, 30*, 181–91.

Venner, K. L., Wall, T. L., Lau, P., & Ehlers, C. L. (2006). Testing of an orthogonal measure of cultural identification with adult Mission Indians. *Cultural Diversity and Ethnic Minority Psychology, 12*, 632–643.

Adolescent Scale Orthogonal Cultural Identification Scale – Adolescent Version

The following questions ask how close you are to different cultures. You may identify with more than one culture, so please mark all responses that apply to you.

Respondents rate each ethnic culture with: 4 = A lot; 3 = Some; 2 = A few; 1 = None at all

1. Some families have special activities or traditions that take place every year at particular times (such as holiday parties, special meals, religious activities, trips or visits). How many of these special activities or traditions does your family have that are based on...
   a. White American or Anglo culture
   b. Black or African-American culture
   c. Asian or Asian-American culture
   d. Mexican-American or Spanish culture
   e. American-Indian culture
2. When you are an adult and have your own family, will you do special things together or have special traditions based on...
   a. White-American or Anglo culture
   b. Black or African-American culture
   c. Asian or Asian-American culture
   d. Mexican-American or Spanish culture
   e. American-Indian culture
3. Does your family live by or follow the...
   a. White-American or Anglo way of life
   b. Black or African-American way of life
   c. Asian or Asian-American way of life
   d. Mexican-American or Spanish way of life
   e. American-Indian way of life
4. Do *you* live by or follow the...
   a. White-American or Anglo way of life
   b. Black or African-American way of life
   c. Asian or Asian-American way of life
   d. Mexican-American or Spanish way of life
   e. American-Indian way of life
5. Is your family a success in the...
   a. White-American or Anglo way of life
   b. Black or African-American way of life
   c. Asian or Asian-American way of life
   d. Mexican-American or Spanish way of life
   e. American-Indian way of life
6. When you are an adult, will *you* be a success in the...
   a. White-American or Anglo way of life
   b. Black or African-American way of life

c. Asian or Asian-American way of life
d. Mexican-American or Spanish way of life
e. American-Indian way of life

Orthogonal Cultural Identification Scale Adult Scale

The following questions ask how close you are to different cultures. When answering the questions about "family," think about the family that is most important to you now. How would you define that family? You can include your current family, your family of origin, or both. Answer the questions keeping that definition in mind. You may identify with more than one culture, so please mark all responses that apply to you.

1. Some families have special activities or traditions that take place every year at particular times (such as holiday parties, special meals, religious activities, trips or visits). How many of these special activities or traditions does your family have that are based on...

   a. White-American or Anglo culture
   b. Black or African-American culture
   c. Asian or Asian-American culture
   d. Mexican-American or Spanish culture
   e. American-Indian culture

2. In the future, with your own family, will you do special things together or have special traditions based on...

   a. White-American or Anglo culture
   b. Black or African-American culture
   c. Asian or Asian-American culture
   d. Mexican-American or Spanish culture
   e. American-Indian culture

3. Does your family live by or follow the...

   a. White-American or Anglo way of life
   b. Black or African-American way of life
   c. Asian or Asian-American way of life
   d. Mexican-American or way of life
   e. American-Indian way of life

4. Do you live by or follow the...

   a. White-American or Anglo way of life
   b. Black or African-American way of life

   c. Asian or Asian-American way of life
   d. Mexican-American or Spanish way of life
   e. American-Indian way of life

5. Is your family a success in the...

   a. White-American or Anglo way of life
   b. Black or African-American way of life
   c. Asian or Asian-American way of life
   d. Mexican-American or Spanish way of life
   e. American-Indian way of life

6. When you are an adult, will *you* be a success in the...

   a. White-American or Anglo way of life
   b. Black or African-American way of life
   c. Asian or Asian-American way of life
   d. Mexican-American or Spanish way of life
   e. American-Indian way of life

Measures of Ethnocultural Empathy

Scale of Ethnocultural Empathy (Wang et al., 2003)

The Scale of Ethnocultural Empathy (SEE) measures an individual's empathy (understanding the feelings of others) toward people of different racial and ethnic backgrounds.

Description: The SEE is a self-report measure including 31 items and measuring four ethnocultural empathy dimensions: (1) Empathetic Feelings and Expression or a concern about communication of attitudes or beliefs and responses to the emotions or experiences of people from other backgrounds (EFE; 15 items: 3, 9, 11, 12, 13, 14, 15, 16, 17, 18, 21, 22, 23, 26, 30); Empathetic Perspective Taking or trying to understand other peoples' experiences and feelings by taking their perspective (EP; 7 items: 2, 4, 6, 19, 28, 29); Acceptance of Cultural Differences or understanding, accepting, and valuing other ethnic groups' cultural traditions (AC; 5 items: 1, 5, 8, 10, 27); and Empathetic Awareness or awareness and knowledge about other racial groups' experiences (EA; 4 items: 7, 20, 24, 25). Responses are offered on a 6-point scale ranging from *strongly disagree* (1) to *strongly agree* (6). Nineteen items have a positive wording and 12 items (1, 2, 5, 8, 10, 16, 17, 21, 27, 28, 29, 31) have a negative wording. After reverse coding the 12 negatively worded items, the scores for the SEE are obtained by summing the item responses; higher scores indicate higher levels of ethnocultural empathy. The scale is self-administered.

Sample: The original scale evaluation includes three studies. Study 1: Three hundred and twenty-three undergraduate participants were recruited from three universities in a Midwestern state. The majority of participants were female (66%), had an average age of 19.7 years, and were single (97%). The ethnic/racial distribution among the participants was: 83% Caucasian, 6% African American, 5% Asian American or Pacific Islander, 2% Latino/Latina, 1% Native American, and 2% biracial. Study 2: The sample included 340 undergraduate students recruited from two large Midwestern universities. Most were female (63%), single (92%) and their average age was 20.8. Among the participants, 79% were White, 14% were African American, 2% were Asian American or Pacific Islander, 2% were Latino/Latina, less than 1% was Native American, and 2% were biracial. Study 3: The sample included 51 undergraduate students, 33 of whom were women, with an average age of 20.6 years. Most respondents were White (88%). There were no Latinos/Latinas or Native Americans in the sample. Only 41 respondents completed the scale at twice.

Reliability: Study 1 Cronbach's alphas for the SEE total scale was .91 and the four subscales were .90 (EFE), .79 (EPT), .71 (AC), and .74 (EA). The 2-week test–retest reliability estimates (Study 3) for the SEE total score and subscales were: SEE ($r = .76$), EFE ($r = .76$), EP ($r = .75$), AC ($r = .86$), and EA ($r = .64$).

Validity: Exploratory factor analysis established a 4-factor structure with moderate inter-factor correlations (Study 1). Factorial validity was established as the 4-factor structure was confirmed as was the hierarchical structure, that is, one overriding factor explaining the relationships of the subscales (Study 2). There is mixed evidence of discriminant validity as the total scale score and two of the three subscales were not statistically significantly correlated with the BIDR Impression Management Subscale, a measure of social desirability, in Study 1, but there were small yet statistically significant associations with three of the SEE scales in Study 2. Convergent validity was established as the SEE total score and subscales were statistically significantly associated with total and subscale scores of the Miville-Guzman Universality-Diversity Scale (assesses awareness and acceptance of similarities and differences among people) and the Davis Interpersonal Reactivity Index (measures of general empathy) (Study 2). Criterion validity was established through the analysis of total score and subscale scores by several demographic variables. As hypothesized, women, non-White students, degree of diversity represented in family members, number of friends from diverse backgrounds, and diversity of high school or neighborhood were all related to higher empathy scores (Study 2).

Comments: The SEE should be evaluated with wider population groups. There is evidence of reliability and validity. Additional evidence of the reliability of the total scale scores with youth ages 11–15 years was reported by Le, Lai, and Wallen (2009) and similar reliability statistics for the total score and subscale scores were found with college students by Cundiff and Komarraju (2008). Additional construct validity was evident in the hypothesized relationships of gender differences in empathy as measured by the SEE to attitudes toward women in leadership positions (Cundiff & Komarraju, 2008). Cundiff, Nadler, and Swan (2009) reported evidence for convergent validity and discriminant validity as higher SEE scores were related to more positive attitudes toward different cultural groups and the SEE scores were distinct from scores about attitudes toward diverse groups. The SEE avoids a response set by using positively and negatively worded questions.

Location: Wang, Y., Davidson, M. M., Yakushko, O. F., Savoy, H. B., Tan, J. A., & Bleier, J. K. (2003). The scale of ethnocultural empathy: Development, validation, and reliability. *Journal of Counseling Psychology, 50*, 221–234.

Selected Publications

Cundiff, N. L., & Komarraju, M. (2008). Gender differences in ethnocultural empathy and attitudes toward men and women in authority. *Journal of Leadership and Organizational Studies, 15*, 5–15.

Cundiff, N. L., Nadler, J. T., & Swan, A. (2009). The influence of cultural empathy and gender on perceptions of diversity programs. *Journal of Leadership and Organizational Studies, 16*, 97–110.

Le, T. N., Lai, M. H., & Wallen, J. (2009). Multiculturalism and subjective happiness as mediated by cultural and relational variables. *Cultural Diversity and Ethnic Minority Psychology, 15*, 303–313.

Scale of Ethnocultural Empathy (SEE)

Please respond to each item using the following scale:

1 = Strongly disagree; 2 = Moderately disagree; 3 = Slightly disagree; 4 = Slightly agree; 5 = Moderately agree; 6 = Strongly agree

1. I feel annoyed when people do not speak standard English (R).
2. I do not know a lot of information about important social and political events of racial and ethnic groups other than my own (R).
3. I am touched by movies or books about discrimination issues faced by racial or ethnic groups other than my own
4. I know what it feels like to be the only person of a certain race or ethnicity in a group of people.
5. I get impatient when communicating with people from other racial or ethnic backgrounds, regardless of how well they speak English (R).
6. I can relate to the frustration that some people feel about having fewer opportunities due to their racial or ethnic backgrounds.
7. I am aware of institutional barriers (e.g., restricted opportunities for job promotion) that discriminate against racial or ethnic groups other than my own.
8. I do not understand why people of different racial or ethnic backgrounds enjoy wearing traditional clothing (R).
9. I seek opportunities to speak with individuals of other racial or ethnic backgrounds about their experiences.

10. I feel irritated when people of different racial or ethnic background speak their language around me (R).
11. When I know my friends are treated unfairly because of their racial or ethnic backgrounds, I speak up for them.
12. I share the anger of those who face injustice because of their racial and ethnic backgrounds.
13. When I interact with people from other racial or ethnic backgrounds, I show my appreciation of their cultural norms.
14. I feel supportive of people of other racial and ethnic groups, if I think they are being taken advantage of.
15. I get disturbed when other people experience misfortunes due to their racial or ethnic background.
16. I rarely think about the impact of a racist or ethnic joke on the feelings of people who are targeted (R).
17. I am not likely to participate in events that promote equal rights for people of all racial and ethnic backgrounds (R).
18. I express my concern about discrimination to people from other racial or ethnic groups.
19. It is easy for me to understand what it would feel like to be a person of another racial or ethnic background other than my own.
20. I can see how other racial or ethnic groups are systematically oppressed in our society.
21. I do not care if people make racists statements against other racial or ethnic groups (R).
22. When I see people who come from a different racial or ethnic background succeed in the public arena, I share their pride.
23. When other people struggle with racial or ethnic oppression, I share their frustration.
24. I recognize that the media often portrays people based on racial or ethnic stereotypes.
25. I am aware of how society differentially treats racial or ethnic groups other than my own.
26. I share the anger of people who are victims of hale crimes (e.g., intentional violence because of race or ethnicity).
27. I do not understand why people want to keep their indigenous racial or ethnic cultural traditions instead of trying to fit into the mainstream (R).
28. It is difficult for me to put myself in the shoes of someone who is racially and/or ethnically different from me (R).
29. I feel uncomfortable when I am around a significant number of people who are racially/ethnically different than me (R).
30. When I hear people make racist jokes, I tell them I am offended even though they are not referring to my racial or ethnic group.
31. It is difficult for me to relate to stories in which people talk about racial or ethnic discrimination they experience in their day-to-day lives (R).

Original Scale References

Crandall, C. S., Eshleman, A., & O'Brien, L. (2002). Social norms and the expression of prejudice: The struggle for internalization. *Journal of Personality and Social Psychology, 82*, 359–378.

Dunton, B. C., & Fazio, R. H. (1997). An individual difference measure of motivation to control prejudiced reactions. *Personality & Social Psychology Bulletin, 23*, 316–332.

Godfrey, S., Richman, C. L., & Withers, T. N. (2000). Reliability and validity of a new scale to measure prejudice: The GRISMS. *Current Psychology, 19*, 3–20.

Hegarty, W. H., & Dalton, D. R. (1995). Development and psychometric properties of the organizational diversity inventory (ODI). *Educational and Psychological Measurement, 55*, 1047–1052.

Krieger, N., & Sidney, S. (1996). Racial discrimination and blood pressure: The CARDIA study of young black and white adults. *American Journal of Public Health, 86*, 1370–1378.

Krieger, N., Smith, K., Naishadham, D., Hartman, C., & Barbeau, E. M. (2005). Experiences of discrimination: Validity and reliability of a self-report measure for population health research on racism and health. *Social Science and Medicine, 61*, 1576–1596.

Lee, M. Y., Sapp, S. G., & Ray, M. C. (1996). The reverse social distance scale. *The Journal of Social Psychology, 136*, 17–24.

Montei, M. S., Adams, G. A., & Eggers, L. M. (1996). Validity of scores on the attitudes toward diversity scale (ATDS). *Educational and Psychological Measurement, 56*, 293–303.

Neville, H. A., Lilly, R. L., Duran, G., Lee, R. M., & Browne, L. (2000). Construction and initial validation of the color-blind racial attitudes scale (CoBRAS). *Journal of Counseling Psychology, 47*, 59–70.

Oetting, E. R., Swaim, R. C., & Chiarella, M. C. (1998). Factor structure and invariance of the orthogonal cultural identification scale among American Indian and Mexican American youth. *Hispanic Journal of Behavioral Sciences, 20*, 131–154.

Oetting, E. R., & Beauvais, F. (1990–1991). Orthogonal cultural identification theory: The cultural identification of minority adolescents. *The International Journal of the Addictions, 25*, 655–685.

Paniagua, F. A. (1998). Assessing and treating culturally diverse clients: a practical guide (2nd ed.). Newbury Park, CA: Sage.

Phinney, J. S. (1992). The multigroup ethnic identity measure: A new scale for use with adolescents and young adults. *Journal of Adolescent Research, 7*, 156–176.

Plant , E. A., & Devine, P. G. (1998). Internal and external motivation to respond without prejudice. *Journal of Personality and Social Psychology, 75*, 811–832.

Ponterotto, J. G., Grieger, I., Burkard, A., Rieger, B. P., D'Onofrio, A., Dubuisson, A., et al. (1995). Development and validation of the Quick Discrimination Index (QDI). *Educational and psychological measurement, 55*, 1016–1031.

Roberts, R. E., Phinney, J. S., Masse, L. C., Chen, Y. R., Roberts, C. R., & Romero, A. (1999). The structure of ethnic identity of young adolescents from diverse ethnocultural groups. *Journal of Early Adolescence, 19*, 301–322.

Stephenson, M. (2000). Development and validation of the Stephenson multigroup acculturation scale (SMAS). *Psychological Assessment, 12*, 77–88.

Umaña-Taylor, A. J., Yazedijan, A., & Bamaca-Gomez, M. (2004). Developing the ethnic identity scale using Eriksonian and social identity perspectives. *Identity: An International Journal of Theory and Research, 4*, 9–38.

Unger, J. B., Gallaher, P., Shakib, S., Ritt-Olson, A., Palmer, P. H., & Johnson, A. A. (2002). The AHIMSA acculturation scale: A new measure of acculturation for adolescents in a multicultural society. *Journal of Early Adolescence, 22*, 225–251.

Wang, Y., Davidson, M. M., Yakushko, O. F., Savoy, H. B., Tan, J. A., & Bleier, J. K. (2003). The scale of ethnocultural empathy: Development, validation, and reliability. *Journal of Counseling Psychology, 50*, 221–234.

References

Abad, N. S., & Sheldon, K. M. (2008). Parental autonomy and ethnic cultural identification among second-generation immigrants. *Journal of Family Psychology, 22*, 652–657.

Amodio, D. M., Harmon-Jones, E., & Devine, P. G. (2003). Individual differences in the activation and control of affective race bias as assessed by startle eyeblink response and self-report. *Journal of Personality and Social Psychology, 84*, 738–753.

Bogardus, E. S. (1925). Measuring social distance. *Journal of Applied Sociology, 9*, 299–308.

Burkhard, A. W., Jones, J. A., & Johll, M. P. (2002). Hierarchical factor analysis of the Quick Discrimination Index. *Educational and Psychological Measurement, 62*, 64–78.

Crandall, C. S., Eshleman, A., & O'Brien, L. (2002). Social norms and the expression and suppression of prejudice: The struggle for internalization. *Journal of Personality and Social Psychology, 82*, 359–378.

Cundiff, N. L., & Komarraju, M. (2008). Gender differences in ethnocultural empathy and attitudes toward men and women in authority. *Journal of Leadership and Organizational Studies, 15*, 5–15.

Cundiff, N. L., Nadler, J. T., & Swan, A. (2009). The influence of cultural empathy and gender on perceptions of diversity programs. *Journal of Leadership and Organizational Studies, 16*, 97–110.

Green, R. G., Kiernan-Stern, M., & Basking, F. R. (2005). White social workers' attitudes about People of Color. *Journal of Ethnic and Cultural Diversity in Social Work, 14*, 47–67.

Gushue, G. V. (2004). Race, color-blind racial attitudes, and judgments about mental health: A shifting standards perspective. *Journal of Counseling Psychology, 51*, 398–407.

Hall, G. C. N., & Allard, C. B. (2009). Application to graduate psychology programs by undergraduate students of color: The impact of a research training program. *Cultural Diversity and Ethnic Minority Psychology, 15*, 223–229.

Hall, G. C., Teten, A. L., Stanley, S., DeGarmo, D. S., & Stephens, K. A. (2005). Ethnicity, culture, and sexual aggression: Risk and protective factors. *Journal of Consulting and Clinical Psychology, 73*, 830–840.

Hausmann, L. R. M., & Ryan, C. S. (2004). Effects of external and internal motivation to control prejudice on implicit prejudice: The mediating role of efforts to control prejudiced responses. *Basic and Applied Social Psychology, 26*, 215–225.

Johnson, M. L., Wall, T. L., Guanipa, C., Terry-Guyer, L., & Velasquez, R. J. (2002). The psychometric properties of the orthogonal cultural identification scale in Asian Americans. *Journal of Multicultural Counseling and Development, 30*, 181–191.

Lam, B. T. (2008). The function of acculturation and collective self-esteem on prejudicial attitudes among Vietnamese American young adults. *Journal of Human Behavior in the Social Environment, 18*, 350–363.

Le, T. N., Lai, M. H., & Wallen, J. (2009). Multiculturalism and subjective happiness as mediated by cultural and relational variables. *Cultural Diversity and Ethnic Minority Psychology, 15*, 303–313.

Liu, W. M., Pope-Davis, D. B., Nevitt, J., & Toporek, R. L. (1999). Understanding the function of acculturation and prejudicial attitudes among Asian Americans. *Cultural Diversity and Ethnic Minority Psychology, 5*, 317–328.

Miville, M. L., & Constantine, M. G. (2006). Sociocultural predictors of psychological help-seeking attitudes and behavior among Mexican American college students. *Cultural Diversity and Ethnic Minority Psychology, 12*, 420–432.

Neville, H. A., Lilly, R. L., Duran, G., Lee, R. M., & Browne, L. (2000). Construction and initial validation of the Color-Blind Racial Attitudes Scale (CoBRAS.). *Journal of Counseling Psychology, 47*, 59–70.

Neville, H., Spanierman, L., & Doan, B. -T. (2006). Exploring the association between color-blind racial ideology and multicultural counseling competencies. *Cultural Diversity and Ethnic Minority Psychology, 12*, 275–290.

Neville, H. A., Coleman, M. N., Falconer, J. W., & Holmes, D. (2005). Color-blind racial attitudes and false consciousness among African Americans. *Journal of Black Psychology, 31*, 27–45.

Olson, M. A., & Fazio, R. H. (2004). Trait inferences as a function of automatically activated racial attitudes and motivation to control prejudiced reactions. *Basic and Applied Social Psychology, 26*, 1–11.

Park, R. E. (1924). The concept of social distance as applied to the study of racial attitudes and racial relations. *Journal of Applied Sociology, 8*, 339–344.

Pegg, P. O., & Plybon, L. E. (2005). Toward the theoretical measurement of ethnic identity. *Journal of Early Adolescence, 25*, 250–264.

Plant, E. A., & Devine, P. G. (1998). Internal and external motivation to respond without prejudice. *Journal of Personality and Social Psychology, 75*, 811–832.

Plant, E. A., & Devine, P. G. (2001). Responses to other-imposed pro-Black pressure: Acceptance or backlash?. *Journal of Experimental Social Psychology, 37*, 486–501.

Plant, E. A., & Devine, P. G. (2009). The active control of prejudice: Unpacking the intentions guiding control efforts. *Journal of Personality and Social Psychology, 96*, 64–652.

Ponterotto, J. G., Potere, J. C., & Johansen, S. A. (2002). The Quick Discrimination Index: Normative data and user guidelines for counseling researchers. *Journal of Multicultural Counseling and Development, 30*, 192–207.

Ponterotto, J., Gretchen, D., Utsey, S., Stracuzzi, T., & Saya, R. (2003). The multigroup Ethnic Identity Measure (MEIM): Psychometric reviews and further validity testing. *Educational and Psychological Measurement, 63*, 502–525.

Schlauch, R. C., Lang, A. R., Plant, E. A., Christensen, R., & Donohue, K. F. (2009). Effect of alcohol on race-based responding: The moderating role of internal and external motivations to respond without prejudice. *Journal of Studies on Alcohol and Drugs, 70*, 328–336.

Schwartz, S. J., & Zamboanga, B. L. (2008). Testing Berry's model of acculturation: A confirmatory latent class approach. *Cultural Diversity and Ethnic Minority Psychology, 14*, 275–285.

Schwartz, S. J., Zamboanga, B. L., Rodriguez, L., & Wang, S. C. (2007). The structure of cultural identify in an ethnically diverse sample of emerging adults. *Basic and Applied Social Psychology, 29*, 159–173.

Slaughter, J. E., Sinar, E. F., & Bachiochi, P. D. (2002). Black applicants' reactions to affirmative action plans: Effects of plan content and previous experience with discrimination. *Journal of Applied Psychology, 87*, 333–344.

Spanierman, L. B., Poteat, V. P., Beer, A. M., & Armstrong, P. I. (2006). Psychosocial costs of racism to Whites: Exploring patterns through cluster analysis. *Journal of Counseling Psychology, 53*, 434–441.

Spenser, M. S., Icard, L. D., Harachi, T. W., Catalano, R. F., & Oxford, M. (2000). Ethnic identity among monoracial and multiracial adolescents. *Journal of Early Adolescence, 20*, 365–387.

Strauss, J. P., Connerley, M. L., & Ammermann, P. A. (2003). The "threat hypothesis" personality and attitudes towards diversity. *The Journal of Applied Behavioral Science, 39*, 32–52.

Supple, A. J., Ghazarian, S. R., Frabutt, J. M., Plunkett, S. W., & Sands, T. (2006). Contextual influences on Latino adolescent ethnic identity and academic outcomes. *Child Development, 77*, 1427–1433.

Towles-Schwen, T., & Fazio, R. H. (2003). Choosing social situations: The relation between automatically activated racial attitudes and anticipated comfort interacting with African Americans. *Personality and Social Psychology Bulletin, 29*, 170–182.

Umaña-Taylor, A. J., & Shin, N. (2007). An examination of ethnic identity and self-esteem with diverse populations: Exploring variation by ethnicity and geography. *Cultural Diversity and Ethnic Minority Psychology, 13*, 178–186.

Umaña-Taylor, A. J., & Updegraff, K. A. (2007). Latino adolescents' mental health: Exploring the interrelations among discrimination, ethnic identity, cultural orientation, self-esteem, and depressive symptoms. *Journal of Adolescence, 30*, 549–567.

Unger, J. B., Ritt-Olson, A., Wagner, K., Soto, D., & Baezconde-Garbanati, L. (2007). A comparison of acculturation measures among Hispanic/Latino adolescents. *Journal of Youth Adolescence, 36*, 555–565.

U.S. Census Bureau (2008). *2006–2008 American Community Survey 3-year estimates.* http://factfinder.census.gov

Utsey, S. O., & Ponterotto, J. G. (1999). Further factorial validity assessment of scores on the Quick Discrimination Index (QDI). *Educational and Psychological Measurement, 59,* 325–335.

Venner, K. L., Wall, T. L., Lau, P., & Ehlers, C. L. (2006). Testing of an orthogonal measure of cultural identification with adult Mission Indians. *Cultural Diversity and Ethnic Minority Psychology, 12,* 632–643.

Yancey, A. K., Aneshensel, C. S., & Driscoll, A. K. (2001). The assessment of ethnic identity in a diverse urban youth population. *Journal of Black Psychology, 27,* 190–208.

Chapter 6
Native Americans

Overview

Native Americans are made up of 564 federally recognized tribes, consisting mainly of four tribes: Navajo – 307,000; Cherokee – 262,000; Sioux – 114,000; and Chippewa – 107,000. Native Americans or American Indians along with Alaskan natives make up 1.6% of the US total population or approximately 4.8 million people (U.S. Census Bureau, 2008). At the present time, a slight majority live somewhere other than the reservations, often in big western cities.

Native Americans are a diverse and expansive population covering the entire United States from New York to Alaska. However, they are primarily located in 10 states: California, Oklahoma, Arizona, Texas, New Mexico, New York, Washington, North Carolina, Michigan, and Alaska.

They are, relative to the US population, a young group with a median age of 31 years versus 36 years for America as a whole. Twenty-eight percent of their population is under the age of 18 which is virtually twice that of the rest of the nation. They are less likely to be married than the US population as a whole; 40% versus 49%. Still, their family unions have a high percentage of two-parent families than that of African Americans.

With respect to education, Native Americans are not faring well. Approximately one-fourth of their population has less than a high school diploma as compared to 15% of the US population. In contrast, only 13% of the population has a baccalaureate or higher degree in contrast to 28% of the US population as a whole.

Native Americans are grossly over-represented among America's poor having a per capita income of approximately 62% of the average American while having a greater number of their population living in poverty. While the unemployment rate for Native Americans is not tracked by the Bureau of Labor Statistics as their numbers are too few, the Bureau of Indian Affairs estimates that the unemployment rate is 50%. Not surprisingly, data suggest that their quality of life is consistent with their economic status. They are in poorer health than most Americans, and on average have approximately a 6-year shorter life expectancy than White Americans. The rates for adult smokers are the highest of any group in the country being approximately 32% as contrasted with 18% for the United States They have a 828

L.E. Davis, R.J. Engel, *Measuring Race and Ethnicity*,
DOI 10.1007/978-1-4419-6697-1_6, © Springer Science+Business Media, LLC 2011

per million infant mortality rate which is almost 70% higher than that of White Americans.

Native Americans are a group which is often neglected and overlooked by researchers. This is due in part to their frequent inaccessibility and to their very small numbers. It is clear that greater attention to this population is sorely needed. Indeed, the fact that we have included but one Native American scale for this demographic group suggests that greater attention needs to be given to America's first people.

Measures of Acculturation

Native American Acculturation Scale (Garrett & Pichette, 2000)

The Native American Acculturation Scale (NAAS) measures the degree of acculturation of Native Americans from traditional to assimilated.

Description: The NAAS is adapted from the Acculturation Rating Scale for Mexican Americans and the Suinn-Lew Asian Self-Identity Acculturation Scale. The NAAS includes 20 items designed to assess language (items 1, 2, 15, 16, 17), identity (items 3, 19), friendships (items 6, 7, 8), behaviors such as music, movies, and the like (items 9, 10, 14, 20), generation/geographic background (items 4, 5, 11, 12), and pride (item 18). Questions are answered using a 5-point Likert scale unique to each item. For each item, a score of *1* indicates high Native American identity, *3* indicates bicultural identity, and *5* indicates high American identity. The total score is calculated by summing the 20 items and dividing by 20. Total scores range from 1 to 5; the authors note that scores closer to 1 or 5 are assumed to be providing a more accurate representation of a respondent's identification. The scale is self-administered.

Sample: The study sample included 139 high school students.

Reliability: The alpha coefficient was .91.

Validity: A panel of 10 experts representing different tribal affiliations and professions determined the cut-off score of 3.

Comments: The NAAS exhibits reasonable internal consistency. To our knowledge this instrument has not been evaluated with other age groups and even with the above sample, there is no information about gender or geographic residence. We found only one study (Winterowd, Montgomery, Stumblingbear, Harless, & Hicks, 2008) that provided evidence of discriminant validity in relation to an enculturation scale.

Location: Garrett, M. T., & Pichette, E. F. (2000). Red as an apple: Native American Acculturaion and Counseling with or without reservation. *Journal of Counseling & Development, 78,* 3–13.

Selected Publications

Winterowd, C., Montgomery, D., Stumblingbear, G., Harless, D., & Hicks, K. (2008). Development of the American Indian enculturation scale to assist counseling practice. *American Indian and Alaska Native Mental Health Research, 15,* 1–14.

Native American Acculturation Scale (NAAS)

This questionnaire will collect information about your background and cultural identity. For each item, choose the *one* answer that best describes you by filling in the blank.

1. What language do you speak?
   1. Tribal language only (e.g., Cherokee, Navajo, and Lakota)
   2. Mostly tribal language, some English
   3. Tribal language and English about equally well (bilingual)
   4. Mostly English, some tribal language
   5. English only
2. What language do you prefer?
   1. Tribal language only (e.g., Cherokee, Navajo, and Lakota)
   2. Mostly tribal language, some English
   3. Tribal language and English about equally well (bilingual)
   4. Mostly English, some tribal language
   5. English only
3. How do you identify yourself?
   1. Native American
   2. Native American and some non-Native American (e.g., White, African American, Latino, and Asian American)
   3. Native American and non-Native American (bicultural)
   4. Non-Native American and some Native American
   5. Non-Native American (e.g., White, African American, Latino, and Asian American)
4. Which identification does (did) your mother use?
   1. Native American
   2. Native American and some non-Native American (e.g., White, African American, Latino, and Asian American)
   3. Native American and non-Native American (bicultural)
   4. Non-Native American and some Native American
   5. Non-Native American (e.g., White, African American, Latino, and Asian American)
5. Which identification does (did) your father use?
   1. Native American

2. Native American and some non-Native American (e.g., White, African American, Latino, and Asian American)
3. Native American and non-Native American (bicultural)
4. Non-Native American and some Native American
5. Non-Native American (e.g., White, African American, Latino, and Asian American)

6. What was the ethnic origin of friends you had as a child up to age 6?

    1. Only Native Americans
    2. Mostly Native Americans
    3. About equally Native Americans and non-Native Americans
    4. Mostly non-Native Americans (e.g., Whites, African Americans, Latinos, and Asian Americans)
    5. Only non-Native Americans

7. What was the ethnic origin of friends you had as a child from age 6 to 18?

    1. Only Native Americans
    2. Mostly Native Americans
    3. About equally Native Americans and non-Native Americans
    4. Mostly non-Native Americans (e.g., Whites, African Americans, Latinos, and Asian Americans)
    5. Only non-Native Americans

8. Who do you associate with now in your community?

    1. Only Native Americans
    2. Mostly Native Americans
    3. About equally Native Americans and non-Native Americans
    4. Mostly non-Native Americans (e.g., Whites, African Americans, Latinos, and Asian Americans)
    5. Only non-Native Americans

9. What music do you prefer?

    1. Native American music only (e.g., pow-wow music, traditional flute, contemporary, and chant)
    2. Mostly Native American music
    3. Equally Native American and other music
    4. Mostly other music (e.g., rock, pop, country, and rap)
    5. Other music only

10. What movies do you prefer?

    1. Native American movies only
    2. Mostly Native American movies
    3. Equally Native American and other movies
    4. Mostly other movies
    5. Other movies only

11. Where were you born?
    1. Reservation, Native American community
    2. Rural area, Native American community
    3. Urban area, Native American community
    4. Urban or Rural area, near Native American community
    5. Urban or Rural area, away from Native American community
12. Where were you raised?
    1. Reservation, Native American community
    2. Rural area, Native American community
    3. Urban area, Native American community
    4. Urban or Rural area, near Native American community
    5. Urban or Rural area, away from Native American community
13. What contact have you had with Native American communities?
    1. Raised for 1 year or more on the reservation or other Native American community
    2. Raised for 1 year or less on the reservation or other Native American community
    3. Occasional visits to the reservation or other Native American community
    4. Occasional communication with people on reservation or other Native American community
    5. No exposure or communications with people on reservation or other Native American community
14. What foods do you prefer?
    1. Native American foods only
    2. Mostly Native American foods and some other foods
    3. About equally Native American foods and other foods
    4. Mostly other foods
    5. Other foods only
15. In what language do you think?
    1. Tribal language only (e.g., Cherokee, Navajo, and Lakota)
    2. Mostly tribal language, some English
    3. Tribal language and English about equally well
    4. Mostly English, some tribal language
    5. English only
16. Do you
    1. Read only a tribal language (e.g., Cherokee, Navajo, and Lakota)
    2. Read a tribal language better than English
    3. Read both a tribal language and English about equally well
    4. Read English better than a tribal language
    5. Read only English

17. Do you
    1. Write only a tribal language (e.g., Cherokee, Navajo, and Lakota)
    2. Write a tribal language better than English
    3. Write both a tribal language and English about equally well
    4. Write English better than a tribal language
    5. Write only English
18. How much pride do you have in Native American culture and language?
    1. Extremely proud
    2. Moderately proud
    3. A little pride
    4. No pride, but do not feel negative toward group
    5. No pride, but do feel negative toward group
19. How would you rate yourself?
    1. Very Native American
    2. Mostly Native American
    3. Bicultural
    4. Mostly non-Native American
    5. Very non-Native American
20. Do you participate in native American traditions, ceremonies, occasions, and so on?
    1. All of them
    2. Most of them
    3. Some of them
    4. A few of them
    5. None at all

Reference

U.S. Census Bureau. (2008). *2006–2008 American Community Survey 3-year estimates.* http://factfinder.census.gov

Appendix A

Appendix A: Scales Identified but not Reviewed in this Volume

African-American Scales

Multidimensional Inventory of Black Identity

Citation: Sellers, R. M., Rowley, S. A. J., Chavous, T. M., Shelton, J. N., & Smith, M. A. (1997). Multidimensional inventory of black identity: A preliminary investigation of reliability and construct validity. *Journal of Personality and Social Psychology, 73*, 805–815.

Racial Argument Scale

Citation: Saucier, D. A., & Miller, C. (2003). The persuasiveness of racial arguments as a subtle measure of racism. *Personality and Social Psychology Bulletin, 10*, 1303–1315.

Two Dimensional Model of Black Acculturation

Citation: Cole, E. R., & Jacob Arriola, K. R. (2007). Black students on white campuses: Toward a two-dimensional model of black acculturation. *Journal of Black Psychology, 33*, 379–403.

Asian-American Scales (and Pacific Islands)

Asian American Racism-Related Stress Inventory

Citation: Liang, C. T. H., Li, L. C., & Kim, B. S. K. (2004). The Asian American racism-related stress inventory: Development, factor analysis, reliability, and validity. *Journal of Counseling Psychology, 51*, 103–114.

L.E. Davis, R.J. Engel, *Measuring Race and Ethnicity*,
DOI 10.1007/978-1-4419-6697-1, © Springer Science+Business Media, LLC 2011

East Asian Acculturation Measure (EAAM)

Citation: Barry, D. T. (2001). Development of a new scale for measuring acculturation. The East Asian acculturation measure (EAAM). *Journal of Immigrant Health, 3,* 193–197.

Khmer Acculturation Scale

Citation: Lim, K. V., Heiby, E., Brislin, R., & Griffin, B. (2002). The development of the Khmer acculturation scale. *International Journal of Intercultural Relations, 26,* 653–678.

Na Mea Hawai'i Scale (Hawaiian Ways)

Citation: Rezentes, W. C. (1993). Na Mea Hawai'i: A Hawaiian acculturation scale. *Psychological Reports, 73,* 383–393.

Short Acculturation Scale for Filipino-Americans

Citation: dela Cruz, F. A., Padillia, G. V., & Butts, E. (1998). Validating a short acculturation scale for Filipino-Americans. *Journal of the American Academy of Nurse Practitioners, 10,* 453–460.

Vancouver Index of Acculturation

Citation: Ryder, A. G., Alden, L. E., & Paulhus, D. L. (2000). Is acculturation unidimensional or bidimensional? A head-to-head comparison in the prediction of personality, self-identity, and adjustment. *Journal of Personality and Social Psychology, 79,* 49–65.

Caucasian Scales

The White Privilege Attitudes Scale

Citation: Pinterits, E. J., Poteat, V. P., & Spanierman, L. B. (2009). The White privilege attitudes scale: Development and initial validation. *Journal of Counseling Psychology, 56,* 417–249.

Hispanic Scales

Acculturative Stress Inventory for Children

Citation: Suarez-Morales, L., Dillon, F. R., & Szapocznik, J. (2007). Validation of the acculturative stress inventory for children. *Cultural Diversity and Ethnic Minority Psychology, 13,* 216–224.

Appendix B

Table B.1 Intra-group scales

Intra-group scales = 38					
White (0)	Black (7)	Hispanic (16)	Asian (8)	Generic (6)	Native American (1)
	The African-American acculturation scale	Los Angeles epidemiologic catchment area acculturation scale	The Suinn-Lew Asian self-identity acculturation scale	Multigroup ethnic identity measure	Native American accul-turation scale
	The African-American acculturation scale-R	American Puerto Rican involvement scale	Acculturation scale for Vietnamese adolescents	Ethnic identity scale	
	The multidimen-sional structures of racial identification	Acculturation scale for Mexican Americans	General ethnicity questionnaire	The acculturation, habits, and interest multi scale for adolescents	
	Multi-construct African-American identity questionnaire	Children's acculturation scale	Acculturation scale for Southeast Asians	Scale of eth-nocultural empathy	
	Black ethnocentrism scale		Asian American family conflicts scale	Stephenson multigroup acculturation scale	

Table B.1 (continued)

Intra-group scales = 38

White (0)	Black (7)	Hispanic (16)	Asian (8)	Generic (6)	Native American (1)
	Racial identity for low-income African Americans	Brief acculturation scale for Hispanics	Intergenerational congruence in immigrant families-parent scale		
		Biculturalism and cultural involvement scale	Intergenerational congruence in immigrant families-child scale		
	Racial/ethnic identity scale	The psychological acculturation scale	Race-related stressor scale	Orthogonal cultural identification	
		Abbreviated multidimensional acculturation scale-AMAS-ZABB			
		Acculturation rating scale for Mexican Americans-II			
		Acculturation rating scale			
		Acculturation index for Mexican Americans			
		Short acculturation scale for Hispanic youth			
		Bidimensional acculturation scale (BAS) for Hispanics			
		Short acculturation scale for Hispanics			
		Cultural life styles inventory			
		The societal, attitudinal, familial, and environmental acculturative stress scale			

Table B.2 Inter-group scales

Inter-group scales = 26

White (8)	Black (7)	Hispanic (0)	Asian (0)	Generic (11)
Psychological cost of racism to whites scale (PCRW)	The prejudice perception assessment scale			Color-blind racial attitudes scale (CoBRAS)
The attitude toward Whites	Cultural mistrust inventory			Reverse social distance scale
Attitude toward Blacks scales				
New Racism Scale	Attitude toward Whites			Attitude toward diversity scale
	Attitude toward Blacks			Modified Godfrey-Richman ISM scale
Race and politics survey				Suppression of prejudice scale
	Index of race-related stress			Experiences of discrimination
	Rejection sensitivity race (RS-Race) questionnaire			Self-evaluation of biases and prejudices scale
Being White in America scale	Racism reaction scale			
Modern racism scale				The quick discrimination index
Pro-Black and anti-Black questionnaire				The organizational diversity index
				Motivation to control prejudice reaction scale
				Internal and external motivation to respond without prejudice scale

Table B.3 Total number of scales based on ethnic grouping = 64

White (8)	African American (14)	Hispanic (16)	Asian (8)	Generic (17)	Native American (1)
Psychological cost of racism to Whites scale	The prejudice perception assessment scale	Los Angeles epidemiologic catchment area acculturation scale	The Suinn-Lew Asian self-identity acculturation scale	Multigroup ethnic identity measure	Native American acculturation scale
Attitude toward Whites Attitude toward Blacks	Cultural mistrust inventory	American Puerto Rican involvement scale	Acculturation scale for Vietnamese adolescents (ASVA)	Ethnic identity scale	
New Racism Scale	Attitude toward Whites Attitude toward Blacks	Acculturation scale for Mexican Americans	General ethnicity questionnaire	The acculturation, habits, and interest multi scale for adolescents	
Race and politics survey		Children's acculturation scale	Acculturation scale for Southeast Asians	Scale of ethnocultural empathy	
	Index of race-related stress		Asian American family conflicts scale	Stephenson multigroup acculturation scale	
	Rejection sensitivity race (RS-Race) questionnaire	Brief acculturation scale for Hispanics	Intergenerational congruence in immigrant families-parent scale	Color-blind racial attitudes scale	
Being White in America scale	The African-American acculturation scale	Biculturalism and involvement questionnaire	Intergenerational congruence in immigrant families-child scale	Reverse social distance scale	

Table B.3 (continued)

White (8)	African American (14)	Hispanic (16)	Asian (8)	Generic (17)	Native American (1)
Modern racism scale	The African-American acculturation scale-R	The psychological acculturation scale	Race-related stressor scale (RRSS)	Attitude toward diversity scale	
Pro-Black and anti-Black questionnaire	The multi-dimensional structures of racial identification	Abbreviated multidimensional acculturation scale-AMAS-ZABB		The suppression of prejudice scale	
	Multi-construct African-American identity questionnaire	Acculturation rating scale for Mexican Americans-II		Experiences of discrimination	
	Black ethnocentrism scale	Acculturation rating scale			
	Racial identity scale for low-income African American	Acculturation index for Mexican Americans		Self-evaluation of biases and prejudices scale	
		Short acculturation scale for Hispanic youth			
	Racial/ethnic identity scale	Bidimensional acculturation scale (BAS) for Hispanics		The quick discrimination index	
	Racim reaction scale	Short acculturation scale for Hispanics		The organizational diversity index	
		Cultural life styles inventory		Motivation to control prejudice reaction scale	

Table B.3 (continued)

White (8)	African American (14)	Hispanic (16)	Asian (8)	Generic (17)	Native American (1)
		The societal, attitudinal, familial, and environmental acculturative stress scale		Orthogonal cultural identification Modified Godfrey-Richman ISM scale	
Total = 9					
				Internal and external motivation to respond without prejudice scale	

FSC
www.fsc.org
MIX
Papier | Fördert gute Waldnutzung
FSC® C083411

Kolibri 360 GmbH
Ferdinand-Jühlke-Straße 7
99095 Erfurt, Deutschland
produktsicherheit@kolibri360.de